Relational Databases For Agile Developers

Ron Ballard

Many of the designations used by manufacturers and sellers to distinguish their products are claimed as trademarks. Where those designations appear in this book, and the author was aware of a trademark claim, the designations have been printed with initial capital letters or in all capitals.

The author has taken care in the preparation of this book, but makes no expressed or implied warranty of any kind and assumes no responsibility for errors or omissions. No liability is assumed for incidental or consequential damages in connection with or arising out of the use of the information, scripts or programs contained in this book.

Visit the author's website: http://thedatastudio.net.

ISBN: 978-1-5272-2365-3

Copyright © 2017 by Ron Ballard

Printed and bound in Great Britain by Clays Ltd, St Ives plc

Table of contents

Introduction 7

How To Read This Book 25

Part A - Starting an Agile Database Project 31

Chapter 1 - Learning to Drive Your Database   32
One Value in Each Cell 32
Every Row Has A Unique Key 46
The Whole Key and Nothing But The Key 51

Chapter 2 - The Checklist   57
Has_many 61
Has_one 63
Belongs_to 65
Has_and_belongs_to_many 65
The Database Design Checklist 68
The Checklist 68

Chapter 3 - An Agile Database - Step by Step   70
Iteration 1 71
Iteration 2 89
Iteration 3 92

Chapter 4 - Database Migrations In SQL   97
The Tools You Need 98
Database Migration for Iteration 1 100
Database Migration for Iteration 2 109
Database Migration for Iteration 3 111

Part B - Defending The Quality Of Your Data 113

Chapter 5 - Naming Things   114
How Did We Get into Such a Mess? 114
Be Descriptive 115
Be Economical 119
Be Easy to Read 121
Be Consistent 124

Chapter 6 - Data Types   125
Simple Data-Types 127

Complex Data-Types	136
Large Black Box Types (blobs)	140
Data-Types That Contain Their Own Internal Structure	142

Chapter 7 - Nulls   150

Arithmetic	152
Aggregates	153
Joins	155
...and Set Operators	156
Strings	160
Inserts and Updates	162
Java	163

Chapter 8 - Keys   164

Natural and Surrogate Keys	164
Data-types for Surrogate Keys	166
Allocating Surrogate Key Values	167
Compound Keys	169
The Bottom Line	170

Part C - Getting Data From Your Database   171

Chapter 9 - Select From One Table   172

Your First Select Statement	172
Pattern Matching	176
Sorting	178
Grouping and Aggregating	180
Window Functions	185

Chapter 10 - Select From Many Tables   193

Joining Data from Multiple Tables	193
Joining Incomplete Sets	198
Nested Queries	216
Stick to the Knitting	224

Part D - Populating And Tuning Your Database   226

Chapter 11 - Populating Your Database   227

Insert	227
Update	231
Delete	237
Transactions	238

Chapter 12 - Database Migrations That Preserve Data — 244
- The Process — 245
- Iteration 1 — 246
- Iteration 2 — 246
- Iteration 3 — 262

Chapter 13 - When Things Go Wrong — 264
- Silent Failure — 265
- "Something Went Wrong" — 266
- The Wild Goose Chase — 268
- Crying "Wolf!" — 270
- The Useful Message — 270

Chapter 14 - Tuning — 273
- Do Not Use Abstract Data Models — 274
- Keep Database Navigation in the Database, Not in the Application — 275
- Select Exactly the Columns You Need and No More — 280
- Use the Database Tools to Collect Statistics for the Optimizer — 281
- Indexes — 283
- Transactions — 284
- Don't Use Object-Relational Mapping systems (ORMs) — 285
- Perceived Performance — 285
- Rewrite Complex Queries — 286
- Advanced Database Tuning — 286

Chapter 15 - Metadata — 288
- Basic Metadata — 288
- Accessing Metadata In an Application — 290
- Using Metadata To Profile Your Database — 292

Part E - Some Common Traps To Avoid — 298

Chapter 16 - Universal Data Models — 299
- Abstract Data Models — 299
- Industry Standard Data Models — 307
- Enterprise Resource Planning (ERP) Systems — 308

Chapter 17 - Big Data — 310
- What are Big Data tools good for? — 311
- What are Relational Databases good for? — 313
- What are the downsides of relational databases? — 314
- What are the downsides of Big Data tools? — 315
- Which Approach Should You Use? — 316

Chapter 18 - Database Features To Be Wary Of — 318
- Why Not Use All The Features? — 318
- Views — 319
- User-Defined Functions and Stored Procedures — 321
- Create Table As Select — 325
- Visual Database Tools — 327

Part F - **Wrapping Up** — 329

Chapter 19 - Wrapping Up — 330

Bibliography — *331*

Index — *333*

Introduction

Why Did I Write This Book?

I spend a lot of my time building databases and applications that use them, and I very often find myself helping people to use databases effectively.

I have frequently been asked to recommend a good book to introduce software developers to relational databases, and I've never found one, for this purpose, that I like. C.J. Date's work, *An Introduction to Database Systems*[1], is brilliant, but so detailed and formal. It's a great reference but not the place to start. At the other end of the spectrum are the learn-SQL-in-a-ridiculously-small-number-of-minutes style books. As Goldacre says, *"I think you'll find it's a bit more complicated than that"*[2].

And then there's the Internet. The Internet is wonderful. It has loads of really good information, and access to the thoughts of some very clever people. Unfortunately it has a lot of rubbish too, and it has propaganda from people who are trying to sell something. Sifting out the good stuff from the bad is not always reliable, especially when you are new to a subject.

There are some important things to learn about relational databases. It isn't terribly difficult but it isn't trivial either. Learning about relational databases is an investment of time and effort at the level we should put into learning a new programming language. It's more likely to be months than minutes. If we are going to work on database applications we have a duty to make this investment.

Database design should not be an arcane art practiced in closed offices by database designers, but that's the way it often works. There should be very little design to do. The important thing is to understand how the organization's data works. The database should be a faithful model of the data and the actual business rules that the organization follows. The job of the person creating the database is to really understand what the organization does with its data. Once that is understood, the database designs itself. You need to understand how to use the database to model

---

1. See Bibliography [Date]
2. See Bibliography [Goldacre]

the real world, and that is not difficult. (See *Chapter 1 - Learning to Drive Your Database on page 32* and *Chapter 3 - An Agile Database - Step by Step on page 70*.)

The goal of this book is to provide a level of information that will give interested readers a good understanding of what relational databases are and how to use them effectively. It will also explain when to use a relational database and when to use other tools.

As well as that, I want to explain how to do things well. I have been lucky to work on many good systems and every success has taught me something. I have worked on some bad systems too, and while I think I have always improved them in some way, the ideal thing to do with a bad system is almost always to throw it away and start again. In practice that is difficult. The costs of running a bad system are enormous but often organizations continue with bad systems because they fear that a new one may be worse. "Better the devil you know...." is what they think. We can build good systems. This book is intended to help you do just that.

My intention is to give good, tested, useful information in a form that you can understand.

I want you to get from this book a good understanding of the important things you should take into account when working on a database application. Once you have that, I offer a short simple checklist that you can use to verify the quality of your database design in a few minutes for each table. You don't need a big bureaucracy and you don't need expensive tools.

Why Are They Telling Me That I Must Do It This Way?

Not everything we hear is true. So how, in the field of data management, do we determine what is true and what isn't?

The examples of code (SQL, Ruby on Rails, Java) in this book are true in the sense that I have tested them and they give the results I show. Later releases of the databases and languages may make the current examples untrue, but generally we're on pretty safe ground here.

The rest of the book is based on my opinions. Those opinions are derived from my experience in this field going back to 1973. They are also based on a desire to solve problems that can be addressed in part by using databases and application development software. I also hope to sell some copies of this book, but I am not going to maximize sales by pretending that there is a short cut to learning what you need to know. I'll make it as straightforward as I can to cover everything we need, but no simpler than that.

There is a lot of money to be made from data management software. In some cases there are very significant license fees, but even with open source software such as PostgreSQL and Hadoop, there is still substantial money to be made from consulting. When large sums of money are involved, then there is a conflict of interest between maximizing financial returns and giving the user the advice that is in her best interest. There is always pressure on vendors to err on the side of increasing financial returns. Those that do this best, survive and grow.

I have witnessed vendors making unrealistic assertions and I have been encouraged to do that myself. Where you stand on this dilemma is up to you. In this book I try to give you, as a user of these technologies, some pointers to assess various proposals that will be presented to you and to help you choose those that are best for delivering great systems to your users. This means being a bit skeptical about the assertions made by vendors of software and services. For example, why are they saying that "best practice" is to use their proprietary development language instead of a language that is widely available, widely used, portable and license-free? I think you should be suspicious in these cases.

There are also organizations that purport to offer independent advice. Again, I think you should ask yourself how independent they are. Is it in their interest to give you, as a user, the best advice for you? Do they gain some benefit from being aligned with the biggest and richest vendors?

Finally, there is another source of advice, and I find this one puzzling. It seems to me to be simply fashion. I don't see a clear reason for promoting some particular technologies, but I have met people who promote them with a zeal that is beyond any rational reasoning as far as I can see, and not obviously related to greed. An example is XML. XML is very good for certain applications. This book, for example, is prepared using XML markup and that enables the same source document to produce a paper book and equivalent books for a number of electronic book readers. This is a good system; I can't think of a better way of doing the job. XML is good for documents and messages with format and content that varies within certain bounds. But I meet people who insist that *all* data should be stored in XML, even if it is a file of 10 million records all with exactly the same format. The cost of storing such a file in XML is vastly increased in terms of extra processing and extra storage space. (I talk about this example in more detail in *Data-Types That Contain Their Own Internal Structure on page 142.*)

One fashion that has become elevated to the status of established practice with relational databases is the very bureaucratic methodology surrounding data modeling. This comes from the same philosophical background as the waterfall methodologies for software development. In this approach a team of specialist data modelers follow a lengthy and complex process in an ivory tower. OK, it may actually be a block of desks in the corner of an open plan office, but they are just as unapproachable as if they were in a real ivory tower. They discourage contact with developers and certainly don't want to talk to users.

As with so many things, Tom DeMarco and Tim Lister said it best, in *Peopleware*[3]:

> "[methodologies] force the work into a fixed mold that guarantees
> - *a morass of paperwork*
> - *a paucity of methods*
> - *an absence of responsibility, and*
> - *a general loss of motivation*"

When you follow the data modeling fashion, you get a team of people, each with a tool that costs thousands of dollars per seat. This team produces conceptual data models that never reflect reality and are never used. The conceptual data model often gets printed out and covers a whole wall. You might as well buy some abstract art to put on your wall - it would be no less useful and it could easily be cheaper and prettier.

Then you have another team, with the same (or a different) expensive tool, maintaining a logical data model. This is another piece of useless fiction.

The actual model defined in the database (the physical model) is the

---

3. See Bibliography [DeMarco&Lister]

Introduction

only one you need. You do not need teams of people with expensive modeling tools, but you probably do need to tidy up your actual database and to make sure that the principles that will make it safe and fast are actually applied. They usually are not.

As the authors of the *Agile Manifesto*[4] say:

> *We are uncovering better ways of developing software by doing it and helping others do it.*
>
> *Through this work we have come to value:*
>
> *Individuals and interactions over processes and tools*
>
> *Working software over comprehensive documentation*
>
> *Customer collaboration over contract negotiation*
>
> *Responding to change over following a plan*
>
> *That is, while there is value in the items on the right, we value the items on the left more.*

Kent Beck	James Grenning	Robert C. Martin
Mike Beedle	Jim Highsmith	Steve Mellor
Arie van Bennekum	Andrew Hunt	Ken Schwaber
Alistair Cockburn	Ron Jeffries	Jeff Sutherland
Ward Cunningham	Jon Kern	Dave Thomas
Martin Fowler		Brian Marick

Copyright 2001, the above authors

this declaration may be freely copied in any form, but only in its entirety through this notice.

Go to the web page and read the whole manifesto if you are not already familiar with it. Be sure to read the Twelve Principles of Agile Software. Do it, please! It's only one page.

Then throw the overblown methodologies in the waste bin and make sure that you have a really good understanding of your craft. This is a better way.

A fashion established in the object-oriented world is that there is an **impedance mismatch** between object-oriented programming and relational databases. This is nonsense. Firstly it is nothing to do with impedance (which is a characteristic of electrical systems). Secondly, and much more importantly: there is no mismatch.

There may be a mismatch between the way some people would like to

---

4. See Bibliography [Agile-Manifesto]

write their programs and the best ways of working with a relational database, but there is no mismatch between the technologies. The job of a relational database is to manage large quantities of structured data reliably and efficiently and to present a clean interface to the outside world. Relational databases can do this. The job of an object-oriented programming language, and the good practices that go with it, is to enable us to build applications that delight their users by operating reliably and quickly and doing the job with the least fuss. Object-oriented programming languages can do this. Relational databases and object-oriented programming languages make a good team.

If object-oriented programming languages were unable to operate with relational databases then they would be no use for most commercial applications. Most development of applications is done with object-oriented languages and with relational databases. It works. I do it all the time.

There are many good software engineering ideas in relational database systems and many in object-oriented programming. Ultimately, we are here to solve customers' problems by building applications that work. If our tools get so involved in navel-gazing that they cannot lift their eyes to the problem we are trying to solve, then they just become encumbrances.

Database developers must work to understand the object-oriented design principles, and object-oriented developers must work to understand relational database principles. Both camps use ridiculously flowery language and that does not help. But both camps have come up with really important principles - principles that have been established to overcome actual problems in software engineering. As professionals we need to understand them.

One key concept that unifies relational databases and object-oriented development is the idea that stuff should be organized into groups of things that belong together. The fancy name for this is **cohesion**. In a relational database, each row should contain things that belong together. If there's a record (= row) in a **person** table in a database, and if that row describes me, then it may contain my name, date of birth, nationality, national ID number, and so on, but it should not include the engine size of my car. I might have two cars, or none. There would be a separate record, in a separate **car** table, for each of my cars with make, model, license plate number, engine size, year of manufacture, etc. Then there would be relationships between my person record and each of my cars, if I have any. Similarly, in an object-oriented application `person` and `car` would be different classes, with different properties and different methods.

How we separate the information we are dealing with into different tables or different classes is driven by the principle of cohesion between the elements that make up a class or the columns that make up a table. In later chapters we will talk a lot about the methods we use to decide what things belong together, and to draw the boundaries. The point here is that there is a lot of compatibility between relational databases and object-oriented systems. We can build on this or we can emphasize the differences, by going off into our separate corners muttering about the way the other lot carry out their business.

We have to deal with some parts of our systems not working quite the way we would like. I find the programming interfaces used to build web pages very messy: the mixture of `HTML`, `JavaScript` and `XML` is ugly. The convolutions we have to go through to manage a multi-page transaction (such as buying a book) are very incompatible with the stateless protocol of the Internet, but we make it work. It isn't elegant, but it is the best we have right now and there are countless numbers of successful applications using this structure. There is no unified theory of everything; we just have to live with it.

Ruby on Rails has a nice way of tying all this together. It is a practical approach to using what is common between the components and managing the differences. Ruby on Rails is a great example of high quality practical engineering. It beats the hell out of fighting between ourselves. This is one reason why I use Ruby on Rails to illustrate some of the development of a system using a relational database.

Why Do You Need a Database?

Relational database technology is important. The reason for it being important is *not* that "users like `SQL` because they already know it." If that were a valid reason then we would all still be using `COBOL`. No! I am writing this because relational databases solved some serious problems with the ways data was managed before. Maybe someone will come up with a better way, but whatever new technology comes along, those lessons need to be remembered. Misuse of some technologies have brought those data management problems back to life in some cases. I have had to work with systems where customers' account numbers were duplicated, causing transactions for one customer to be applied to another customer as well, where transactions were lost, where customers were denied bonuses they had earned because their data was not recorded properly. I also worked on a system that took 24 hours to extract the accounting information to go into the general ledger. This was for 150,000 customers, most of whom had only two or three transactions a year. It wasn't high volume. It should have taken seconds to produce this extract. These problems could all have been solved by proper use of a relational database system. If you have a better solution than a relational database, that's great, but please don't ignore the lessons of the past.

You might say that you can make your application work with simpler **persistence** models and you don't need a database. That may be true. Take a windowing operating system, for example. It could be Microsoft Windows, or Apple macOS or X-Windows or some new and even better one. The operating system has to remember which windows are open, what applications are running, where the windows are on the screen, how big they are, which window is in front of which other one, whether they are minimized, which one has the focus, and so on. The operating system would probably hold all this in memory, but if it has the capability to remember what your screen looked like when you switched your computer off, or the battery power ran out, then it has to write that information to some persistent store, your hard disk, or solid-state drive or whatever else has been invented by the time your read this. Then, when the system starts up again it can reset your screen to the state it was in before the crash. The term persistence makes sense for this kind of small, short-term storage.

The systems used in large organizations usually have quite different data storage needs. An application will still need to keep track of the state of each object that is being manipulated, but *it will typically be one of many applications using the same data.*

In a telephone company, for example, the switches will generate hundreds of millions of call data records (**CDRs**) every day and those will be stored in the database. Meanwhile the shops and the call center and the website will be signing up new customers and entering their details into the database. There will typically be tens of millions of customers. Then the billing system will come along, typically every month for each customer, and look in the database to find their CDRs and their customer information to calculate the charges to be applied this month. Many other applications will use this database. There may be payments to infrastructure suppliers, extracts of accounting data for the corporate general ledger, reports to the security services on suspected criminal activity, and many more.

To describe what is happening in cases like this telephone company as "persistence" is technically accurate, but rather misleading. The data takes a much more central role since it is used by many applications and it is large. There is no escape from the fact that we have to look at this company's database very carefully to make sure that the bills come out right and the CDRs can be loaded fast enough, without losing or duplicating any, and the customer's details accurately reflect what the customers have told us most recently, and so on.

This does not mean that such systems cannot be built using an agile development process.

The database can be constructed for the first story and grown one story at a time. But there must be people on the team who understand how to migrate the database from one release to the next while still maintaining a good design that reflects the real data model, maintains the integrity of the data, and ensures the performance and the usability for all the applications that depend on it.

There is no contradiction here. Having skills in relational databases is one requirement of the team in such projects, but we do not need to design the whole database first, in fact that would be a big mistake for exactly the same reasons that we do not design our whole application up front. I have taken the database lead role in several successful agile projects and it works just fine.

But for these big systems you *do* need a database. It must be capable of keeping the data accurate and complete and up-to-date. It must be able to recover from things going wrong. As a customer of a bank or telephone company or your electricity supplier or your health care provider or your online book store or any of the other big organizations you deal with, you expect the data about your use of their services to be 100% accurate and reasonably up-to-date. These are reasonable expectations, and they are achievable with the help of a decent database.

Why Should You Learn about Relational Databases?

When I was in my mid-teens I was quite good at mathematics, not a genius, but consistently in the top 10% of my class at school. My brother, who is four years younger than me, was having trouble with mathematics so my parents thought it would be a good idea for me to help him. We did try, but we would always get to a point where he would say "but why?" and I didn't know how to answer. I didn't care why we should "let x be the number of peas in a pod," it was just an interesting puzzle to me and that was reason enough. As a teenager, I couldn't explain "why" to him.

My brother's favorite subject was biology (and he went on to teach biology very successfully for over 25 years). About the time I went to university, mathematics stormed into biology. The work in evolutionary biology, ecology and many other fields, suddenly became as dependent on mathematics as it had been on classification and cataloging before. Then my brother had an answer to his question, many answers. To work in his subject he needed to master mathematics, and he did. He quickly passed my ability in mathematics and stays ahead of me to this day.

If you are interested in relational databases just because the puzzle of data management is interesting in itself then I hope this book will give you some interesting ideas to think about. But if your interests are elsewhere, in web applications, smartphone apps, graphics, simulation, financial analytics or many other fields, then relational databases may just be a skill you need to master. I shall try to give you reasons why we use relational databases, and I shall try to give reasons for the approaches and techniques I recommend.

Relational databases are powerful tools and we want to get the best out of them. We want the best performance, we want them to be reliable, we want them to be easy to build and easy to change. I will try to explain why in terms that describe real practical benefits and that hopefully will be relevant to you.

Why Is There So Much Terminology?

That's a good question. A cynic might say that it's an example of **Not Invented Here**; each new language or approach requires its own set of jargon. A more generous person might say that the different terms are used to label the nuances of meaning which separate these terms. Here is a very approximate equivalence between the terms used in various ways of looking at data.

File	Object-oriented	Relational database in practice	Relational theory	Spreadsheet	Conceptual	XML
File	Class Object	Table	Relation	Worksheet	Entity (type)	Document
Record	Instance	Row	Tuple	Row	Entity	Element
Field	Property	Column	Domain	Cell	Attribute	Sub-element or Attribute
	Method	Function		Formula		
Save or store	Persist	Commit		Save		

Some of these are very close, for example: `Field`, `Property`, `Column` and `Attribute` are widely interchangeable.

In other cases, my suggestions that some of these concepts are similar could unleash tirades of fury, for example `File`, `Object`, and `Table`. They are different. An object has properties and also the methods that operate on those properties. A file system has no knowledge of the methods that operate on fields in its files. But a relational database does have functions that can be used on particular data-types. We could call `substring` a `method` on the `varchar` class.

To add to the confusion, some terms are used for the thing being described and for its description. When we say `object`, sometimes we mean object class and sometimes we mean object instance; the same thing happens with `entity` and with `column`.

In this book I sometimes use the term `cell` to mean the value of a column in a particular row. This is simply to try to minimize ambiguity.

So, don't take this table as a reference; instead, think of it as a way of getting these terms into the right area in your mind and be prepared to refine these ideas as you read through this book.

Why Is This Book for Agile Developers?

First of all, let us be clear about what Agile Developers are. As far as I am concerned Agile Developers are those who follow the principles summarized in The Agile Manifesto[5]

`Agile` (like `Big Data`) has suffered from the sound-bite phenomenon. A sound-bite is used to capture a large and complex idea in just a few words, often as few as one or two words. What happens is that many recipients of the sound-bite never find out what it means, so they invent the meaning from the sound-bite. This gives the creators of sound-bites huge power to manipulate their audiences.

When many people use or hear `Agile` or `Agile Development` all they understand is the word-association. Agile means quick, nimble, not bogged down with bureaucracy, acting on impulse. Sadly, many software and service providers use the word Agile to suggest to their prospective clients that they can deliver quickly and cheaply without all the fuss and expense of other software solutions. What they deliver is often shoddy, buggy and impossible to maintain. The costs in the long run are often much, much more than promised or anticipated.

This is the sound-bite version and it is million miles from what `The Agile Manifesto` intended. The authors of `The Agile Manifesto` proposed a highly disciplined approach that works by doing all the important things with great care and attention to detail. It also means not doing the things that waste money and time in projects.

The integrity of those responsible for `The Agile Manifesto`, and of those engineers who genuinely follow its principles, is outstanding. Their aim is that we should all be able to deliver the best possible systems at the lowest possible long-term cost.

Over the last 50 years or so we have learned many techniques that work. Kent Beck, in *Extreme Programming Explained*[6], acknowledged this when he said,

> "When I first articulated XP [Extreme Programming], I had

---

5. See Bibliography [Agile-Manifesto]

6. See Bibliography [Beck]

> *the mental image of knobs on a control board. Each knob was a practice that from experience I knew worked well. I would turn all the knobs up to 10 and see what happened. I was a little surprised to find that the whole package of practices was stable, predictable, and flexible."*

The practices he was taking about were things like:

- We know that the best way to remove bugs is through code inspections. So, Beck implemented pair-programming so that every decision and every line of code is inspected at the time it is created. It sounds crazy to have two people working on a job that is normally done by one, but it works, so we need to let the measurable improvements override our unreliable intuition.

- Tests are not used to find bugs because that is not very effective. Instead, tests are used to ensure that we have built all the necessary functionality, and that we have not broken any existing functionality with our latest changes. Agile projects build tests first and then build the code. This is called `Test-Driven Development`. It is counter-intuitive but, again, it works. So this is another dial that gets turned up to 10.

- We also have learned that having an analyst build a 3-inch thick specification, with little reference to the users, guarantees that the system will contain functionality that is unnecessary, does not match what the users want, or has become out of date by the time it is built. This is wasteful, so Agile projects do not do it. Instead they involve the users throughout the project, ideally full-time, every day. The users describe the functionality that is most important to them, the developers build this and show it to the users. This is done every week or two. On each iteration, the users may change what has been done, so long as that is the most important thing to do now.

And several other principles. These are examples; much less than a full description.

You can use relational databases in proper Agile Development projects. There is no conflict. You can have people working in pairs on the database. You can change the database structure on every iteration, and you should be willing to do so whenever a database change is called for. You can build automated tests that include the database processing.

What you cannot do is to have an office full of DBAs (Database Administrators) who jealously guard the database design and never talk to users. If you have a team of people like this you should offer them jobs inside the development teams. Many DBAs are willing to integrate; many of them dislike the over-specialization that plagues our industry as much as real Agile Developers do.

DBAs must give up that title and integrate with the team. They must learn to communicate with users, with object-orient development experts, with web-page designers, with message-processing gurus and many others. While each of us has some areas we know more about and some where we know less, we must all learn enough about the rest of the work to be able to communicate, at least.

And Agile Developers must know about relational databases. It is part of the portfolio of knowledge that we must all build as we go through our careers.

This book is designed to help you learn about relational databases in a practical way, and to cover the topics you really must understand. It also tells you what you can safely ignore. Most relational databases include some features that are far better tackled with other tools. I mention these and I strongly suggest that you ignore them. For example, do not waste a second of your time learning how to manipulate XML using SQL. There are much better tools than SQL for manipulating XML, and much better places to do so than in the database.

Hasn't All This Been Said Before?

There are many books about designing relational databases and using SQL. I try to offer a very practical way to learn the important techniques and to use them for the benefit of your customers. There are certainly topics covered here that I have never seen anywhere else. But I did find, quite recently, a very interesting online article by Martin Fowler: *Evolutionary Database Design*[7]. Martin Fowler is one of the signatories to the *Agile Manifesto*[8], and I have drawn on his work in several places in this book, so I was pleased to find a significant overlap with the ideas that I have been developing.

---

7. See Bibliography [Fowler-evodb]
8. See Bibliography [Agile-Manifesto]

Why Bother? It All Looks Very Simple from the Examples

I hope the examples do look simple. I try to make them understandable, and one way of doing this is to make the numbers of rows (or records) very small. For small examples you may find yourself thinking that a spreadsheet would be easier. That may be true, but what seems simple with small examples, rapidly gets out of hand as the volume increases. Diagrams, spreadsheets, slides and code examples are all manageable if they fit on a page or two; beyond that we need some powerful tools to help us.

In the real world of banking or insurance or retail or telephone or railway systems (and many, many others) we will be looking at tens of millions, hundreds of millions or even billions of rows. This sheer scale makes a huge difference to our ability to understand the data. Relational databases, and the disciplines that go with them are fine tools to help us manage such complexity.

Why Are There Examples in SQL, XML and Ruby on Rails Before They Have Been Explained?

In Part A of this book I want to focus on the design of a relational database, the way that the relational database creates a model of the real world.

So don't worry if you don't understand all the code in the examples; the code should not be essential to the ideas we are going through in the early chapters.

The SQL examples in the early parts of the book are very simple. Later chapters do explain SQL in detail. It is possible to do some quite complex things in SQL and those will take some explanation.

The XML examples should be fairly self-explanatory. This book does not attempt to explain XML, but you do need to understand XML to work in this area. If you feel that you need help with XML I would recommend W3Schools[9] and *Effective XML*[10].

---

9. http://www.w3schools.com/xml/

I use Ruby on Rails for some of the early examples, because I think it is straightforward way to give examples that work. You should easily be able to see what is happening in these examples. You can go as far as running all the examples on your own computer if you want to, but it isn't necessary. In later chapters we cover the use of SQL for creating database objects and for manipulating them. The relational database is more than SQL. (You could say "not only SQL" but that tag has been appropriated by the Big Data people.) The first thing we want to do is to understand what relational databases are and how they represent real-world data. Having established these concepts, we can move on to using the de-facto standard language to interact with our database. That language is SQL.

Acknowledgements

As I worked through this big project I have been overwhelmed by the level of encouragement and support I received from the people mentioned here, for something that is really my pet project. They have been very generous.

The ideas I have were formed largely through my interactions with these people. That doesn't mean that we agree about all of the things in this book, we cannot blame any of these good people for any of my ideas. I take full responsibility for the end result as it exists on these pages. I do thank all the people mentioned here for helping me to get to this point.

Patti Whaley has supported me in every way while I have been working on this book, with comments on technical content, style, grammar, tone, structure. She has fed me, encouraged me, introduced me to people who could help me, discussed ideas for the book at any time they popped into my head or hers. Patti even worked through the whole draft converting the formatting from Microsoft Word to XML and converting the spelling from UK to American English. (I am very fond of UK English, but far more of the potential readers of this book speak American English, so let's call this a democratic decision.) And Patti has kept me sane with long walks, music, films, gardening, travel and wonderful food.

I have worked with David Walker for over 20 years. When I met him, I thought I was a database expert - I had already worked for database vendors for 15 years - but he taught me more and kept on doing so. David

---

10. See Bibliography [Harold]

is the only person I know who can work with the CEO of a multi-national corporation and the junior programmer trying to make a shell-script work, and teach both of them valuable lessons. Very many of the ideas in this book came from David or were improved by discussions with him.

Mike Tanner and I first worked together in 1982. Back then, on the rare occasions when we disagreed, Mike would say "you're the boss" and that told me that I really should think about this one a bit more. Mike has always been a very creative developer with the ability to think through issues and avoid a problem before the rest of us knew there might be one. So when I chose not to implement one of Mike's review comments I heard that voice in my head again, and gave it a bit more thought.

Paul Beckford taught me what Agile Development is all about. He ran one of the most successful projects I have ever been part of. Officially I was in charge, but Paul made it work for our users and I did my best to make sure he had room to do his job. We have had many discussions since then, on the ways to make projects successful, and specifically on the contents of this book. Paul has been an active reviewer, a supporter of what I have been trying to do and a provider of other sources of valuable information.

Oliver Courtney and I worked together on a few Data Quality and Governance jobs and have had many long talks about how to make projects work and how to improve data quality. Olly's contributions appear in many of these pages.

Dave Rees tested some early drafts especially the technical sections, offering encouragement and helping to make the technical explanations more approachable.

Deniz İşcen read the complete draft. She gave enthusiastic support and made suggestions that led to significant improvements in two chapters.

Dakota Segura made a project of the dialog chapter ("An Agile Database Step by Step") and provided detailed corrections and suggestions, with an impressive level of attention to detail.

I would also like to thank the people listed in the *Bibliography on page 331*. Some of them have taught me in courses and seminars. Others have been generous enough to get involved in conversations, mostly by email. The resources cited here have all been very helpful to me as I tried to improve the way I worked. Some of them have had a fundamental and long-lasting impact on the way I think - you'll see which from the individual citations and quotes.

There have been many other people who taught me by their good example. They all helped to paint the picture as I see it now.

I have enjoyed making this book; I hope you enjoy it too.

How To Read This Book

Part A - Starting an Agile Database Project

This part is about organizing your data in a relational database so that your databases:

- are easy to understand
- are easy to use in your applications
- are easy to change as your applications develop and change, from the first iteration, to the live release, to later enhancements and fixes.
- keep your data safe for your users, so that they get accurate data at the level of each data item and when they follow relationships between items.
- perform well, from the early tests with a few records, to live running with thousands, millions or even billions of records

Organizing your data is a process that is too often wrapped up in time-consuming processes using expensive tools. In this book I propose an agile approach to database design, one that relies on continuous user input to grow the design one iteration at a time. This does not mean a free-for-all approach; it is actually highly disciplined, just as agile code development should be highly disciplined. The results are spectacular compared with traditional `waterfall` development. We get better results this way and we get them more quickly. Part A explains how.

If you are responsible for designing your database then this part of the book is for you. It explains, in plain language, and with examples using familiar real-world data, how to make a good design that takes advantage of any of the relational database systems that are available to you now.

If you are writing applications, or developing analytics or visualizations on an existing database, this part will be useful for you to understand how the database has been designed. It will also help you to spot poor design in existing databases and tell you what problems the poor design may cause, so that you are able to defend against these issues in your code.

If you are managing a database development, this section will help you to understand how your team members are building the database and to challenge any decisions or practices that you feel may not be heading in the right direction.

In this part I start by explaining how to go about organizing your data. We look at common ways of representing data and explain problems that often occur and how to arrange things to overcome these problems. We develop simple, consistent structures that are easy to work with.

Next we look at the links between data objects. We use the plain-English terminology from Ruby on Rails to describe the four kinds of links that we can build.

We offer you a nine-point checklist that you can use to test your database design to ensure that it will work well now and in the future. There is some terminology in the checklist. If you are tempted to jump to the checklist and skip the rest of this part, it may still help you but you will get most out of it, and avoid being puzzled by some of the terms used in it, if you read the rest of Part A first.

Next we give you a worked example in the form of a dialog. If you have worked on an agile project, this should sound familiar as you observe the meetings and discussions that lead to user stories and the early iterations in the development of a new application. This shows the techniques described in Part A in a real world situation and can be a model for your work with your users.

If you are not using Ruby on Rails, you can still use migrations to refactor your database at every iteration and keep the design clean, clear and efficient. We show you how to write migrations in **SQL**. This is your easy reference for defining the tables, columns and relationships in a relational database.

Part B - Defending the Quality of Your Data

We have already seen how to build tables that work well together as a model of the data in your organization, and in the worked example and the checklist we mentioned some other details that we need to think about. In Part B we are going to look more closely at some decisions we must take for each column in our database. These decisions concern naming, data-types, nulls and keys. Together they help us to maintain the quality of our data.

- *Naming* is actually a data quality issue. Vague, cryptic and misleading names often lead to the wrong data being stored in a column. The developer may be rushed, or may have tried and failed to find out what a cryptic name means. So he guesses, and his guess may be wrong leading him to assign the wrong data value or to skip the validation. We give 15 practical suggestions to help you design more meaningful names. Actually, naming applies to tables as well as columns. You should also find this chapter useful for naming objects in your applications.

- Choosing the right *data-type* is very important. For example, if you define a column as a date, then only valid dates can be stored in it, and the powerful date manipulation that comes as part of your database will always work. We tell you which data-types to use and which to avoid, and we explain why. The result will be more robust applications with better performance.

- No one would guess the behavior of *nulls* in a relational database; we just have to learn them. When we understand nulls, they can be very useful, but without understanding we all make mistakes that give our users the wrong answers. The chapter on nulls gives you practical examples and shows you what happens in each case so that you can use nulls with confidence.

- Choosing good *keys* ensures that the database can manage the links within your data and make sure that there is always a valid link where there should be one. We explain the advantages of each approach, helping you to make the best choices for your database and your application.

Part C - Getting Data From Your Database

You may want to grab one existing record to show it to the user or allow her to edit it. You may be writing a report to give the sales team daily tracking of sales by territory. You may have worked out a way to carry out some innovative analytics to tell your boss something he didn't know about the operation of your company. You may be producing some fancy visualization for a presentation to your customers. For any of these you will use the `SQL select` statement.

The `SQL select` statement can be very simple or very powerful. In Part C we build up your expertise, starting with the simplest possible `select` statements and progressing to sophisticated analytical statements. There are real-world examples all the way through so that you can develop your skills one step at a time. This has been the most popular chapter with spreadsheet gurus who want to move on to analyzing huge data sets.

Part D - Populating and Tuning the Database

In this part we look at getting data into the database and changing data once we have inserted it.

The first chapter in this section describes the `data manipulation` (DML) SQL statements: `insert`, `update` and `delete`. These are the commands you need to understand to be able to store data in your database and to change or delete elements of it. We also discuss `transactions` which enable you to group changes to make sure that related changes happen as one reliable unit.

Now that we have covered all the `data manipulation` statements we can talk about Data Migrations That Preserve Data. This is what you will need to do as you refactor from one iteration to the next. We describe testing techniques to ensure that your migrations are correct and then build some actual migrations to show how the tests and the migration support one another, so that you can keep your database in top condition without fear of breaking your applications.

When populating a database, we must check that we have changed the data as we intended. *Chapter 13 - When Things Go Wrong on page 264* talks about the importance of trapping exceptions and reporting them in ways that make it easier to recover from any failure. This can save you, and your colleagues, from long late-night sessions trying to puzzle out what went wrong.

Next we look at tuning your database for performance. If you have followed the design patterns described in Part A of this book, and refactored your database to keep a good design, you will already have tackled the most common reasons for poor performance. We give some tips about writing code to access databases efficiently. We then look at the tools that come with database products to optimize the performance. We all know how annoying slow applications can be. With modern relational databases, and the advice we give here, you can get sparkling performance in all but the most extreme situations.

Finally in this part we show how to access the database metadata. This is particularly useful if you inherit a poorly documented database and you have to find out what it contains and how it works. You may find yourself in this situation because you are being asked to produce reports from an existing database, or load its contents into a `data warehouse` or add a new application that uses existing data.

Part E - Some Common Traps to Avoid

Strangely there are some common practices that consistently cause problems, and yet there are those who promote them, often for no apparent personal gain. We look at some of the worst offenders, describe the arguments used for them, and explain why they are, in fact, counter-productive.

It is very likely that you will come across some of these. You may feel uncomfortable about them but you may be unsure about how to counter their plausible claims. I have been there many times, so I hope you can use my experience to avoid situations that would otherwise result in disappointment and unnecessary cost for you and your users.

We look at some bad design ideas that are common even though they usually fail, specifically: abstract data models and views.

We look at some `silver bullets` that may be very effective in some areas, but that should never be applied in some others, despite what the nice salesperson says. Big Data is a prime example.

We look at some tools that seem very appealing, but only tie us in to a certain vendor and make it very difficult to move on to better systems, specifically stored-procedure languages and visual database tools.

Code and Data Samples

Throughout this book you will see code samples like this:

download: select_like_zip_code.sql

```
select
    first_name,
    family_name,
    telephone_number,
    city,
    state,
    zip_code
from
    person
where
    zip_code like '412%';
```

If you are using an electronic copy of this book you can simply click on the link following "download: " and you should be taken to the web page that contains the code.

If you are using a paper copy of this book you can go to the URL *http://www.thedatastudio.net/ downloads/books/relational_databases_for_agile_developers/ select_like_zip_code.sql*. Just substitute the name of the file you are interested in at the end of the URL. Alternatively, you can go to the home page of The Data Studio (*http://www.thedatastudio.net*) and follow the link to *Downloads* from there.

Part A - Starting an Agile Database Project

When you start an agile development to build an application using a database, you develop the database and the code at the same time. This is the best way to "design" your database. As you grow your database, iteration by iteration, you need to understand how the database works. For this, the first chapter is all the foundation you need. The design principles described here are important because they will make your database robust and easy to change as it grows with your application. You will learn how to build your database and how to refactor it as you understand more and more about the application you are building.

Chapter 1 - Learning to Drive Your Database

It's a great feeling when you first get your driver's license. You've learned how to make the car do what you want it to and how to avoid injuring yourself and others. And suddenly you have freedom. There are so many places you can go to when you want to go, and you can take your friends with you. Learning took a little while and some study and some practice, but it was worth while.

Learning how to use a relational database may not be so good for your social life as learning to drive, but otherwise it is not so different. You do need to study a bit and you do need to practice, but it isn't so difficult, and once you can do it, the database is a tool that will help you to build amazing applications. Work through this chapter and you will be able to use the database to help you build your application, adapting the database on every iteration to make it exactly what your users need. This is just a few pages to explain the main controls and the most important rules of the road before you settle in behind the wheel and set off on your journey.

When we build a relational database the data may come from many places. There may be an online application which captures data that users enter, and stores it in the database. We may load data from other systems, and this data may arrive in XML files, csv files, messages, other databases, and so on.

In this and the following chapters we use various straightforward examples to illustrate data that we might want to store in our database.

We then run some checks to see if the data is structured in a way that will help the applications that use it to avoid mistakes, over-complex processing and inefficiency.

We will often restructure the data in ways that help us to achieve these goals, without losing any information. Don't worry, it isn't so complicated, as you will see from the examples.

One Value in Each Cell

In a relational database, we are looking at data in tables. A table looks like a very simple spreadsheet. Here's an example, which describes policies in an insurance system.

	A	B	C	D	F
1	policy_number	inception_date	expiry_date	premium	voucher_number
2	XYZ/00149204	17-Nov-2011	16-Nov-2012	544.87	2308388
3	XYZ/00063742	11-Apr-2011	10-Apr-2012	665.12	2129304
4	XYZ/00025348	20-Nov-2010	19-Nov-2012	275.27	2334157
5	XYZ/00014769	20-Nov-2010	19-Nov-2012	644.93	2334064
6	XYZ/00126466	29-Sep-2011	28-Sep-2012	309.56	2266203
7	XYZ/00007196	3-Jul-2010	2-Jul-2012	235.80	2005019
8	XYZ/00008156	13-Jul-2010	12-Jul-2012	742.12	2158468
9	XYZ/00023318	9-Nov-2010	8-Nov-2012	51.81	2224457

Data is in columns and rows. Each column has a heading and the values in that column are described by the heading. For example, every value in column B is a valid `inception_date` (the date when the policy came into force). Every row has the same five fields. Every cell has exactly one value in it.

Of course, spreadsheets can be much more complicated than this, but we want our database tables to follow this simple format, because organizing our data in this way makes it easy to process and helps us to avoid making mistakes. This is database design *on rails*. We do the important things and we do them the same way every time. We deliberately avoid the many features that vendors have added and that make their products more complex. We reduce flexibility and choice because flexibility and choice are not the most important things to us. What we do want is robustness, efficiency, productivity, reliability and most of all the ability to meet our users' needs. We do everything we need to do to achieve these aims and we avoid everything that adds unnecessary complexity. If you're a Ruby on Rails fan you will understand this. I have to use the tools my clients specify and Ruby on Rails is not often on that list. But the lessons I learned from the Rails approach are things I apply on every project. If you don't use Ruby on Rails you can still learn from the principles that have made it such a success. We'll cover several of those principles here.

Rails and Agile are not the same thing, but they are often used together for very good reasons. Both are focused on delivering great applications to users. Both cut out unnecessary bureaucracy and grandstanding so that they can get on with the job. Here we are interested in getting on with the job.

Let's look at the characteristics of our simple table in a bit more detail.

This data is organized so that:

- All rows in the table (except the header, row #1) have the same layout
- Every cell in the table has only one value
- There are no repeating groups within a row

All Rows in One Table Have the Same Layout

This means that every record in the file must have the same fields in the same order. Another way of saying this is that there is only one record type per file.

In the spreadsheet the first row is a special record containing headings which tell us what the content of each column means. These headings are examples of `metadata`. Metadata is information about the actual data, for example, looking at the first column, the values starting XYZ/00... are policy numbers and the heading tells us that. `Policy_number` is metadata that describes the data in column A.

In relational databases, the metadata is stored separately from the data. The important thing about this is that a table in a relational database contains only the data. Rather than adding an extra row to name all the columns, the relational database remembers the column names for you.

Because of this, in a relational database we do not have to write special code in our application to exclude the header when we are counting the number of policies, because there is no header.

Every Cell in the Table Has Only One Value

While it might seem convenient sometimes to store multiple pieces of information in one field, some examples will show that this complicates your processing tasks and makes errors more likely.

Here is part of a file created by an application as a feed to an accounting system.

download: compound_field.xml

```
<posting>
  <EffectiveTime>2014-05-31 11:00:16</EffectiveTime>
  <amount>-186.08</amount>
  <description>
    Top-up|Chevrolet Captiva Sport RHB 624|Finch, Basil|DEF/425770
  </description>
  <policyNumber>DEF/425770</policyNumber>
  <policyDate>2013-09-03 18:56:12</policyDate>
</posting>
```

The <description> element contains several fields separated by vertical bars, and within some of these fields there are sub-fields (for example: vehicle make, model and license number). This is bad practice in XML, in relational databases and in any other format.

There are two reasons why this is bad practice:

- It makes the data more difficult to process
- It makes it more likely that this field will represent different objects in different records

The <description> element is more difficult to process because we cannot simply use our favorite XML parser to pick out the vehicle make, for example. We have to get the description and then pick out the first word following the "|" delimiter. In this case, the first word is "Chevrolet" (which is the make of the car) and this is followed by "Captiva Sport" (which is the model). But what if the make is "Alfa Romeo" and the model is "Giulietta"? The make is two words and the model is one. How can we write a program that reliably gets the make as one field and the model as another? Maybe we could compare against a list of known makes. So then we have extra coding and a list that needs maintaining as new car makers enter the market. This is all extra work, which costs money and, really, don't we have more interesting things to do?

Now maybe our developers, despite indications of poor design skills, are very disciplined and *always* create the description field as:

```
transaction_type|make model license_number|family_name, first_name|policy_number
```

Well, the XML file in this case is based on a real-world example and the developers' discipline levels did match their design skills, so we had other postings, that looked like this:

```
Breakdown|Webb, Reisha|93351|09/17/1986|PQR/408734
```

So here we have:

```
transaction_type|family_name, first_name|zip_code|date_of_birth|policy_number
```

Imagine how complex your code has to be to accurately sort out such an XML file.

The XML file should have been designed like this.

download: atomic_fields.xml

```xml
<posting>
  <EffectiveTime>2014-05-31 11:00:16</EffectiveTime>
  <amount>-186.08</amount>
  <TransactionType>Top-up</TransactionType>
  <VehicleMake>Chevrolet</VehicleMake>
  <VehicleModel>Captiva Sport</VehicleModel>
  <VehicleLicenseNumber>RHB 624</VehicleLicenseNumber>
  <Familyname>Finch</Familyname>
  <FirstName>Basil</FirstName>
  <DateOfBirth />
  <PostCode />
  <policyNumber>DEF/425770</policyNumber>
  <policyDate>2013-09-03 18:56:12</policyDate>
</posting>
```

In this example, each field contains only one value. It is not more difficult for the developer to create the record like this and it is certainly easier for an application or a human being to read the record and find exactly the item of data that is needed.

This is why we say "only one value in one cell", because it makes life easier for our users and for the other applications that use our data. We restrict flexibility and gain productivity and reliability by keeping our design *on rails*.

Another way of storing multiple values in one field is to use an array, like this:

family_name	first_name	shop_visits	date_of_birth
Walters	Ann	[2014-05-17,2014-07-23,2014-11-22]	1993-10-05
Bellamy	Jim	[2013-12-05]	1962-05-21
Millward	Steph	[2013-09-27,2014-06-26]	

This is slightly easier to deal with than the previous example, but still has several undesirable characteristics. We still have to parse the array to find each individual `shop_visit` date. If we want to work out the number of `shop_visits` for each person, we will have to parse every array in the table. Also, we cannot take advantage of the database's date data-type, which ensures that `shop_visits` are actually dates and makes it easy for us to work out time between visits, or the most busy day of the week, or any other date processing.

We can make our database easier to use, and more reliable, by restructuring the table like this:

family_name	first_name	shop_visits	date_of_birth
Walters	Ann	2014-05-17	1993-10-05
Walters	Ann	2014-07-23	1993-10-05
Walters	Ann	2014-11-22	1993-10-05
Bellamy	Jim	2013-12-05	1962-05-21
Millward	Steph	2013-09-27	
Millward	Steph	2014-06-26	

This is better, but it does duplicate some names. We'll come back to that.

We have referred to our separate fields as *atomic* fields. Atoms can be split, of course, and it is possible to split the fields in the example. We could split the policy numbers into the alphabetic prefix and the numeric part. We could split the dates into day, month and year. How we choose to create atoms of data is really down to the use of each field.

Dates are better kept as dates. There are many operations which we need to do on these special data-types treating them as dates rather than as days, months and years. Our relational databases, and strongly-typed languages (Java, for example) provide useful functions to compare dates and pull out the parts such as the day name or the month number. This has proved to be the best compromise over the years.

The same argument applies to timestamps.

For business keys, such as the policy number in an insurance system, it is not so clear cut. Business system designers often choose keys with embedded structure and meaning. (They are mistaken to do so, but that's another story.) The policy number prefix might refer to a business division such as car insurance, house insurance, or travel insurance. Generally, if the policy number is the `natural` key, the identifier of the object being described, then it makes sense to treat it as one field. But if you find that you are always splitting out the prefix in your application code then it might be more effective to keep the prefix separate from the number.

Whatever you decide, be consistent. So if you decide to store the policy number as one field, then wherever the policy number is used in your system, always store it as one field. Then, if you are searching for matching policy numbers, you don't have to worry about whether you have to split one of them or concatenate two parts.

No Repeating Groups

Here is a list of the fields in another car insurance table. This list is shown vertically rather than horizontally because it is too wide; it is just a list of the column headings for the table.

Chapter 1 - Learning to Drive Your Database

Field Name
policy_number
vehicle_license_number
effective_start_date
policy_holder_name
zip_code
policyholder_drivers_license_number
number_of_named_drivers
named_driver_1
named_driver_date_of_birth_1
named_drivers_license_number_1
named_driver_2
named_driver_date_of_birth_2
named_drivers_license_number_2
named_driver_3
named_driver_date_of_birth_3
named_drivers_license_number_3

The problems with this table are:

- it stores an extra field to record the number of named drivers
- it limits the number of named drivers to 3
- it is not clear whether the policyholder should be repeated as the first named driver
- it is difficult to count the number of drivers on each policy. Do we have to check name, date_of_birth and driving_license_number to see if an entry is used or not?

The number of named drivers has been included by the designer to overcome the problem of counting drivers, but this breaks the *Don't Repeat Yourself* principle described in *The Pragmatic Programmer* [11]. *Don't Repeat Yourself* says that you should not have the same piece of information in two places. Here we have the number_of_named_drivers in one field, and we could work this out by inspecting how many of the named driver slots are actually used. The application which maintains the table has to keep the number_of_named_drivers in step with the number of entries actually used. Deleting, adding and changing named drivers is an awkward process with this structure, resulting in more code than is

---

11. See Bibliography [Hunt&Thomas]

necessary, which means more cost and more potential for errors.

The insurance company has presumably decided that three named drivers is enough. But, when a competitor offers a similar policy with the possibility of more named drivers, then this insurance company may decide that it needs to respond, resulting in database and code changes, delaying implementation and introducing further opportunities for error.

The table with repeating groups should be restructured as two tables, like this:

Policy Table
policy_number
vehicle_license_number
effective_start_date
policyholder_name
policyholder_date_of_birth
zip_code
policyholder_drivers_license_number

Driver Table
policy_number
named_driver_name
named_driver_date_of_birth
named_drivers_license_number

With the original table split into two, it is now easy to count the number of named drivers on each policy. Here is a possible way to do this:

download: count_drivers_by_policy.sql

```
select
    policy_number,
    count(named_drivers_license_number)
from
    driver
group by
    policy_number;
```

There is no separate `number_of_named_drivers` field to maintain, and the insurance company can have policies with as many named drivers as it likes without any changes to database structure or code.

Only One Record Type in One Table

Here is a fragment of an `XML` file, again from an accounting system, but with some `account` elements as well as the `posting` elements.

download: accounts_and_postings.xml

```xml
<account>
  <name>Policy Premium</name>
  <accountCode>NPP</accountCode>
  <balance>100487.24</balance>
  <balanceAt>2014-05-31 23:59:59</balanceAt>
</account>
<posting>
  <EffectiveTime>2014-05-31 11:00:16</EffectiveTime>
  <amount>586.08</amount>
  <TransactionType>New Business</TransactionType>
  <FamilyName>Finch</FamilyName>
  <FirstName>Basil</FirstName>
  <policyNumber>DEF/425770</policyNumber>
  <policyDate>2013-09-03 18:56:12</policyDate>
</posting>
<posting>
  <EffectiveTime>2014-05-31 11:00:16</EffectiveTime>
  <amount>1532.00</amount>
  <TransactionType>Renewal</TransactionType>
  <FamilyName>Finch</FamilyName>
  <FirstName>Basil</FirstName>
  <policyNumber>DEF/425770</policyNumber>
  <policyDate>2013-09-03 18:56:12</policyDate>
</posting>
<account>
  <name>Mileage Top-up</name>
  <accountCode>MTU</accountCode>
  <balance>7250.00</balance>
  <balanceAt>2014-05-31 23:59:59</balanceAt>
</account>
<posting>
  <EffectiveTime>2014-05-31 11:00:16</EffectiveTime>
  <amount>-186.08</amount>
  <TransactionType>Top-up</TransactionType>
  <FamilyName>Finch</FamilyName>
  <FirstName>Basil</FirstName>
  <policyNumber>DEF/425770</policyNumber>
  <policyDate>2013-09-03 18:56:12</policyDate>
</posting>
```

We would need two tables in our relational database to store this data, like this:

Accounts Table
id
account_name
account_code
balance
balance_at

Postings Table
account_id
effective_time
amount
transaction_type
family_name
first_name
policy_number
policy_date

The XML format may seem more flexible, in that you can put whatever you like in the file and make it conform to standard XML. For this system, though, we are dealing with very structured data. It is an accounting system, dealing with amounts of money. The numbers need to be correct and will need to be assigned to the right accounts. In this case consistency is more important than flexibility. We really do want our accounting systems to be *on rails*. If the format needs to change (to add a new field, for example) then that will require a controlled new release of the database and the code that works with it. A new release implies tested, reliable code, so that our users can trust the data we hold and the applications they use on it.

Sequence by Value, Not by Position

The XML file we looked at before is not ideal. It doesn't make it clear which account each posting belongs to. Possibly there is some mapping through `TransactionType` or possibly the postings that follow an `account` element, belong to that account. We would need to talk to the owners of that file to find out how it works. The owners may be the accounts team or the team that developed the application that produces the file. If the mapping is by the sequence of elements, then they should really include the `posting` elements inside the `account` element like this:

download: postings_within_accounts.xml

```
<account>
  <name>Policy Premium</name>
  <accountCode>NPP</accountCode>
  <balance>100487.24</balance>
  <balanceAt>2014-05-31 23:59:59</balanceAt>
  <posting>
    <EffectiveTime>2014-05-31 11:00:16</EffectiveTime>
    <amount>586.08</amount>
```

```xml
      <TransactionType>New Business</TransactionType>
      <FamilyName>Finch</FamilyName>
      <FirstName>Basil</FirstName>
      <policyNumber>DEF/425770</policyNumber>
      <policyDate>2013-09-03 18:56:12</policyDate>
    </posting>
    <posting>
      <EffectiveTime>2014-05-31 11:00:16</EffectiveTime>
      <amount>1532.00</amount>
      <TransactionType>Renewal</TransactionType>
      <FamilyName>Finch</FamilyName>
      <FirstName>Basil</FirstName>
      <policyNumber>DEF/425770</policyNumber>
      <policyDate>2013-09-03 18:56:12</policyDate>
    </posting>
  </account>
  <account>
    <name>Mileage Top-up</name>
    <accountCode>MTU</accountCode>
    <balance>7250.00</balance>
    <balanceAt>2014-05-31 23:59:59</balanceAt>
    <posting>
      <EffectiveTime>2014-05-31 11:00:16</EffectiveTime>
      <amount>-186.08</amount>
      <TransactionType>Top-up</TransactionType>
      <FamilyName>Finch</FamilyName>
      <FirstName>Basil</FirstName>
      <policyNumber>DEF/425770</policyNumber>
      <policyDate>2013-09-03 18:56:12</policyDate>
    </posting>
  </account>
```

Whatever the rules are, we must build code which interprets the file we are given and captures the actual meaning of the data and the relationships between items.

The physical sequence of records in a relational database is always undefined, and this is by design. This may seem strange, but it is important.

We are used to inferring sequence from position. The words in this sentence are an example of this. However, a database is not a document. One very smart thing the designers of the relational database approach did was to strictly limit the ways we can store information, and this enables a small number of constructs that we need to do all the data manipulation we can think of. We are *on rails* again.

The way sequence is handled in a relational database is the way every other kind of information is handled: by data values. If you need to see the data in the sequence it was entered, then you need to have a column which contains a sequence number. Relational databases offer simple tools to help with this.

The physical sequence of the records in the database is now irrelevant, and you can easily see the records in many different sequences. You sequence the data when you read it from the database. Here are three (of many) possible sequences:

by `policy_number`:

download: order_by_policy_number.sql

```
select
    policy_number,
    effective_time,
    transaction_type,
    amount
from
    postings
order by
    policy_number;
```

by `effective_time` within `transaction_type`:

download: order_by_transaction_type_and_effective_time.sql

```
select
    policy_number,
    effective_time,
    transaction_type,
    amount
from
    postings
order by
    transaction_type,
    effective_time;
```

by **amount** with the highest **amount** first and the lowest last:

download: order_by_amount_descending.sql
```
select
    policy_number,
    effective_time,
    transaction_type,
    amount
from
    postings
order by
    amount desc;
```

It is important to remember that tables in relational databases have no defined sequence. When you select the data without an `order by` clause you may get the data in the sequence you expect, but usually you will not. Also, the next time you select the data without an `order by` clause it may well be returned in a different sequence.

What Have We Done So Far?

What we have described is `First Normal Form`. The formal definition from *An Introduction to Database Systems*[12] is:

> "*First Normal Form*: a relvar is in 1NF[13] if and only if, in every legal value of that relvar, every tuple contains exactly one value for each attribute."

Relvar? 1NF? tuple? What is he talking about? We should remember that the inventor of the relational database, Ted Codd, and his colleague, Chris Date (who, between them, published many books and papers on the subject) were grappling with real problems in data management. They were trying to overcome what we now call `data quality issues`, such as "Why has the electricity company got my address wrong?" or "Why does this transaction appear twice on my credit card bill?"

Codd and Date came up with formal definitions to help them understand the common problems in data management and to develop rigorous ways to avoid these problems. They distilled the many ways of managing data down to one simple set that meets the requirements of all but the most unusual of real-world applications. This is the relational database model. Nearly 40 years later David Heinemeier Hansson described the

---

12. See Bibliography [Date]
13. 1NF = First Normal Form. A gratuitous abbreviation, sorry, I'm quoting Date literally.

principles he applied to Ruby on Rails. Those principles are the same. We choose a simple way of doing something and then we *always* do it that way. Then we can ignore all the other possible ways and focus on solving our users' problems. Relational databases are *Data Management on Rails*. We can now use the good work done by Codd and Date to explain, in more everyday language, good patterns for building robust database applications.

As described in this chapter, a table is in First Normal Form if:

- Every row in the table has the same cells in the same order
- Every cell in the table has one and only one value
- Each cell appears only once in each row; we do not have repeating groups
- There are no hidden values, for example no implied sequence from one row to the next

Every Row Has A Unique Key

In the previous section we left the shop_visits table with the comment that it needed some more work. Here it is again:

family_name	first_name	shop_visits	date_of_birth
Walters	Ann	2014-05-17	1993-10-05
Walters	Ann	2014-07-23	1993-10-05
Walters	Ann	2014-11-22	1993-10-05
Bellamy	Jim	2013-12-05	1962-05-21
Millward	Steph	2013-09-27	
Millward	Steph	2014-06-26	

The problem with this table is that it duplicates data; the `last_name`, `first_name` and `date_of_birth` appear for every `shop_visit`, even when there are several visits per customer. This wastes space, which might not be a big problem if the table is quite small. What is a problem though is keeping the customers' details up-to-date. Suppose Ann Walters gets married and changes her family name to Ayres. We have to update every record for every visit that she has made. And what if we find that in some records her name is "Walters" and in some it is "Waters." Is it the same person? Which name is correct? Somehow, in big systems, duplicated data does become inconsistent. I don't know how, but it does.

In this section we are going to fix this problem.

What Is A Key?

Firstly we have to talk about keys. We are very familiar with keys, or identifiers, as they are also known. We have bank accounts that are identified by account number, insurance policies that are identified by policy numbers, credit cards have unique numbers, we have numerous online accounts that may be identified by our email address or some other key. Our cars have unique license numbers, our mobile phones have unique numbers, we have social security numbers, our houses have ZIP Codes and street addresses. Many things in our lives have identifiers.

When we look at the `shop_visits` table we assume that we are looking at three people. Normally in a small group we identify people by their name and this works fine. We could say that the person's name is a `candidate key`. In a bigger group of people we soon find two people with the same name, and in large commercial systems, there are many people who share their name with several other people in the same system. In these cases, a person's name is not a good key. Date of birth is even worse. Date of birth combined with name reduces the duplication, but it is not enough.

In the `shop_visits` table, we say that `last_name`, `first_name` and `date_of_birth` are *natural keys* (or *natural candidate keys*) because they are attached to the person without any computer system having to create a key.

In most database systems we need to create a `surrogate key`, some identifier that the system uses to identify one particular person, one particular account, one particular policy, and so on. The usual way of doing this is to use a unique integer and to call it `id`. There are other ways of generating unique keys and other naming conventions, but we'll follow the usual pattern here.

Let's add surrogate keys for our customers, like this:

id	family_name	first_name	shop_visits	date_of_birth
53	Walters	Ann	2014-05-17	1993-10-05
53	Walters	Ann	2014-07-23	1993-10-05
53	Walters	Ann	2014-11-22	1993-10-05
54	Bellamy	Jim	2013-12-05	1962-05-21
55	Millward	Steph	2013-09-27	
55	Millward	Steph	2014-06-26	

What Does The Key Identify?

Now we know that all three rows for Ann Walters refer to the same person, but this has not solved the main problem.

Looking at this table again, we can see that there is one row per visit, so it is a table of visits, not a table of customers.

What we need to do is to take out the customer data and put it in a separate table, like this:

Table: customers

id	family_name	first_name	date_of_birth
53	Walters	Ann	1993-10-05
54	Bellamy	Jim	1962-05-21
55	Millward	Steph	1985-03-19

Table: shop_visits

customer_id	shop_visits
53	2014-05-17
53	2014-07-23
53	2014-11-22
54	2013-12-05
55	2013-09-27
55	2014-06-26

Quite a lot has happened here.

We have separated the customer data into a `customers` table and given each customer a surrogate key called `id`. This `id` is called a **Primary Key**. Primary keys are very important in relational databases, and there are some rules that they must follow:

- A primary key must be unique. No two rows can share the same primary key. This means, in this case, that every customer has only one row in the `customers` table and every customer has a unique `id`.
- Every row must have a primary key. It would not be acceptable to have a customer without an `id` in this table. This means that the

system must generate the `id` when a new customer is added to the table.
- A primary key lasts for the life of the object. You don't change your bank account number every year, or every time the bank does a software upgrade. You keep it until you close the account.

Relational database systems, and the relational database theory, do not require every table to have a primary key. In this book though, we are talking about what works well, and we suggest that every table you ever create must have a primary key.

Relational databases let us define primary keys, and if we do, then the database enforces the rules listed above.

Now let's look at the `shop_visits` table.

The `customer_id` identifies the row in the customer table that relates to this visit. In the `shop_visits` table, `customer_id` is called a `foreign key`. A foreign key must match a primary key in a specified table. Relational databases enforce this for us if we define the `foreign keys`.

In our example, every `shop_visit` record must link to a customer in the `customer` table.

So, what is the primary key of the `shop_visits` table? Every combination of `customer_id` and `shop_visit` is unique so we have a compound primary key; the combination of `customer_id` and `shop_visit` could be the primary key.

It is possible that a customer could visit twice on the same day, in which case our `shop_visits` table will not work as we have described it because we cannot have duplicate primary keys. It would be very inconvenient if we did have two `shop_visits` with the same key. How would we know which was which? Maybe there was a bigger charge for one than the other. Maybe what happened in those two visits had to happen in a particular sequence.

We should make the `shop_visits` column a timestamp to allow for multiple visits on the same day.

So what we have is valid, but since this book is recommending ways to make your databases work well, we will create a surrogate key for shop_visits too. Also, now that we're clear that we have a shop_visits table, we'll improve the naming a bit. This refactoring is important to keep the database design in line with the application we are building as we develop our understanding of it.

Table: customers

id	family_name	first_name	date_of_birth
53	Walters	Ann	1993-10-05
54	Bellamy	Jim	1962-05-21
55	Millward	Steph	1985-03-19

Table: shop_visits

id	customer_id	visit_date_time
237	53	2014-05-17 16:00:00
321	53	2014-07-23 09:15:30
239	53	2014-11-22 10:35:10
240	54	2013-12-05 09:35:25
322	55	2013-09-27 13:53:02
323	55	2014-06-26 11:55:20

A Tidier Version

The naming we are using for primary and foreign keys follows the standards used in *Agile Web Development with Rails 4*[14]. You don't have to name them this way, but it's a fine standard and worth following.

What we have now is a much easier structure to deal with. When Ann Walters gets married and changes her family name, we only have to update one record in the customer table. All shop visits still refer to the correct person with the correct name. There cannot be any ambiguity because there is only one record for Ann Walters. We also do not waste space by repeating the same names and dates of birth over and over again.

What we have described in this chapter is `Second Normal Form`.

Second Normal Form says that every row must have a unique key that distinguishes the row from every other row in the table. Then we must make sure that every other column in the table is dependent on that key, and not on something else.

This helped us to understand that we were looking at two things instead of one: `customers` and `shop_visits`. And this enabled us to get rid of duplication and makes it much easier to keep our data clean and tidy. It also helped us to understand the many ways that we can use this data.

The Whole Key and Nothing But The Key

If you have structured your data as we have described up to this point, then your database will already be healthier than most databases in use in the world today. What we have described so far is definitely beneficial. There are clear reasons why following the principles of First and Second Normal Forms is worthwhile, and I hope I have explained those.

You can go further, but we are already getting to the situations which are less common and where you might not want to restructure the database further even if you detect one of these situations. We will talk about `Third Normal Form` and mention some of the higher normal forms, but beyond that we have to construct very contrived examples to illustrate

14. See Bibliography [Ruby]

problems that we can fix with yet another Normal Form. This may sound like heresy to some database designers but, really, "You Ain't Gonna Need It". [15]

Let's look at the next case.

Links Within A Record

Here is a table that we might find in the membership database of a sailing club.

id	family_name	first_name	main_interest	locker	street_address	city	state	zip_code
108	Redding	Nadia	catamarans	F237	1203 Albert Parkway	Alexandria	VA	22376
109	Redding	Michael	catamarans	M234	1203 Albert Parkway	Alexandria	VA	22376
77	Hillman	Sunita	cruisers	F15	1943 Beveridge Street	Huntington	VA	22303
19	Chapman	Adrian	asymmetrics	M45	3702 52nd Street	Washington	DC	20007
214	Tinsley	Marcus	dinghies	M133	1906 Valley Drive	Brookmont	MD	20832
685	Willis	Alison	dinghies	F176	726 Hickory Drive	Rose Hill	VA	22323

This seems to follow all the rules we have described so far.

There is some duplication because Nadia and Michael live at the same address, so that appears twice. That isn't going to waste a huge amount of space in the database. If the two addresses are slightly different (maybe one of them writes it with the county included and one doesn't) and we send letters by post, they will still get there. If Nadia and Michael are mother and son, and Michael goes off to college and changes his address, this is easy: we just update the address fields in Michael's record. We can say that the address depends on, or belongs to, the member.

These addresses have ZIP Codes. The ZIP Code depends on the street address, city and state. Because the ZIP Code and the address are related, this means that we have some structure inside each record, and this structure is recording some extra information. If we wanted to, we could use this table to find the relationship between address and ZIP Code (but only for addresses of members of the sailing club).

If Adrian Chapman decides to leave the club, then we delete his record from the database. Let's assume no other member shares his address. So

---

15. This expression, often abbreviated to "YAGNI" (but not by me) is attributed to Kent Beck in *Extreme Programming Explained*. See Bibliography [Beck]

we have lost the information about Adrian Chapman, as we intended, but we have also lost the information that the address "3702 52nd Street, Washington, DC" belongs to ZIP Code "20007".

We should always be aware of the possibility of losing information, because that can often be a very bad thing. But, in this case, do we care? I don't think so. If we want to look up a ZIP Code we will go to the official source. There is unlikely to be any requirement to look in the membership database for the ZIP Codes for addresses of non-members. (In the real world, I would check with the users, of course. Just because I can't think of a requirement doesn't mean that there isn't one.)

To get this data into Third Normal Form we would have to separate addresses into another table, because Third Normal Form says that every column value must be dependent *only* on the primary key. In this case `zip_code` depends on `street_address`, `city` and `state`, as well as depending on the member's `id`.

This is very sensible. My address will continue to exist in the real world and have a ZIP Code whether I live there or not. It is clearly an object that is independent of me. At any given time (if I manage to avoid being homeless) there will be a relationship between me and my current, primary address.

Table: member					
id	family_name	first_name	main_interest	locker	address_id
108	Redding	Nadia	catamarans	F237	646
109	Redding	Michael	catamarans	M234	646
77	Hillman	Sunita	cruisers	F15	182
19	Chapman	Adrian	asymmetrics	M45	174
214	Tinsley	Marcus	dinghies	M133	98
685	Willis	Alison	dinghies	F176	328

Table: address				
id	street_address	city	state	zip_code
646	1203 Albert Parkway	Alexandria	VA	22376
182	1943 Beveridge Street	Huntington	VA	22303
174	3702 52nd Street	Washington	DC	20007
98	1906 Valley Drive	Brookmont	MD	20832
328	726 Hickory Drive	Rose Hill	VA	22323

This shows the club membership database converted to Third Normal Form. I must admit that I find this more pleasing than having members and addresses in one table, as we had before. However, this may be because of the many years I have spent normalizing databases. The important thing is not how I feel about it, but how well it suits its purpose. Let's see what happens when we consider how this database will be used.

When we add a new member, with the single table version, we just collect the fields from the screen and insert the record into the database. With the two-table (normalized) version, we must start a transaction, insert the address details capturing the `address id`, insert the member details linking to the address record we just inserted, and end the transaction. It isn't a big deal, but it is more code.

If we want to keep the `address` table free of duplicates then we must also check to see whether the address details are already there. If they are, then we link the member to the existing `address` record, if not then we insert a new `address` record and link to that. This is more functionality, and it's functionality that we could not do before, but it may not be necessary.

When we want to delete a member, with the single-table version, we just delete the record for that member. With the two-table version, we can just delete the member record too, but then we have an address sitting in the database with no member attached to it. We might re-use it later, but then we would have to do extra checking. If we want to keep the database clean, we will need to remember the `address id` from the member record, check whether that address is still being used by somebody else, and, if not, use the saved `address id` to delete the address.

When a member wants to update her address, with the single-table version, we just update the record for that member. With the two-table version, we create a new **address** record and update the **member** record to point to the new address. That's OK, but we now have, possibly a duplicated **address** record (if the member's new address was already in the database) and possibly a redundant address (if no-one else was sharing the member's old address). There's quite a bit of processing to sort that out.

For a sailing club database, which might have about 1,000 records, and would have fairly simple processing, the move from Second Normal Form to Third Normal Form is just not worthwhile. We have no interest in building up our own ZIP Code database, and it does cause extra work. In this case I would stick with Second Normal Form.

However, if we were looking at a telephone company's database, it could be a very different story. The major telephone companies each have millions of customers. It is quite likely that when one person closes an account at a particular address, the next person at that address will open an account with the same company. Because the landline is attached to the address, the address takes on much more importance to the telephone company, so in a similar situation for the telephone company, the Third Normal Form approach would probably be better.

The lesson we can learn from this is that there is not one right answer that applies to people and addresses; it depends on the ways in which the data will be used. The thought process that we use to check whether a database is in Third Normal Form is worthwhile because it prompts us to ask our users questions that will help us to understand their data better.

Third Normal Form says that every field in a record must depend on the primary key of that record and not on any other field in the record. If there is a relationship between non-key fields in a record then we lose that relationship if we delete the record. This may or may not be a problem. We need to be able to identify this type of situation. We can then decide whether this is important to our users. If it is important, then we should split the table into two, so that it is in Third Normal Form. If it isn't important then we may decide to leave it in Second Normal Form, and that is OK.

There are further Normal Forms, but we really don't need to worry about those. This may sound strange coming from someone who is so adamant about the necessity of being disciplined about database design. The thing is that the higher normal forms are so academic and apply to very, very few cases in the real world. The only examples I have ever seen were very contrived and I can think of more straightforward ways of modeling those situations.

If you are interested in these higher normal forms then you could look at the excellent, but very formal, discussion in *An Introduction to Database Systems*[16].

What Have We Learned?

We have now learned how to design a relational database. That's it. If you follow the principles described here you will have a well-structured database. You can apply these principles on the first iteration of your agile development and on every iteration. You do not have to design your whole database up front, in fact, if you do, then you will be wasting your time because your design will be wrong. Nobody is clever enough to get any serious application design completely right before building it. Building your database one step at a time you can keep it true to the needs of your users *and* keep your database design clean at every iteration. If you do that, your database will be better than almost every other database in existence.

So are we all done here? Well, you could work out the rest for yourself, but I'd like to offer you some more help. The next chapter shows you some typical patterns that will emerge in your data as you apply the principles we have covered already. At the end of the next chapter we give you a simple checklist to help keep your database in good shape. In the chapter after that we run through the first few iterations of a typical agile development project so that you can see how this works in practice.

---

16. See Bibliography [Date]

Chapter 2 - The Checklist

We are now going to look at some of the common patterns that arise in database designs, and at ways of representing them. We will end up with Third Normal Form structures, but we don't have to go through a big heavyweight process to get there.

I see normalization of relational databases as a checklist that helps to get the database into good shape. Good shape means a design that helps the developers and the users to avoid problems. You could apply a similar checklist to object design, or `XML` file design, or many other areas that we work in.

Normalization is often presented as a rigid process that fits into the bureaucratic `waterfall` methodologies. Working this way, teams of designers start with what they call a *conceptual* model, develop a *logical* model from that and then develop a *physical* model from that. You will hear these terms, but I'm not even going to explain them because they represent an approach that is costly and wasteful. Conceptual and logical models are always wrong; a physical model derived from such a logical model is also always wrong. No-one is clever enough to do all this up-front. There is a better way - let's explore it.

What we do is to work closely with the users, in an iterative process that reflects how we learn about the characteristics of the data and what the users want to do with it.

I often make sketches of parts of the database that are developed as we build each story. They get amended, crossed out, torn up and thrown away until we have something that accurately reflects the data in the story. The final one in each story is used to build the database and code for the current iteration.

Anything can happen to the database design from one iteration to the next. Sometimes the database design does not change. Usually, the changes are small and incremental, but the database design is the servant of the application we are building. It is not sacred, and the right thing to do, once in a while, when we realize we have gone down the wrong path, is to tear up the database design and start again.

The definition of the database with its tables and its primary and foreign keys is the only design we need. Tuning options, such as indexes, partitioning, and other physical storage options, do not disrupt the design. One of the fundamental principles of relational databases is that the physical storage is controlled separately from the logical structure. You do not have to change the way you access the database when you add a new index, for example.

There are often multiple teams using the databases we build. We may be building an Internet sales application, and we will be focused on making life easy for customers who want to buy our products. If we are very successful, the Finance Team will want to get data about what has been sold (and returned), and the Marketing Team will want to extract all kinds of data about our customers and what they buy. We might want to send data directly to our suppliers to reorder items before they are sold out.

Users of our database may use different tools from those we use to build the application, and they need an easy way to understand what is in the database. Good diagrams can help, especially if we have organized and named our data well, as we do, of course.

I do often use a low-cost database diagramming tool. I do not use it for designing the database - that design emerges from each story. I find the diagrams useful for communicating with other users of the database, but only when those diagrams are small. A **database schema** diagram that covers a wall of your offices and has a thousand tables is of no real use.

We have to be careful to avoid having two parallel realities: the database in the diagram and the database in the application. Fortunately, we can generate the diagram from the database.

The database design that is in the database is the real one. If a diagram helps us to visualize parts of the database, that can make it worth using. The tool must be our slave, not our master. In this book you will see some diagrams from the tool that I often use.

Let's remind ourselves of why we use the normalization design patterns:

- To enable straightforward navigation around the data model
- To remove duplication
- To give us more flexibility if we need to expand the data model later
- To make managing the data, and especially updating it, much less

Chapter 2 - The Checklist

likely to introduce errors
- To make the database run efficiently
- To make it easy to enforce some important integrity constraints, so that the database software keeps the data accurate for us
- To produce a design that is a good model of the real world.

The last point may not be obvious, but it is true. I used to think that data was infinitely variable in structure as well as content. I have been lucky to work with David Walker[17] for many years. David writes and publishes many papers on data management and data warehousing. In recent years I have been a regular reviewer for him. David asked me to review a draft white paper called *How Data Works*. My first reaction was: "this is silly; you can't just say how data works in a few pages." But I was wrong; this paper really does describe how data works.

You should read the whole paper, but one important aspect of it is the `Volume-Complexity Curve`. And to summarize this small part of the paper brutally, high volume data tends to have a very consistent structure whereas lower volume data often has a more complex and variable structure.

Relational databases are best suited to highly structured data, and this can be very high volume indeed. If we look at data from banking transactions, telephone call data records, `telematics` devices (delivering location and movement information from vehicles and ships) and pretty much any data from the `Internet-of-Things`, then we are looking at highly structured data.

A Third Normal Form representation of any of this data will organize the data into its separate objects, and enable us to identify each object and to record its relationships with other objects. There are large areas of overlap between database design and object design. This should not be surprising, since we are all trying to model the real world in ways that can be managed by computers, but it has been the subject of many heated arguments.

I'm all for peace.

Ruby on Rails is a good example of an object-oriented development language that recognizes the relational database as its friend. `ActiveRecord` is the `Object-Relational Mapping (ORM)` layer built into

---

17. http://datamgmt.com

Ruby on Rails and available in Ruby. Martin Fowler described and named this approach in *Patterns of Enterprise Application Architecture*[18] and David Heinemeier Hansson brought it to life in Ruby on Rails.

> "David Heinemeier Hansson, of Active Record fame, has always argued that if you are writing an application backed by a relational database you should damn well know how a relational database works." [19]

I couldn't agree more. For many, many applications, including those built with object-oriented tools, relational databases are the best way of storing the data. I hope this book is a relatively painless way to get to know how a relational database works, and how to use it with your favorite application development tools.

Let's take a look at the way Ruby on Rails describes relationships between tables in a relational database. I find this a good way of describing the structures we use, and it fits well with the database design principles we have already described.

Ruby on Rails classifies **associations**, the relationships between tables, as:

- has_one
- has_many
- belongs_to
- has_and_belongs_to_many

Has_and_belongs_to_many may seem to be a bit of a mouthful at first, but it is accurate and, in fact, these four ways of describing relationships between tables are a very neat summary of what we need. It isn't difficult once you get familiar with it.

These associations assume that the relationship has a direction, and this is how relational databases describe relationships too. There are many metaphors used to describe such relationships: parent-child, component-sub-component, owner-thing_owned. Actually I've never heard people talk about the "thing_owned," but people do talk about owners, and "has_" and "belongs_" suggest this metaphor. In relational databases the relationship is implemented by the Primary Key at the

---

18. See Bibliography [Fowler]
19. http://java.dzone.com/articles/martin-fowler-orm-hate

parent end matching the Foreign Key at the child end. Some examples should make this clearer.

Has_many

What you will see most frequently is the `has_many` type of relationship.

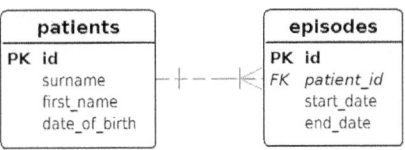

This shows a database that stores details of hospital patients and episodes of treatment in the hospital. This diagramming style is common in tools used for documenting database designs. These diagrams are useful because they do tell us a lot in a simple picture. What this one tells us is:

- There is a table called `patients` and another one called `episodes`.
- Both tables have a Primary Key called `id`.
- The `episodes` table has a Foreign Key called `patient_id`.
- There is a relationship between these two tables.
- Every row in the `patients` table has one or more rows in the `episodes` table. The `crow's foot` (the little 3-pronged thing at the episode end of the relationship) indicates the `many` end of the relationship.

In the diagramming tool (but sadly not in the diagram itself) we can see that the way these two tables are linked is by the Primary Key of the `patients` table matching the Foreign Key of the `episodes` table. It would be easy to guess that this is the relationship, but guesswork and database application development do not make a happy couple. In this case we have followed the Ruby on Rails naming conventions for the Primary Key and Foreign Key so this indicates the relationship: `patients.id` matches `episodes.patient_id`. The "dot" notation is widely used. In this case it means <table>.<column> so `patient_id` is a column in the table `episodes`.

The way Ruby on Rails names things is an example of `Convention over`

Configuration. The idea of Convention over Configuration is that if you follow some consistent patterns in naming objects and in structuring your application, you can free yourself to think about the important things, like your users' requirements. The conventions you follow mean that you always solve similar problems in the same way. You could choose the flexibility of configuring every solution in a unique way, but this flexibility, which sounds attractive, just adds to your workload and distracts you from more important things. Flexibility is not always a benefit. Convention over Configuration is something that you'll keep running across if you work with Ruby on Rails and other well-designed approaches. In particular, Convention over Configuration applies to relational databases. The database vendors have given us many options that we must refuse to use. The simple principles of relational databases enable us to apply Convention over Configuration to make our applications simple and robust.

Referring to Ruby on Rails conventions:

- The relationship from patients to episodes is described as patient has_many episodes.
- The reverse relationship, from episodes to patients, is described as episode belongs_to patient.

Of course, you can use relational databases with most programming languages. The reason we refer to the Ruby on Rails and ActiveRecord approach so much is because it is a very nice way of building the interface between the database and the application.

Chapter 2 - The Checklist

Table: patients			
id	family_name	first_name	date_of_birth
263	Smith	Julia	2001-02-15
736	Jones	Michael	1946-12-03

Table: episodes			
id	patient_id	start_date	end_date
1057	263	2014-03-21	2014-03-23
2883	263	2014-04-21	2014-04-21
1276	736	2012-06-15	2012-06-15
2784	736	2013-02-12	2013-06-18
3321	736	2014-10-23	2014-11-02
4354	736	2014-12-05	2014-12-06

We said that there is at least one episode for every patient. This suggests that a person who has never had an episode is not considered to be a patient. That could be a valid rule for the way the hospital applications, and the hospital database, work.

However, this is not always the case; in the has_many type of relationship, many can mean "zero or more." So the parent may have no children. However, the child must always have a parent, exactly one parent. (Parent:child is commonly used terminology to describe relationships between tables, but it isn't actually a very good analogy, so best not to think about it too much.)

An example of a one-to-many relationship, where the many could be zero or more, would be insurance_policy to claim. Most policies would have no claims. Some policies would have one claim and a few would have more than one claim. So policy to claim is a has_many relationship where many means zero or more. The claim must have a policy though. I don't know of any insurance company that will accept a claim without a policy, and that rule must be reflected in the database that supports the claims system.

Has_one

The has_one type of relationship is actually quite rare. If there is a strict one-to-one relationship between two objects, are they actually separate objects? Sometimes it does make sense to model them as one object; sometimes it is better to model them as two.

Let's look at an insurance example again. Suppose our car insurance policies are always one car per policy. So we could store the car details with the policy as shown here:

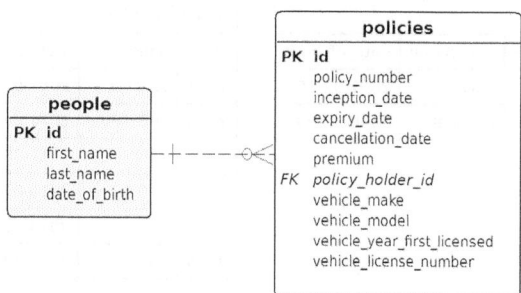

This would work, and might well be our first iteration, but it doesn't seem right. I am thinking of a vehicle as being a different object from a policy, not just attributes in a policy. I felt the need to prefix the vehicle fields with "vehicle_" because they are not describing a policy; they are clearly describing a vehicle. I therefore want to make the vehicle a separate table. The data model is supposed to be a representation of the real world, and in the real world vehicles exist independently of policies.

Also this is an example of moving from Second to Third Normal Form. This particular vehicle belongs to the policy and therefore it does depend on the policy `id` (the Primary Key) of the `policy` table. But the `vehicle_make`, `vehicle_model` and `vehicle_year_first_licensed` depend on the `vehicle_license_number`. I could go to a website, look up the car using its license number and find out the make, model and year first licensed. The license number is therefore a natural key for the vehicle.

Ultimately though, the data model depends upon the stories we are implementing. We should not guess what complications might arise in future. Relational database models are easy to change and we should always be prepared to migrate from the model that supports the stories so far implemented to the model we need when we include the next story. We should follow the rules of data normalization, as described in *Chapter 1 - Learning to Drive Your Database on page 32*, but we should not build some idealized version of the real world.

Chapter 2 - The Checklist

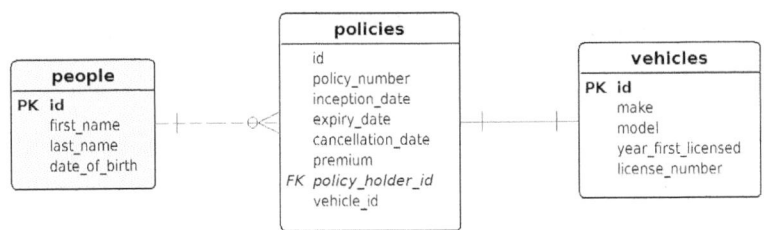

Whether we would build it this way or not, this shows `vehicles` as a separate table with a one-to-one relationship between `vehicles` and `policies`. If this meets the needs of the insurance company, then it is fine. Each table is properly structured and the relationships between them are implemented using primary and foreign keys, as they must be.

Notice that in this version the line showing the relationship between `policies` and `vehicles` does not have a crow's foot at either end, it just has a single bar across the relationship line at each end. This indicates a one-to-one relationship.

Belongs_to

We have shown the `belongs_to` type of relationship as the reverse of `has_many` and the reverse of `has_one`. The entity that is described as `belongs_to` is the table with the Foreign Key, pointing back to the parent entity. The one described as `has_many` or `has_one` contains the Primary Key that matches the Foreign Key in the child table.

Has_and_belongs_to_many

`Has_and_belongs_to_many` is also known as a `many-to-many` relationship. We often find situations where we need this kind of relationship.

Those of us who use iTunes playlists are very familiar with the many-to-many relationship. A playlist can have many songs, or course, but the really useful feature of playlists is that a song can be on many playlists, as shown below.

Let's look more closely at some of the data in this structure. I have three playlists:

- Nice jazz, for when I just want to relax and not concentrate too hard
- Saxophone solos, for when I want to hear the experts play what I am trying to learn
- Trumpet stars, just because they are brilliant

playlists	
id	playlist
23	Nice Jazz
97	Saxophone solos
64	Trumpet stars

playlists_songs	
playlist_id	song_id
97	644
97	372
97	549
97	723
23	723
23	644
23	426
23	372
23	295
23	483
23	549
64	723
64	483

songs		
id	artist	song
723	Miles Davis	Blue in Green
644	John Coltrane	My Favorite Things
426	Abdullah Ibrahim	Water From An Ancient Well
372	Stan Getz	Stella by Starlight
295	Ellis Marsalis	Delilah
483	Dusko Goykovich	Simona
549	Wayne Shorter	Virgo
133	Gato Barbieri	Circulos

Each list has several songs (they could have just one, or even none, if they are lists I have defined but not added any songs to yet). And each song can be on zero or more lists. *Blue in Green* by Miles Davis is on all three lists, *Virgo* by Wayne Shorter is on two lists, *Delilah* by Ellis Marsalis is just on one list and *Circulos* by Gato Barbieri is not on any playlist. If you look at the way the `ids` match, you can see how adding a song to `playlists_songs` is not constrained by whether that song is on any other playlist. Easy, isn't it?

Of course, the application which manages my playlists makes it even easier: I just drag songs to playlists. But whatever that application is doing to add an entry to playlists_songs, it isn't doing anything to songs or playlists.

Back in the world of the insurance company, if we think carefully about (or get our users to explain) the policies-to-vehicles relationship we find that this is a many-to-many relationship too.

A policy may have only one vehicle at a time, but people do change their cars, so over the life of the policy there may well be more than one car covered by the policy. So one policy can have many cars. Also, sometimes one policyholder will sell a car to another policyholder with the same insurance company. In this case a car has more than one policy over time.

The insurance company must keep a record of all cars that have been associated with all policies because claims are often made late, and the company must be able to go back through the records to confirm which car was covered on which policy when.

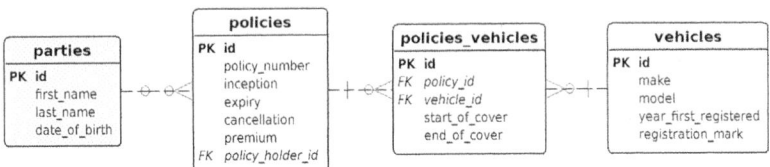

This diagram shows how we would implement this many-to-many relationship in the database. There are a few things to notice:

- We have introduced a new table policies_vehicles that holds the relationships between policies and vehicles.
- There is a one-to-many relationship from policies to the policies_vehicles table, so that each policy can have many relationships to vehicles.
- There is also a one-to-many relationship from vehicles to the policies_vehicles table, so that each vehicle can have many relationships to policies.
- Every relationship must point to an existing policy record and to an existing vehicle record.
- We have added two timestamps to the policies_vehicles table: start_of_cover and end_of_cover. These enable us to see which cars were covered on which policies when. These fields belong to the

relationship, not to the `policy` nor to the `vehicle`.

The Database Design Checklist

If you have read this far, you should now have a good idea of how relational databases work. This will be reinforced, in *Chapter 3 - An Agile Database - Step by Step on page 70*, and by later chapters that describe accessing the data.

We mentioned at the beginning of this chapter that relational database design has been, and continues to be, a very bureaucratic process in many organizations. This really is not necessary. When you understand the principles, you can get to a good design very quickly and adapt it to changing needs without turning the world upside down.

Rather than slavishly going through stages of conceptual, logical and physical design, as well as the normal forms, I find it more effective to go straight to a physical design and then run through this checklist for each table.

The Checklist

1. Is every column atomic? (No compound fields.)
2. What is the Primary Key?
3. Does every other column depend on the Primary Key?
4. Does any column depend on another column that is not the Primary Key?
5. Are there any repeating groups?
6. Does every column have the most restrictive data-type possible for the data it holds?
7. Does the name of the column accurately describe the data that will be stored in it?
8. Are Foreign Keys defined in all cases where there is a relationship?
9. Are nullable columns genuinely OK to be null? This applies to data columns and to Foreign Keys.

The disciplines are worthwhile, and this is a quicker way to apply them. The checklist covers not only normalization, but also some other sadly neglected disciplines such as:

Chapter 2 - The Checklist

- naming things helpfully (*Chapter 5 - Naming Things on page 114*)
- using the appropriate data-types (*Chapter 6 - Data Types on page 125*)
- not allowing nulls in columns that are actually mandatory (*Chapter 7 - Nulls on page 150*)

After a while these become second nature and you automatically design your databases this way. But the checklist is still useful. Just as the pilot of an airliner, even though he or she knows very well how to fly, follows a checklist on every flight[20] so we too should follow this checklist for every table in every database we design.

If you follow this checklist your databases will work much better than almost everyone else's.

---

20. In fact the pilot follows various checklists depending on the situation, see *The Checklist Manifesto: How To Get Things Right*; Bibliography [Gawande]

Chapter 3 - An Agile Database - Step by Step

This chapter includes a little play about developing an insurance claims system. It shows you a practical demonstration of building a database through a series of iterations, as part of the development of an application that uses this database.

You will learn about the practical application of the ideas we have covered in the first two chapters. You will see how a database design can grow from the stories we develop with our users, and how the design can be refined at each iteration.

To keep things simple in this chapter we use Ruby on Rails **migrations** to show what is changing in the database in each iteration. The intention is to show you what a migration is before we get into the syntax of SQL. In *Chapter 4 - Database Migrations In SQL on page 97* we will see how to build migrations using SQL. SQL will work with any relational database and no matter what programming languages you are using.

The database design should grow and change with the application design, both always driven by the users' needs. **Migrations** are important because they give you a way to make these frequent changes while protecting the integrity of your database design.

The development team has been asked to build this system because the company has outgrown its spreadsheet solution and a promised new system has been put on hold indefinitely. The development team expects to build the solution using Ruby on Rails and a relational database: PostgreSQL.

Cast of characters:

- Annie: Developer. Speaker for development team (on this occasion)
- Bal: Developer
- Carla: Developer
- Doug: Claims Manager
- Ella: Actuarial analyst and spreadsheet wizard
- Faisal: Claims Handler
- Gina: the IT boss (not present)

Chapter 3 - An Agile Database - Step by Step

Iteration 1

Annie: Hello Doug, hello Faisal, hello Ella. Thanks for taking the time to talk to us about helping you with the Claims system. Bal and Carla will be working with me to build the system for you, so it's best if we all talk to one another so that we're all heading in the same direction.

As we mentioned last time, we'll build the system in stages. You'll probably hear us call these stages *iterations* - if we start using terminology that doesn't make sense, please ask what we're talking about. I expect we'll have to ask you about some insurance terminology too.

So, maybe you could just start telling us what you do with claims.

Doug: Yes, well I hope you can help us. We went through it all with the SnakeOilSystems (**SOS**) guys, but frankly, we didn't get much out of that. It has never worked properly.

Annie: Well we'll try to do better, and we'll show you what we're doing at each stage so you can keep us on track if we start going off in the wrong direction.

Doug: OK. We do need something, because with the spreadsheet Ella is taking nearly the whole month to produce the monthly report.

Annie: Let's see if we can fix that for you then. So, where do we start? Maybe you can tell us how a claim first appears.

Doug: Right, so the first important thing we have to capture is **FNOL**.

Bal: Sorry Doug, what's "effnol"?

Doug: [Raising his eyebrows.] Yes we have our jargon too. **FNOL** is First Notification of Loss. It's the first time we hear about a claim.

Annie: And that can be by phone? Letter? Do people claim by email as well?

Doug: Well, they can, but we want them to call us as soon as possible. We want to get control of the process. You know, someone will turn up with a breakdown truck and offer to take care of everything and then we have trouble controlling the costs. So, on the website it says "Call us first, we want to help." Then we get our own people involved.

Annie: I see. So you've had the First Notification of Loss, what happens then?

Doug: We need to find out if the claimant is our policy holder or a third party. We need car license numbers for any cars involved. We need to find out what the incident was and when it happened. The caller usually just starts talking about the claim - it often doesn't make much sense because they may be a bit shaken up by a crash or something, but we always capture what they say - we can fill in the details later.

We need to find out what they are claiming for, it could be damage to vehicles, or property, it could be bodily injury (that's where we can have really big claims), it could be theft, it might just be a windshield. We have to get everything under the right Claim Heads.

Then we need to make sure the PH[21] was covered at the time.

Bal: Do the people in the call center have a checklist?

Doug: Yes, and it's on the web site for customers too.

Annie: Right. Bal: can you get that page up? Would that be useful?

Doug: Yes, or you could look at the spreadsheet, it's all in there. But there's lots of other stuff in the spreadsheet too.

Bal: I've found the checklist. This is what it says:

- *Other drivers' details.* Make sure you get the name, phone number, email and address of anyone else involved in the accident. Call us as soon as possible.

---

21. "PH" = policy holder. Like many real users, Doug is addicted to abbreviations. The team is being sensitive about not interrupting him all the time, but they will come back to confirm their understanding later.

- *Stay calm and polite. Get all the details you can, but do not admit liability.*
    - License numbers of vehicles involved.
    - Insurance company and policy number from all the drivers involved.
    - Contact details of any witnesses.
    - Use your smartphone to take photos of the cars involved, before they are moved, if possible. Also take photos of the accident scene, any road signs and any damaged property.
    - Count number of passengers in each vehicle; note how old you think each one is.
    - Note any injuries to people.
    - Note any damage to vehicles and property.
    - Make a note of the weather conditions and time of day. Is it wet, icy, dark?
    - If you can, make a sketch of the accident while it is fresh in your mind.
    - If the police are involved, ask for the incident reference number.

Doug: The Claim Handler enters what he can in the SOS system, but he also has to take notes because SOS doesn't have fields for everything, and sometimes the system is so slow that we have to just write it down and enter it afterwards.

The Handler has to copy it all into the spreadsheet anyway. The claimant has to send us photos and drawings separately, if they have them.

Then another Handler has to go through it all and usually get back to the claimant for more details. When people first make a claim they are often very stressed, and if they call from the scene of the incident, then they may have to get any injuries attended to, get the vehicles moved, maybe talk to the police.

Then we can start thinking about reserves. There may be a hire car, repairs, legal fees, doctor's consultations. Do you want to go into that now?

Annie: Well, we will need to go into all that, of course. Maybe we can go over what we've talked about so far and then work out what we can do in our first iteration so that we have something to show you next week. We can then see if that is on the right lines, make any fixes and move on to the next bit. Is that OK with you?

Doug: Sure. We're keen to see something concrete out of this.

Annie: OK, good. We probably have some questions on what you've said so far. Anyone?

Carla: [writing on whiteboard] We seem to have a few things to record: CLAIM, the fact there has been a claim; INCIDENT, the incident that gave rise to the claim; POLICY, the policy the claim relates to; CLAIMANT, the claimant (who may or may not be the policy holder). Oh yes can I check that "PH" means policy holder?

Doug: Yes, that's right.

Carla: There's also a CLAIM HANDLER, more than one on each claim, maybe?

Doug: Yes, always, well, nearly always.

Bal: You also mentioned Claim Heads, Doug. What does that mean?

Doug: Claim Heads are very important. Every reserve and every payment has to be under a Claim Head, and we have to know whether it's for the PH or a TP.

Bal: TP?

Doug: Yeah, sorry, that's Third Party.

Annie: You mentioned that this all gets captured in SOS, but you have a spreadsheet too.

Faisal: Yes, I spend my whole life entering data that I've entered somewhere else already.

Doug: That's a sore point. Originally SOS said they could build all the Claims functionality.

Chapter 3 - An Agile Database - Step by Step

Faisal: But now we have to type all this stuff in and, as far as I can see, it just goes into a black hole.

Annie: So I understand that the SOS Claims functionality is on hold indefinitely, and that is where we come in.

Faisal: Are we going to have to enter everything three times now?

Annie: That would be a big mistake in my opinion. We'll do our best to make sure you don't. We can always extract data from our system to send to SOS if they really need it. I'll talk to Gina to make sure that's clear.

What we need to do now is to get some "stories" written down and work out which we are going to do first.

So let's start with FNOL.

Annie writes on the whiteboard:

"I, as a Claims Handler, want an easy way to capture the data from the First Notification of Loss (FNOL), so that we can start the claim process for a customer."

Annie: As I explained, Doug, we write it this way to identify who needs the functionality, what it is, and why it is needed. So does that look right?

Faisal: Well, it's a very short description, but it's right as far as it goes.

Doug: Yeah, the Claims Handler needs it, but I need to see this too.

Annie: How about if we write another story for you to cover what you need to see as a result of capturing the FNOL data? I guess you don't actually take these calls do you? You need to manage the process, right?

Doug: Yes, that's right, it's the Claim Handlers who do this.

Annie: What about the "so that..." part, can we make that stronger.

Faisal: I'd say, "so that we capture some key information at the earliest opportunity in the claim process."

Doug: Yes, that's better, but we need to say what that key information is.

Faisal: The trouble is that the caller may be very stressed. We obviously need something to identify them: name or license number or Policy number (but they probably don't know their policy number). We usually can see the number they are calling from, but it might be a phone that they have borrowed from someone else.

Annie: OK, I understand, we get what information we can, but we have to accept incomplete information at this point. I've changed the "so that..." part to what you suggested. Now we can use the list of things you want to capture to build the acceptance criteria.

Annie writes on the whiteboard:

Must be able to capture:

- *First Notification of Loss (date & time)*
- *Details of caller*
    - *Family name*
    - *First name*
    - *Telephone number*
    - *Email address*
    - *Is the caller the policy holder?*
    - *Was the caller the driver?*
    - *Policy number*
    - *License number of vehicle*
    - *Postal address*
    - *Number of passengers*
    - *For each passenger:*
        - *Any injuries?*
        - *Approximate age*
    - *Description of damage to vehicle*
- *Details of other driver(s) (There may be more than one.)*
    - *Family name*
    - *First name*
    - *Telephone number*
    - *Email address*

Chapter 3 - An Agile Database - Step by Step

- - Name of insurance company
    - Policy number
    - License number of vehicle
    - Postal address
    - Number of passengers
    - Ages of passengers
    - For each passenger:
      - Any injuries?
      - Approximate age
    - Description of damage to vehicle
- Details of witnesses (There may be more than one.)
  - Family name
  - First name
  - Telephone number
  - Email address
  - Postal address
- Date and time of incident
- Property damage
- Police reference
- Photos to follow?
- Sketch to follow?
- Weather conditions

Doug: If we get all of that we'll be doing really well.

Faisal: Some of it needs to be free text, because claimants do ramble on sometimes.

Annie: From what you've said, none of this is mandatory. We need to capture whatever they can tell us and accept the notification whatever is missing.

Faisal: Yeah, but we have to have something to let us get back to them.

Annie: OK, so that's one of our acceptance criteria: we must be able to capture whatever they tell us, no matter which bits are missing. Is that right?

Doug: Yes, I'm afraid so.

Meanwhile Bal has written each data item to be captured on a separate post-it note.

Annie: OK, so Bal has made all these post-it notes, let's imagine that the left side of the whiteboard is your screen and see how you'd like the fields laid out.

There is then a discussion with several people getting up to shuffle things around on the whiteboard. When it seems to have stopped changing, Bal takes a photo with his smartphone.

Carla has written the first story on an index card, with the first acceptance criterion on the back.

Carla: Can we see if we can get any more acceptance criteria?

Doug: I need to be able to see what the Claims Handlers have entered.

Carla: OK, that's another story.

She picks up a blank index card and starts writing:

Carla: "I, as the Claims Manager, want to be able to see all the claims data that has been captured, so that..." Doug, can you finish that for us?

Doug: So that I can check that these guys are doing their job! No, just kidding. Um... "so that I can assess the claims volume for the day, and how much follow-up we will need to do."

Carla writes this on the card.

Carla: Does the system allocate a claim number at this stage?

Doug: Yes, and we'll need a different range so that we can tell which system they were entered in.

Carla: Do we need to migrate the existing claims into the new system?

Chapter 3 - An Agile Database - Step by Step

Doug: If it works, yes. Sorry, I'm sure you guys will do a good job, but we've had a lot of promises and two failed claims systems so far.

Annie: We understand. We don't expect you to take anything on trust, so we'll show you what we're doing every week and hopefully we'll all get more confident as we go along.

Doug: Sure. Well, it will be nice to see what's happening.

Carla: Are the claims numbers, just numbers? I mean, do they have a prefix, like the policy numbers, for example?

Doug: No, they are just six-digit numbers. The current system is up to nearly 003000.

Carla: Let's go back to the list of fields we need to capture and get some acceptance criteria for those. **FNOL**: that's a date and time?

Doug: Yes, to the nearest minute.

Carla: We can put that on the form automatically when the handler brings up the screen.

Faisal: Yes, but we have to be able to change it. What if we're entering something from notes taken on paper?

Carla: Well, it would be nice to eliminate that all together, but we can make it so that you can adjust the date and time.

Faisal: Yes, please.

Carla: Family name of caller. Can we say that's mandatory?

Faisal: I wish we could, but actually, no.

Carla: OK.

The team works through the list of fields, finding out whatever constraints can be applied to each one and writing acceptance criteria to describe them.

* * * *

After the meeting, Annie, Bal and Carla decide that the first iteration can provide the forms to enter the **FNOL** data and store this data in a database. They can then run queries to show that the data is present in the database and can be accessed.

Carla sketches out the database.

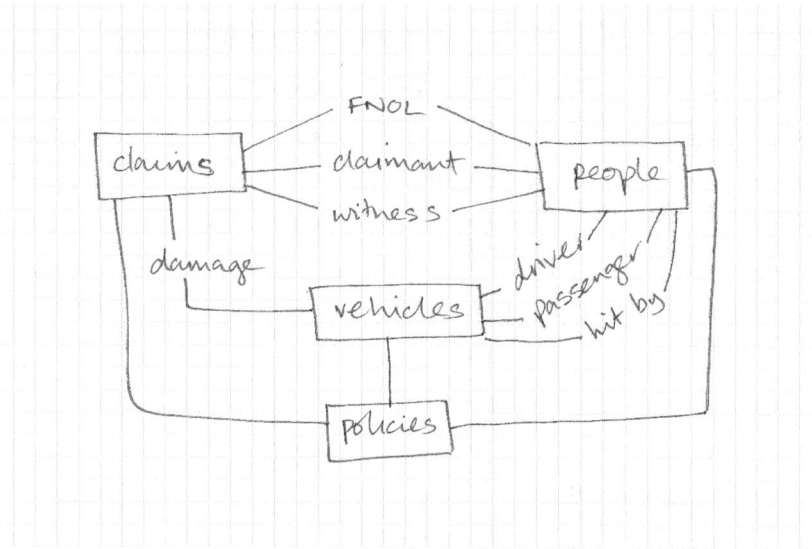

Carla has clearly done this before...but has she got carried away?

Carla: It's only four tables, and some of them won't have many columns yet, but there are quite a few relationships.

Bal: Did you get all that from what Doug said? We have to remember to implement only what we've been asked for, not what we think we might need.

Carla: [smiling] Yeah, OK, you're right. Doug didn't say anything about people being hit by cars, but it does happen doesn't it? We should ask him about it next time, but it shouldn't go into this iteration. Are we all happy that there are four main entities: claims, vehicles, people and policies?

Bal: Well, there are different kinds of people: the person making the call, the claimant (who may be the same person), the policy holder (who may be the same person), plus third parties (who could be other drivers, passengers, or witnesses). So you've put them all as people because...well, they are people, and each person may have several roles, and be linked to other entities.

Carla: Yes, it is a judgment call, so it's right to question it. Looking at the checklist they use, the claims team members capture a lot of the same things about each person, so we can show that on one form in the application. We can then link each person to the claim and show their role on the link. People will be linked to vehicles, and some will be linked to the policies as well. We need to come back to policies, by the way.

Bal: Yes, it makes sense to have an object called person. So what are you thinking about policies?

Carla: There's a big difference between our policies and the policies that third parties hold with other insurers. We know a lot more about our policies. For third party policies probably the most we will get will be the name of the insurance company and maybe the policy number. I guess they will want to refer to all sorts of things about our policy: when it expires, what level of cover they have, excess, replacement car. But, I'm guessing again. These are things we must ask Doug but they won't be in this iteration. For now, the only thing we need to capture is the policy number.

Bal: FNOL is different from claimant and witness, isn't it? A claim can have only one first notifier but it can have several claimants and several witnesses ... if they're lucky.

Carla: Yes, that's right. Let's make sure we model it that way.

Bal: OK, that all makes sense to me. Shall we do the Rails scaffolds?

Bal and Carla work on the Rails scaffolding to define the data model and give them a basic application that they can refine. Here is what they come up with:

download: scaffold_iteration_1.sh

```
rails generate scaffold Person \
  family_name:string \
  first_name:string \
  telephone_number:string \
  email_address:string \
  address_line_1:string \
  address_line_2:string \
  city:string \
  state:string \
  zip_code:string \
  date_of_birth:date \
  approximate_age:integer \
  name_of_insurance_company:string \
  policy_number:string

rails generate scaffold Policy \
  person:belongs_to \
  policy_number:string

rails generate scaffold Claim \
  policy:belongs_to \
  person:belongs_to \
  first_notification_of_loss:timestamp \
  date_and_time_of_incident:timestamp \
  police_reference:string \
  photos_to_follow:boolean \
  sketch_to_follow:boolean \
  description_of_weather:string \
  description_of_incident:string \
  description_of_property_damage:string

rails generate scaffold Vehicle \
  policy:belongs_to \
  license_number:string \
  state_where_licensed:string

rails generate scaffold Claimant \
  claim:belongs_to \
  person:belongs_to

rails generate scaffold Witness \
  claim:belongs_to \
  person:belongs_to

rails generate scaffold Driver \
  vehicle:belongs_to \
  person:belongs_to \
  from_date_time:timestamp \
  to_date_time:timestamp

rails generate scaffold Passenger \
  vehicle:belongs_to \
  person:belongs_to \
  from_date_time:timestamp \
```

Chapter 3 - An Agile Database - Step by Step

```
    to_date_time:timestamp

rails generate scaffold Damage \
    vehicle:belongs_to \
    claim:belongs_to \
    description:string
```

Bal and Carla have decided which fields belong in each table and given them appropriate data-types. They have also defined the relationships with the `belongs_to` method.

Carla has created the development **PostgreSQL** database, run the scaffold scripts and run the Rails command to create the database tables:

```
    rake db:migrate
```

Carla then uses a database diagramming tool to examine the database they have created and show the database structure as a diagram. Carla uses the Datanamic tool[22], but there are many alternatives.

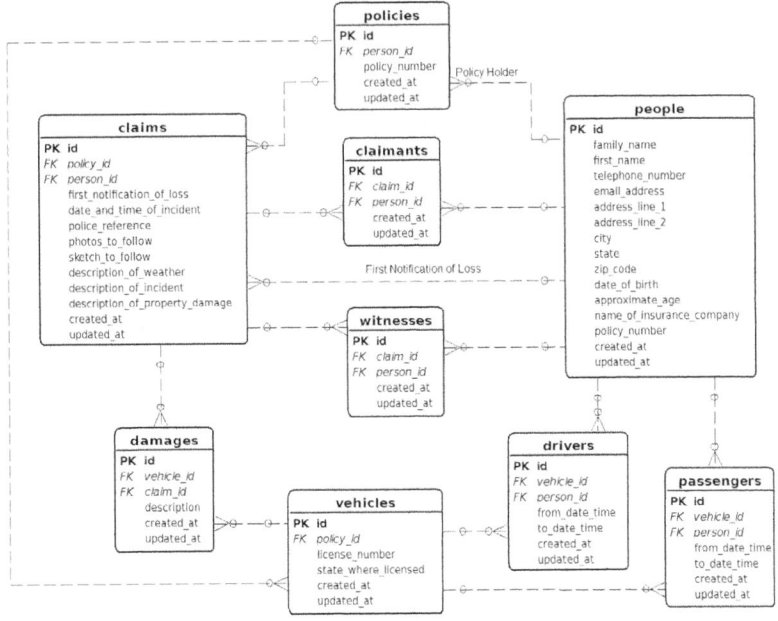

Bal: *[Looking at the data model diagram] Why do you do that?*

---

22. http://www.datanamic.com

Carla: The diagram? Don't you like it?

Bal: I kind of like your drawing better

Carla: Thanks, but that was just a sketch without the detail. Gina told us that other people will use this database. The policy system will look up claims here, especially when it is doing renewals. And the Customer Portal will let customers see some of the data too. And the Tableau[23] guys will do reports for Finance and for the actuaries so it's useful for them to see how the database works without having to look at our code. They can look at the code if they want, but not many of them understand Ruby, or Rails.

Carla: Will you run through the database checklist with me?

Bal: Sure.

Carla: OK, `policy` table first:

- Is every column atomic? Yes, there aren't any compound fields.
- What is the Primary Key? `id`
- Does every other column depend on the Primary Key? `Policy_number` belongs to `policy` and there had better be an exact one-to-one relationship between `id` and `policy_number`, so Yes. The timestamp columns from Rails always depend on the `id` of the table they are in, so they are OK too.
- Does any column depend on another column that is not the Primary Key? We're only looking at `policy_number` and that is OK.
- Are there any repeating groups? No
- Does every column have the most restrictive possible data-type for the data it holds? We need to limit the size of the `policy_number` column to ten characters. Can you fix that now, Bal?

Bal: Sure.

Bal generates a new Rails migration:

---

23. Tableau is a Data Visualization (reporting) tool. See http://www.tableau.com

Chapter 3 - An Agile Database - Step by Step

```
rails generate migration limit_policy_number_size
```

and edits it to look like this:

download: LimitPolicyNumberSize.rb

```
class LimitPolicyNumberSize < ActiveRecord::Migration
  def change
    change_column :policies, :policy_number, :string, limit: 10
  end
end
```

and runs the Rails command to migrate the database:

```
rake db:migrate
```

Bal: Done.

Carla: Thanks Bal. The other columns are fine: `id` is integer and the timestamps are timestamps.

- *Does the name of the column accurately describe the data that will be stored in it?* `policy_number` *sounds good to me.*
- *Are Foreign Keys defined in all cases where there is a relationship? A policy belongs to a person - the Policy Holder - so we have the Foreign Key* `person_id`.
- *Are nullable columns genuinely OK to be null? Check data columns and Foreign Keys.*
  - `id, created_at` *and* `updated_at` *are all managed by Rails and are not null.*
  - *Even* `policy_number` *may be null. We might have the policy holder details, but not the policy number.*
  - *We have to make the* `person_id` *optional, even though it's a Foreign Key to* `People`, *because they told us that we may not even know the Policy Holder.*

Bal and Carla work through the checklist for the other tables. They identify a few more cases where stronger data-types are needed. They also notice some areas that they expect to change. However, the database design stands as a suitable model for the first iteration.

We'll just eavesdrop on the discussion for the `people` and `claimants` tables.

Carla: OK, the people table:

- *Is every column atomic? Yes.*
- *What is the Primary Key?* id *generated by Rails, it's also necessary because there is no other reliable primary key for a person.*
- *Does every other column depend on the Primary Key? [checks each column] Yes.*
- *Does any column depend on another column that is not the Primary Key? The* approximate_age *and the* date_of_birth *are obviously linked. But I don't think we'd have both for one person. The person making the first notification of loss may estimate the ages of some of the people involved, but if we get the actual date of birth, I guess we calculate the age from that.*

Bal: You said "I guess" again...

Carla: Yes, and that means we have to check with Doug and his team to find out what they actually do.

- *Continuing with: "Does any column depend on another column which is not the Primary Key?" The ZIP Code and address are related. Are we going to do ZIP Code look-up? We need to check.*
- *Are there any repeating groups? No, that's fine.*
- *Does every column have the most restrictive data-type for the data it holds?*
  - telephone_number *should be limited. How do they enter them? Numbers only? With international dialing code? We'll have to check. If it's numbers only we could make it a* bigint *(*integer *is ten digits, and that isn't enough). Otherwise it has to be a* string. *Do we have a standard way of doing this?*

Bal: Unfortunately not.

Carla: OK, we'll have to check that.

- - `Email_address`: *well, it has to be a string, but we do have standard validation for email addresses.*
  - *Address and ZIP Code. We have to check if they want to do ZIP Code look-up. For this iteration we are OK.* `zip_code` *can't be more than five characters, so we can limit that.*
  - `Date_of_birth` *is a date already, but there are some constraints on that. We need to check if they have standards. The* `people` *table could hold information about babies and very old people as passengers, so it should probably be something like "a date that gives an age between 0 and 120 on the day of the incident." We do need to check though.*
  - `Name_of_insurance_company`. *This could be any insurance company; we'll have to check what the maximum length is.*
  - `Policy_number` *is the policy number (one of ours or from some other insurer). Again we'll need to check what the maximum can be.*
- *Does the name of the column accurately describe the data that will be stored in it? I'm happy with those, are you?*

Bal: Yes, sensible names as usual.

Carla: OK, thanks.

- *Are Foreign Keys defined in all cases where there is a relationship?*
  - *A person may have any or all of the following relationships:*
    - *First_notification_of_loss (the person as notifier)*
    - *Claimant*
    - *Witness*
    - *Policy*
    - *Driver*
    - *Passenger*

These are all relationships from `person` *so* `person.id` *is the Primary Key and the Foreign Keys have to be at the other end. We'll check each of those tables when we get to them.*

- *Are nullable columns genuinely OK to be null? Check data columns and Foreign Keys.*
    - *The users have said that any of the data can be missing, so this is going to be quite loose.*
    - *id is the Primary Key, so not null.*
    - *last_name can be null, hopefully not, but it could be.*
    - *first_name could be null.*
    - *telephone_number could be null.*
    - *email_address could be null.*
    - *Address could be null, so that's address_line_1, address_line_2, city, state and zip_code, all nullable.*
    - *date_of_birth could be null.*
    - *approximate_age could be null.*
    - *name_of_insurance_company could be null.*
    - *policy_number could be null.*
    - *created_at and updated_at are managed by Rails; they will be not null.*

Bal: *A few questions to ask the users, but otherwise all OK.*

Carla: *The claimants table:*

- *Is every column atomic? Yes.*
- *What is the Primary Key? id generated by Rails.*
- *Does every other column depend on the Primary Key? A particular claimant role, identified by claimant.id, relates a particular person, as claimant, to a particular claim. Created_at and updated_at are the timestamps showing when the claimant role was created or changed. That's all OK. This relationship (claimant role) means that one person can be a claimant on more than one claim, which is true. It also means that one claim can have several claimants, which is true. It also means that the same person could have more than one claimant role on the same claim. I'm not sure about that one. We must check with Doug.*
- *Does any column depend on another column that is not the Primary Key? No, so that's OK.*
- *Are there any repeating groups? No, that's fine.*

- *Does every column have the most restrictive data-type for the data it holds? Yes, these are all strong data-types and the most appropriate ones.*
- *Does the name of the column accurately describe the data that will be stored in it? Yes, all absolutely standard.*
- *Are nullable columns genuinely OK to be null? Check data columns and Foreign Keys.* Id, created_at *and* updated_at *are all* not null *already, as generated by Rails.* Claim_id *and* person_id *must be* not null, *because a claimant role is a link between a person and a claim. If either the person or the claim does not exist, or is not known, then the role cannot exist. Will you make* claim_id *and* person_id not null, *please Bal?*

Bal: Sure, that makes sense.

Bal generates a new Rails migration and edits it to look like this:

download: ClaimantsClaimIdAndPersonIdNotNull.rb

```
class ClaimantsClaimIdAndPersonIdNotNull < ActiveRecord::Migration
  def change
    change_column :claimants, :claim_id, :integer, null: false
    change_column :claimants, :person_id, :integer, null: false
  end
end
```

He then runs the Rails command to migrate the database:

```
rake db:migrate
```

The data model and the generated Ruby on Rails objects are fine as a starting point for the first iteration. The team works through the tests and the user interface in the first week, without changing the data model.

Iteration 2

At the next meeting with Doug and his team, the developers present what they have done. There are a few layout changes that the users want and they add some extra fields to `vehicle`: make, model and the year when the vehicle was first licensed. The users want to record some more information about the incident too. This gives the development team enough stories for the second iteration.

Bal and Carla generate a migration to add the extra columns to `vehicle`.

download: AddColumnsToVehicle.rb

```ruby
class AddColumnsToVehicle < ActiveRecord::Migration
  def change
    add_column :vehicles, :make, :string, limit: 40
    add_column :vehicles, :model, :string, limit: 40
    add_column :vehicles, :year_first_licensed, :integer
  end
end
```

and a new scaffold for a separate `incident` model and `incidents` table:

download: scaffold_iteration_2.sh

```
rails generate scaffold Incident \
  date_and_time_of_incident:timestamp \
  description_of_incident:string
```

and a migration to remove redundant columns from claims:

download: RemoveIncidentColumnsFromClaim.rb

```ruby
class RemoveIncidentColumnsFromClaim < ActiveRecord::Migration
  def change
    remove_column :claims, :date_and_time_of_incident, :timestamp
    remove_column :claims, :description_of_incident, :text
  end
end
```

and a migration to add the new foreign key from `claims` to `incidents`:

download: ClaimBelongsToIncident.rb

```ruby
class ClaimBelongsToIncident < ActiveRecord::Migration
  def change
    add_column :claims, :incident_id, :integer
    execute %{
        alter table claims
        add constraint fk_claims_incidents
        foreign key (incident_id) references incidents(id);
    }
  end
end
```

Chapter 3 - An Agile Database - Step by Step

This last migration executes some `SQL` explicitly. We will cover this in *Chapter 4 - Database Migrations In SQL on page 97*. The migration also assumes that there is no data in the `claims` table.

The resulting data model is:

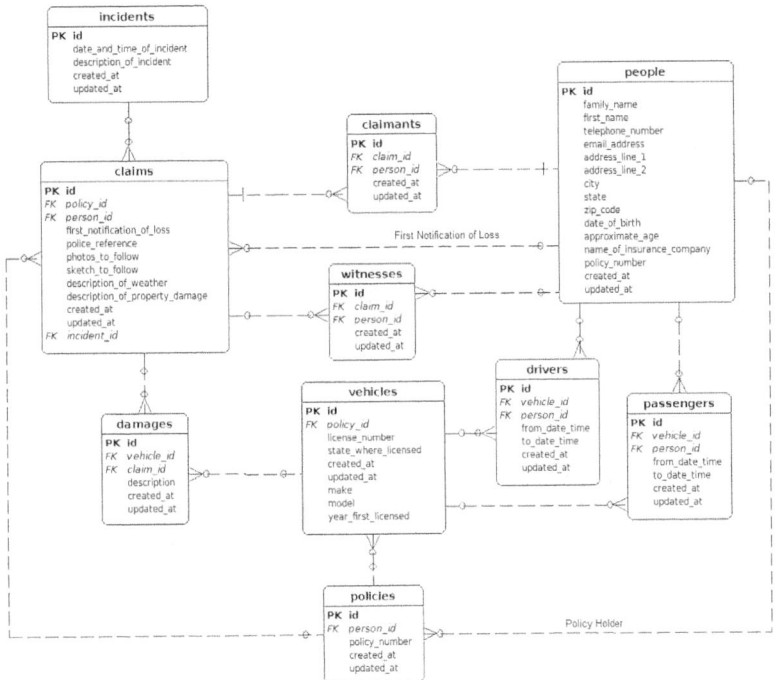

The migrations we have done do not attempt to preserve any data already in the database. In *Chapter 12 - Database Migrations That Preserve Data on page 244*, we will explain what to do if there is data to migrate. Also, we have not thought about making the migrations reversible. At this stage in the development, this is usually appropriate. The tests at this stage will start with an empty database and populate the tables as the different tests run. The application will have to change to deal with some fields moving from `claims` to `incidents`. The tests will need to take account of the new limits on field lengths, and should check that the application behaves in a friendly way when the constraints on field sizes are breached, even if we never expect this to happen in the real world. See *Chapter 13 - When Things Go Wrong on page 264*.

Iteration 3

Doug and his team are now happy that they can capture what they refer to as **FNOL**, and this is already much better than what they had been using previously. But now they want to start managing the claim.

Doug starts talking about "the bordereau."

Bal asks what a bordereau is and Doug explains that they have to report to the "capacity provider." Bal asks who the capacity provider is and Doug gives the name of the company that Bal knows to be the reinsurer: the company that ultimately takes the risk. Doug appears a little impatient, so Bal takes a different tack and asks if they can have a sample of a bordereau so that the new system can re-create it the way the users like it. This seems much more acceptable.

Meanwhile, Carla searches for bordereau on the internet and finds the following definition[24]:

> "*Bordereau (plural: bordereaux)*
>
> "*A report providing premium or loss data with respect to identified specific risks. This report is periodically furnished to a reinsurer by the ceding insurers or reinsurers.*"

The sample bordereau is more helpful than the definition. The bordereau turns out to be a report in which there is one line for every change in any amount of money against a claim, a claimant and a claim head.

In fact, every amount of money in the claims system must be linked to a claim, a claimant and a claim head. This is an important discovery, and it takes a while for the insurance people and the software developers to reach a common understanding.

This is quite normal, of course, and we must expect it and welcome it. Different disciplines build up concepts and terminology to describe the work they do. The terminology is necessary, in order to train new people and to communicate within that discipline to improve the work that they do. This applies to medicine, accountancy, police work, house

---

24. http://www.irmi.com/online/insurance-glossary/terms/b/bordereau.aspx

building, railway engineering, musical performance, and every other field of human activity. As software developers, we must enjoy learning about other fields of activity so that we can help the people who work in those areas with systems that help them do their jobs more effectively. It is often quite difficult, and it is usually very rewarding.

In discussing the bordereau, the team has learned several things about how claims work:

- A claim can have many claimants.
- Each claimant can claim under many claim heads (such as damage to car, hire of replacement car, medical fees, legal fees, etc.).
- Every financial transaction in the claim is assigned to a claimant and a claim head.
- Financial transactions can be amounts paid to claimants or amounts recovered from third parties.
- Financial transactions can also be **actuals** or **reserves**. Actuals are amounts that are actually paid or recovered; reserves are what the claims handlers expect to be paid or recovered. Reserves are a bit like budgets in normal accounting systems, but reserves can change very frequently, sometimes more than once a day.

Carla and Bal look at the data model to see what they have to change. We already have a table for claimants, and each row in this table is a relationship between a person and a claim. The same person who is a claimant on one claim might also perform other roles in the system and might be a claimant on another claim. That all works fine. If we attach a transaction to a claimant then we will have identified the claimant and the claim that is affected by the transaction. The application must be coded to ensure that the claimant record - for the right policy and the right claim - is the correct one to attach any transaction to.

For `claim_heads` we need a new table. The users have insisted on having codes for each of the claim heads. These codes are abbreviations based on the description of the claim head; for example, "Third Party Property Damage" has the code `TPPD`. Doug has given the team a list of codes and descriptions.

Carla and Bal create a scaffold for the new `claim_heads` table:

download: scaffold_iteration_3_claim_head.sh

```
rails generate scaffold Claim_head \
  code:string \
  description:string
```

and then a scaffold for the **transactions** table:

download: scaffold_iteration_3_transaction.sh

```
rails generate scaffold Transaction \
  claimant:belongs_to \
  claim_head:belongs_to \
  actual_or_reserve:string \
  payment_or_recovery:string \
  amount:decimal
```

and some migrations to restrict the data-types:

download: LimitClaimHeadCodeAndDescription.rb

```
class LimitClaimHeadCodeAndDescription < ActiveRecord::Migration
  def change
    change_column :claim_heads, :code, :string, limit: 8
    change_column :claim_heads, :description, :string, limit: 40
  end
end
```

download: LimitTransactionColumns.rb

```
class LimitTransactionColumns < ActiveRecord::Migration
  def change
    change_column :transactions, :actual_or_reserve, :string, limit: 7
    change_column :transactions, :payment_or_recovery, :string, limit: 8
    change_column :transactions, :amount, :decimal, precision: 8, scale: 2
  end
end
```

The revised data model is:

Chapter 3 - An Agile Database - Step by Step

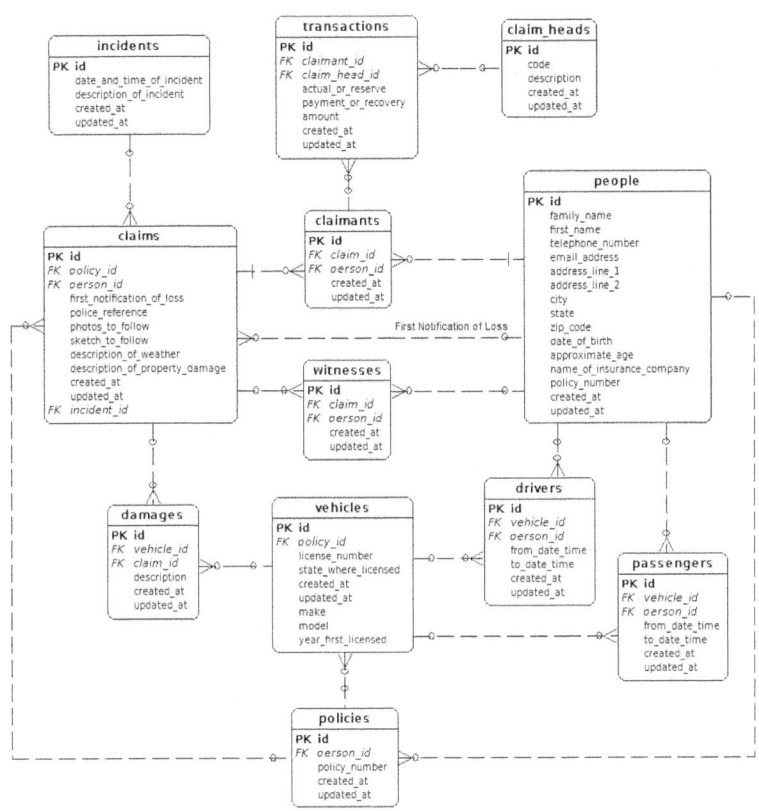

Bal and Carla run through the checklist on the new tables. There are some interesting decisions to be made about data-types. The column `actual_or_reserve` will be a string (`character varying`, or `varchar` in SQL terminology) and will take the values **Actual** and **Reserve**. The column `payment_or_recovery` will be similar, taking the values **Payment** and **Recovery**. One could argue that integer codes would be more efficient, but I would challenge anyone's ability to measure the difference with any of the modern relational databases. The big advantage of naming and recording the columns like this is that their meanings are really obvious.

The data-type of the amount is very important. Because it is money, is must be a fixed precision exact value. Floating point numbers must never be used for money. The fixed-precision decimal data-types map to the `BigDecimal` class in Ruby and the `BigDecimal` class in Java.

As with Iteration 2, the migrations do not attempt to preserve any data already in the database and we have not thought about making them reversible. At this stage in the development, this is still appropriate. The tests at this stage will start with an empty database and populate the tables as the different tests run.

Making migrations reversible is usually not worth the effort. The development usually proceeds forwards and migrating to an earlier version is quite rare. When we do need to go back to an earlier version, we can invest the effort at that point.

However, preserving existing data becomes essential as soon as a live system has been released. Users do not take kindly to re-entering data, and, in many cases, would not have the records to do so accurately. We will look at migrating databases while preserving existing data in *Chapter 12 - Database Migrations That Preserve Data on page 244*.

Our Claims application and the database that will support it are taking shape. We have seen how the database can grow in complexity over some early iterations. There is no need to be afraid of changes; relational databases make change quite easy. In contrast, trying to get every detail correct before starting to develop the application is, in any real application, impossible.

Chapter 4 - Database Migrations In SQL

The chapters up to this point have been focused on the *principles* we use to structure data in a relational database. These principles organize the data in a logical way that helps us to process the data simply, consistently, efficiently and safely. I hardly mentioned SQL because I wanted to get the ideas behind relational databases established without relying on SQL. SQL is a layer built on top of the relational database. It is important to understand how the database works before we get into the syntax of SQL.

In earlier chapters we have used Ruby on Rails Migrations to create the initial tables in our database and to change them as the database design emerged. You may not be using Ruby on Rails. I often use other development languages and tools. But I do emulate the idea of migrations, even when I am not using Ruby on Rails. This chapter will show you how to achieve the same effect using SQL.

In the past there have been other languages for defining and manipulating relational databases, but in practice, SQL is now the only one. Now that we have worked through the relational database ideas, we will focus on SQL. It is important to learn SQL thoroughly if we want to work in this area.

The SQL language is divided into two parts:

- Data Definition Language (DDL)
- Data Manipulation Language (DML)

Data Definition Language is about creating, altering and dropping database objects. You will see many SQL statements which start with the commands create, alter and drop. These statements deal with database object definitions; we can think of them very much like class definitions. When we define the person table, we are defining a class. The rows in that table are instances of the class person

In this chapter we will cover the most important parts of the SQL Data Definition Language (DDL). We will be using the create, alter and drop commands to build the definitions of the database. In later chapters we will use Data Manipulation Language (DML) commands to populate the tables with rows of data and to manipulate those rows.

The Tools You Need

First of all let's look at the tools you need. These tools are free or very low-cost, a tiny fraction of the cost of tools used in a typical `waterfall` project. The tools are essential if you want to run your database application development as an agile project.

Plain Text

You must create every change to the database structure, every migration, as a plain text script file. This must be stored in the version control system. Then you will have a record of what you did and, most importantly, you can run exactly the same change on your development, test and live databases. If you tick boxes and type the changes into your interactive administration tool, you will have to type them three times and you will make mistakes. You will miss something or you will introduce some subtle difference that will cause a failure in the applications which depend on the migration.

I create every `SQL` statement in a text editor. I sometimes use interactive tools for running `SQL` statements, but I never type the `SQL` command in the `SQL` window of these tools; I have a text editor window open, I type the commands there and I copy and paste them into the `SQL` tool. I do not edit the `SQL` in the `SQL` tool; I edit it in the text editor and copy the changed statement into the `SQL` tool. I can use the text editor to save the `SQL` statement I have developed and give it a name that describes what it does. It is amazing how often these statements get re-used.

I never use `SQL` query builders. I need to know what joins I am doing and why. It isn't hard to write them. Any illusion that a visual programming tool is easier or more efficient is simply that - an illusion. The only purpose of visual programming tools is to sell products to people who think they can save on programming costs by having their team draw pictures instead of writing code. This works well for simple demonstrations, but makes real-world complex tasks much more difficult for skilled developers. It also makes a lot of money for the vendors of such tools. You might as well buy snake oil.

Get yourself a decent text editor and start enjoying Plain Text.

For more on the virtues of plain text, read the chapter called "The Power of Plain Text" in *The Pragmatic Programmer* [25]. For more on the dangers of query builders see the section called "Evil Wizards" in the same book, and *Visual Database Tools on page 327.*

Version Control

Another absolutely essential tool for any development is a version control system. That is for *any* development. I worked for years without one, but I will not do so now.

In a lot of organizations developments are done without a version control system. In such an organization every document contains a long table near the beginning with a row for every change, the name of the person who made the change and the date when it was made, and of course there will be a version number for every change. Usually the version number has at least two parts.

Also, the file name will have the version number in it, such as: "Some Formal Document v1.3a.doc."

Is that a version which supersedes v1.3, or precedes it, or what? Is there a later v1.3b?

Traditionally (over the last 20 years or so) the files are stored in a Windows share. There will also be copies on local drives on various individuals' PCs. How often do we find that different people have different versions and they all believe them to be the latest?

Now, many organizations are waking up to the benefits of version control systems. However, they then usually do two misguided things. The first is that they buy a version control system and the second is that they use their expensive version control system as if it were a Windows share.

You don't need to buy a version control system. You almost certainly don't need to buy a *Software Configuration Management* system, nor do you need to buy an *Application Lifecycle Management* system. The best version control systems are free and they are called Subversion[26] and

---

25. See Bibliography [Hunt&Thomas]

Git[27].

Using these tools is easy and simple. Discipline is necessary to get the best out of them, but you don't need a massive amount of training. If you are really keen (as I'm sure you are) you could read *Pragmatic Guide to Subversion*[28].

And you can minimize your chances of going off the rails by following these simple recommendations:

- Let the version control system do the work!
- Remember that the version in the version control system is the master version; any file on your local disk is not the master until you check it in to the version control system.
- Do not change the name of a file from one version to another; all versions of one file go in the same folder, under the same name. Then you can see the change history in the version control system.
- If you do need to change the name of a file or folder, do it using the version control system client, not on the working file on your local disk. If you do it in the version control system it will change the working file for you and everything will stay in sync.
- Never, never, never put a version number, or date, or time in a file name - this is a version control system, not a Windows share! The version control system has the definitive values for version number, date and time of each file.
- Check-in atomic units - one component per file - do not check in `zip` files or `tar` files.
- The version numbers in the version control system are trusted over any version information recorded inside a file - so do not record version information inside the file.
- The version control system keeps a log of your versions, so don't keep an incomplete and out-of-date one in the document. Delete that big table from the front of your document - you really do not need it.

Database Migration for Iteration 1

We will look at the database migrations in the Claims system we built in

---

26. http://subversion.apache.org
27. https://git-scm.com
28. See Bibliography [Mason]

Chapter 3 - An Agile Database - Step by Step on page 70, but this time we will build them using **SQL**.

Here is the first migration, which creates the tables for iteration 1 in an empty database.

download: person.sql

```
create table person
(
    id                               serial      not null,
    family_name                      varchar(40),
    first_name                       varchar(40),
    telephone_number                 varchar(16),
    email_address                    varchar(200),
    address_line_1                   varchar(60),
    address_line_2                   varchar(60),
    city                             varchar(60),
    state                            varchar(2),
    zip_code                         varchar(5),
    date_of_birth                    date,
    approximate_age                  integer,
    name_of_insurance_company        varchar(60),
    policy_number                    varchar(40),
    created_at                       timestamp   not null default now(),
    updated_at                       timestamp,
    constraint primary_key_person    primary key(id)
);
```

download: policy.sql

```
create table policy
(
    id                               serial      not null,
    person_id                        integer     not null,
    policy_number                    varchar(10),
    created_at                       timestamp   not null default now(),
    updated_at                       timestamp,
    constraint primary_key_policy    primary key (id),
    constraint foreign_key_policy_person
        foreign key (person_id) references person(id)
);
```

download: vehicle.sql

```
create table vehicle
(
    id                               serial      not null,
    policy_id                        integer,
    license_number                   varchar(8),
    state_where_licensed             varchar(2),
    created_at                       timestamp   not null default now(),
```

```
        updated_at                      timestamp,
        constraint primary_key_vehicle  primary key (id),
        constraint foreign_key_vehicle_policy
            foreign key (policy_id) references policy(id)
    );
```

download: claim.sql

```
    create table claim
    (
        id                              serial      not null,
        policy_id                       integer,
        person_id                       integer     not null,
        first_notification_of_loss      timestamp,
        date_and_time_of_incident       timestamp,
        police_reference                varchar(40),
        photos_to_follow                boolean,
        sketch_to_follow                boolean,
        description_of_weather          varchar(2000),
        description_of_incident         varchar(2000),
        description_of_property_damage  varchar(2000),
        created_at                      timestamp   not null default now(),
        updated_at                      timestamp,
        constraint primary_key_claim    primary key(id),
        constraint foreign_key_claim_policy
            foreign key (policy_id) references policy(id),
        constraint foreign_key_claim_person
            foreign key (person_id) references person(id)
    );
```

download: claimant.sql

```
    create table claimant
    (
        id                              serial      not null,
        claim_id                        integer     not null,
        person_id                       integer     not null,
        created_at                      timestamp   not null  default now(),
        updated_at                      timestamp,
        constraint primary_key_claimant primary key (id),
        constraint foreign_key_claimant_claim
            foreign key (claim_id)   references claim(id),
        constraint foreign_key_claimant_person
            foreign key (person_id) references person(id),
        constraint unique_claim_person  unique (claim_id, person_id)
    );
```

download: witness.sql

```sql
create table witness
(
    id                       serial       not null,
    claim_id                 integer      not null,
    person_id                integer      not null,
    created_at               timestamp    not null default now(),
    updated_at               timestamp,
    constraint primary_key_witness       primary key (id),
    constraint foreign_key_witness_claim
        foreign key (claim_id) references claim(id),
    constraint foreign_key_witness_person
        foreign key (person_id) references person(id)
);
```

download: driver.sql

```sql
create table driver
(
    id                       serial       not null,
    vehicle_id               integer      not null,
    person_id                integer      not null,
    from_date_time           timestamp,
    to_date_time             timestamp,
    created_at               timestamp    not null default now(),
    updated_at               timestamp,
    constraint primary_key_driver        primary key (id),
    constraint foreign_key_driver_vehicle
        foreign key (vehicle_id) references vehicle(id),
    constraint foreign_key_driver_person
        foreign key (person_id) references person(id)
);
```

download: passenger.sql

```sql
create table passenger
(
    id                       serial       not null,
    vehicle_id               integer      not null,
    person_id                integer      not null,
    from_date_time           timestamp,
    to_date_time             timestamp,
    created_at               timestamp    not null default now(),
    updated_at               timestamp,
    constraint primary_key_passenger     primary key (id),
    constraint foreign_key_passenger_vehicle
        foreign key (vehicle_id) references vehicle(id),
    constraint foreign_key_passenger_person
        foreign key (person_id) references person(id)
);
```

download: damage.sql

```
create table damage
(
    id                      serial      not null,
    vehicle_id              integer     not null,
    claim_id                integer     not null,
    description             varchar(2000),
    created_at              timestamp   not null default now(),
    updated_at              timestamp,
    constraint primary_key_damage  primary key (id),
    constraint foreign_key_damage_vehicle
        foreign key (vehicle_id) references vehicle(id),
    constraint foreign_key_damage_claim
        foreign key (claim_id) references claim(id)
);
```

download: migration_001.sql

```
\i person.sql
\i policy.sql
\i vehicle.sql
\i claim.sql
\i claimant.sql
\i witness.sql
\i driver.sql
\i passenger.sql
\i damage.sql
```

The last of the scripts above is the migration script to run all the `create` statements to set up the database for Iteration 1. These examples are all written for `PostgreSQL`. They also work for the appliance formerly known as `Netezza`.

For other databases it is necessary to tweak some of the data types as we note in *Chapter 6 - Data Types on page 125*. Also, the `\i <file name>` command to include the referenced files is different in other databases' SQL command line processors. For example, Oracle's `SQL*Plus` uses the @ sign in front of the file name, without any spaces in between, to tell the command processor to execute the contents of the file.

You may notice that the tables in this version of the migration are named in the singular, not in the plural as we did before. I think that Ruby on Rails is a very good implementation of the interface between the application and the database. I have just one preference for one thing different from the Ruby on Rails standards. If I am working in a project which is using Ruby on Rails for some or all of the application development I will follow the Ruby on Rails standards with no hesitation.

However, if I am working in a project that is not using Ruby on Rails then I will make the table names singular because they are almost always shorter and because I like the references to use consistent names. In the `policy` table in this chapter, `person_id` matches `id` in the `person` table. In the Ruby on Rails version, `person_id` in the `policy` table matches `id` in the `people` table.

Here are the two alternatives side by side.

My Preferred Style	Ruby on Rails Style
| ```
select
    policy.policy_number,
    person.last_name
from
    policy,
    person
where
    policy.person_id = person.id;
``` | ```
select
    policies.policy_number,
    people.last_name
from
    policies,
    people
where
    policies.person_id = people.id;
``` |

The examples in the migration above give you models to use for most of what you will ever need to create tables in your database. This is how they work.

We give the new table a name:

```
create table policy
```

And then we list the columns and constraints separated by commas and enclosed in parentheses. The statement is finished with a semi-colon.

```
create table <table_name>
(
  <column definitions>
  <constraints>
);
```

We give each column a name and a data-type and we specify whether it is allowed to be null or not.

Names must be meaningful, not case sensitive, with words separated using underscores. See *Chapter 5 - Naming Things on page 114*. You can make names case sensitive in most databases, but that means you have to enclose every name in double quotes or square brackets or backticks. It is much easier to write and to read if you make everything lowercase and use underscores to separate words. Please never put a space in a table name or column name. The mess you make of your SQL to enable you to use spaces in names is really not worth it. What possible benefit would you get from having spaces in your table and column names anyway?

The data-type `serial` is specific to `PostgreSQL`. It is similar to the `auto-increment` and `identity` columns in other databases. It is simply an integer column that is given a new value when a row is inserted. It can therefore be used to allocate unique primary keys.

`Bigserial` works in the same way, but creates a `bigint` rather than an `integer`.

By default every column is allowed to be null, so I don't specify those explicitly. However, it is important to highlight those columns which cannot be null.

We want as many columns as possible to be `not null`. Of course, if the application needs them to be nullable, then we must allow that, but where the column is mandatory we must say `not null` so that the database enforces this for us.

I have included the columns that Ruby on Rails includes by default because I think it's usually a good idea. These are `created_at` and `updated_at`. `Created_at` has a default value of `now()`. The `now()` function returns the current timestamp, and sets the `created_at` column for us whenever we insert a new row. It is a default and we could override it, but why would we do that? When we update a row we must always populate the `updated_at` column using the `now()` function. Some other databases have the `now()` function; most have `current_timestamp` meaning the same as `now()`.

There are cases where you would not want `created_at` and `updated_at`. You can leave them out if you do not need them.

Following the list of column definitions there are column constraints.

There should be a primary key constraint on every table. Relational databases do not insist that you have a primary key on every table, but you should always define one. With primary keys defined, the database will enforce this aspect of data integrity for you. The primary key constraint identifies the column (or columns) which form the primary key.

It is quite valid for a primary key to consist of more than one column, but if it does then the combination of those columns must be unique and no column in the primary key can be null.

Then there are foreign key constraints wherever the table `belongs_to` another table. If there is a foreign key relationship then we must always specify it so that the database checks it for us every time.

The foreign key constraint specifies the foreign key in the table we are creating, and the table and column that the foreign key refers to.

The table being referenced must have been created already, so the scripts create the tables in the order necessary to define foreign keys. It is possible to create the tables first and add the constraints afterwards (using the `alter table` SQL command). I prefer to add the constraints at the time the table is created so that the whole definition of each table stays in one script.

Foreign key columns can be allowed to be null, if it makes sense for a row to exist without a parent. This does happen sometimes. In *Chapter 3 - An Agile Database - Step by Step on page 70*, we say that a claim belongs to a policy, but when the claim is first reported then we may not know the policy. We will have to find out the policy before we pay out on the claim, so there should eventually be a foreign key pointing from the claim to the policy, but we have to allow it to be null initially.

The examples you have seen so far in this chapter cover most of what you need to know about creating tables in a relational database. In the documentation of every database you will find an overwhelming mass of options. You can safely ignore most of them. In fact your databases will be better architected if you do ignore most of them.

The SQL examples shown in this book follow a style that I use because it is easy to read without missing anything important. The benefit of this grows over time. When you come back to a table that you have not worked on for two years, then you want to be able to grasp the definition as easily as possible.

SQL scripts, like most programming languages, treat any white space as being acceptable separators between words, so one or more spaces or tabs are treated as white space. Also, a single newline is treated as a unit of white space. Unfortunately many SQL interfaces get upset by multiple newlines together, in other words, they treat a blank line as the end of the statement. This is a mistake since SQL statements are defined to be terminated by a semi-colon, so blank lines should not be a problem, but they usually are. Believe it or not, there are also situations where your SQL statement will fail if you include the semi-colon terminator. Oracle's JDBC interface will tell you that your statement has an "invalid character" if you include the semi-colon!

We can use white space to lay out our SQL statements to help the reader. Some *unhelpful* habits, in my opinion are:

- Typing keywords in capitals
- Putting list separators (commas, and, or, etc.) at the start of each item in the list (except the first), rather than where they belong, just after each item in the list (except the last),
- Putting several comma-separated items on the same line
- Indentation schemes that put most of the code way over on the right hand side of the page.
- Open brackets placed at the end of a line so that they do not align with the close brackets. This seems to be a *de facto* standard with Java and other tools but on projects where I set the standards I put open brackets on a new line because it is easier to see the open and close brackets and the blocks of code that they delineate.

Here is a collection of my pet formatting dislikes. I shall stick to my way for the rest of this book. I hope you like it.

```
What you often see

CREATE TABLE passenger (id SERIAL NOT NULL
                       ,vehicle_id INTEGER NOT NULL
                       ,person_id INTEGER NOT NULL
                       ,from_date_time TIMESTAMP
                       ,to_date_time TIMESTAMP
                       ,created_at TIMESTAMP NOT NULL
                       ,updated_at TIMESTAMP NOT NULL
                       ,CONSTRAINT primary_key_passenger PRIMARY KEY (id)
                       ,CONSTRAINT foreign_key_passenger_vehicle
                                               FOREIGN KEY (vehicle_id)
                                               REFERENCES vehicle(id)
                       ,CONSTRAINT foreign_key_passenger_person
                                               FOREIGN KEY (person_id)
                                               REFERENCES person(id));
```

Chapter 4 - Database Migrations In SQL

```
My preferred style

create table passenger
(
    id                                      serial      not null,
    vehicle_id                              integer     not null,
    person_id                               integer     not null,
    from_date_time                          timestamp,
    to_date_time                            timestamp,
    created_at                              timestamp   not null default now(),
    updated_at                              timestamp,
    constraint primary_key_passenger        primary key (id),
    constraint foreign_key_passenger_vehicle
        foreign key (vehicle_id) references vehicle(id),
    constraint foreign_key_passenger_person
        foreign key (person_id) references person(id)
);
```

We have seen that it is easy to create tables using the SQL Data Definition Language (DDL). Once the script is correct, you can run it in every environment and know that it will behave in the same way.

Database Migration for Iteration 2

At this stage in the process we are assuming that we do not need to preserve any data that is already in the database. Our test cases would populate the database from scratch for every iteration. Once there is a quantity of data in the database, we may want to preserve it across migrations. When the system goes live, we will certainly want to keep all the data. There are techniques for doing this and we will discuss them in *Chapter 12, Iteration 2 on page 246*, after we have looked at SQL Data Manipulation statements.

In this chapter we will focus on the SQL Data Definition statements and simply migrate the database definitions.

In Iteration 2, as described in *Chapter 3 - An Agile Database - Step by Step on page 70*, Iteration 2, the users want to:

- add some extra fields to describe each vehicle: make, model and year_first_licensed
- record some more information about the incident.

The team decides to make the incident a separate table. After discussion with the users they understand that an incident could result in more than one claim, or may be reported but without a claim being raised. Incident is therefore a separate object. The claim will refer to an incident, although this data for the incident may not be available at the first notification of loss.

Here is the migration script to change our database from the Iteration 1 version to the Iteration 2 version.

download: migration_002.sql

```
alter table vehicle
    add column make                 varchar(40),
    add column model                varchar(40),
    add column year_first_licensed  integer;

create table incident
(
    id                         serial       not null,
    date_and_time_of_incident  timestamp,
    description                varchar(2000),
    created_at                 timestamp    not null default now(),
    updated_at                 timestamp,
    constraint primary_key_incident primary key (id)
);

alter table claim
    drop column date_and_time_of_incident,
    drop column description_of_incident,
    add column incident_id  integer,
    add constraint foreign_key_claim_incident
        foreign key (incident_id) references incident(id);
```

The SQL Data Definition statements here are quite straightforward. We have:

- added the extra columns to the vehicle table
- created the new incident table
- dropped the incident columns from the claim table (because they are now in the separate incident table)
- added the incident_id to the claim table. It is allowed to be null because in some cases we will create a claim without any incident details, although these will be required later.
- defined incident_id as a foreign key pointing to the incident table.

Database Migration for Iteration 3

In Iteration 3 we are adding a table for Claim Heads and a table for transactions. Every transaction references a claim head and a claimant.

Here is the migration script for iteration 3.

download: claim_head.sql
```
create table claim_head
(
    id                          serial      not null,
    code                        varchar(8)  not null,
    description                 varchar(64) not null,
    created_at                  timestamp   not null default now(),
    updated_at                  timestamp,
    constraint primary_key_claim_head primary key (id)
);
```

download: transaction.sql
```
create table transaction
(
    id                          serial      not null,
    claimant_id                 integer     not null,
    claim_head_id               integer     not null,
    actual_or_reserve           varchar(7),
    payment_or_recovery         varchar(8),
    amount                      numeric(8,2),
    created_at                  timestamp   not null default now(),
    updated_at                  timestamp,
    constraint primary_key_transaction primary key (id),
    constraint foreign_key_transaction_claimant
        foreign key (claimant_id) references claimant(id),
    constraint foreign_key_transaction_claim_head
        foreign key (claim_head_id) references claim_head(id)
);
```

download: migration_003.sql
```
\i claim_head.sql
\i transaction.sql
```

We're all done here.

When we want to release our system to the test or the live environment, we can simply extract our migration scripts from the version control system, at the appropriate revision level for the release.

We can then run the migration scripts in order in the test or live database, and the tables will be set up exactly as they were in our development database.

In this system, as in most, we will have some reference data to set up, for example the codes and descriptions for `claim_head`. Loading these must also be scripted, so that we can have exactly the same data in every environment.

Part B - Defending The Quality Of Your Data

We have already seen how to build tables that work well together as a model of the data in your application. We also showed how you can build your database one iteration at a time, without creating a grand design up-front. Using this agile approach we must use good design patterns at every step and we must be prepared to refactor ruthlessly to keep improving our design. In Part B we are going to look more closely at some decisions we must make as we create every table and every column. These decisions concern naming, data-types, nulls and keys. Together they help us to maintain the quality of our data and the robustness of our database.

Chapter 5 - Naming Things

Does it really matter how we name things? It certainly does! Poor naming causes data quality issues and really ramps up the cost of future development on the application as later developers struggle to find out how the system works. Follow this guide to learn how to be nice to your co-workers and save money for your organization.

Business processes describe named objects and the functions that are performed on them. For example: a *customer buys* a *policy, commission* is *paid* to a *business partner*. The highlighted words are objects and functions that need to be named. This is true whether the business process is manual, assisted (by a spreadsheet for example) or fully automated.

Good naming conventions use names that accurately and unambiguously describe the objects they refer to, and the functions being performed.

Good naming conventions make the processes easier to understand, and understanding is key to successful systems. An analyst, developer or user has a much better chance of completing her task accurately if she has a clear and precise view of the process she is trying to model. Obscure or misleading names add unnecessary difficulties to a task that is already complex.

How Did We Get into Such a Mess?

On a recent project I was working with a team of six analysts to understand the data in an old mainframe system that is to be used to populate our data warehouse. The typical name of a table in this system is seven characters long. The first three characters are the same for every table so we have four uppercase alphabetic characters to tell us what each table holds. There are 193 tables in this system. The names might as well be in code. When we get to the column names it is just as bad. We have one column called `TRAN_IND`. Nobody knows what it means. This is in the `transaction` table and every column name in that table starts with `TRAN_`.

This effort has cost at least $200,000. We have not been able to answer all the questions, and I estimate that at least two-thirds of the time has been spent trying to track down the meanings of cryptic names. It has been a frustrating job and a terrible waste of money.

Another recent project using the same data just copied the old names to the new database (making a few transcription errors in the process). The pain is perpetuated.

I would like to be able to say that this is just an error of the past and that we do things better now. In some cases this is true, but in the new system in the same organization they continue with misleading names. In one table there is one column called TD_SECURE_ACCOUNT and another called TD_ACCOUNT_SECURE. Can you guess the difference in meaning? Neither could we. In a customer address table we found a column called STREET_ADDRESS containing email addresses. There are many other examples.

Some packaged software still uses very short names. Sometimes developers create cryptic names because the examples they saw when they were learning suggested that this is the way to do things. Some tools restrict the length of names. Some vendors' "best practice" guidelines suggest wasteful and unnecessary schemes of prefixes on every name.

A source we find very useful is *The Pragmatic Programmer* [29]. Chapter 8.44 *It's All Writing* is particularly relevant to naming conventions.

Most modern systems support long names; the better ones have a limit of 128 characters or more. Sometimes we need a long name to describe a column or an object or a method precisely, but length is not the most important criterion of course. We want names in our systems to be descriptive, economical, easy-to-read and consistent.

Here are some tips to help you achieve these goals.

Be Descriptive

Use natural language

Whatever natural language is being used in your project, use real, correctly spelled words from that language.

---

29. See Bibliography [Hunt&Thomas]

Object names should be made up of words that can be found in an official dictionary for the language you are using. Avoid jargon: both industry-specific jargon and computer jargon. When a technical term cannot be avoided, make sure that it is in the `Business Definitions Dictionary` in your wiki. (You do have a wiki, don't you? You should. The best ones are free and the cost of not having one is ridiculously high.)

Words must be spelled correctly. The reason for this is simply to avoid ambiguity and mistakes. If a word is spelled wrongly, it may indicate another meaning, or a maintenance programmer may subconsciously correct the spelling, leading to an error in his code when the name does not match.

Concrete

There is no rule that you must deal in abstract, generalized concepts. In almost all applications we are dealing with concrete, real objects. We are not dealing with an "event" we are dealing with a payment or a customer call, or an address change or some other kind of event. Yes, these may all be events, but we have to process each one in its own way. We just make things more difficult for ourselves by trying to treat different things as if they were all some generic thing.

Within an object, each of the attributes is a specific thing and it is OK, in fact I would say it is mandatory, to name all those things specifically. Take a look at one of your credit cards. You will see that it belongs to a scheme: MasterCard, Visa, American Express, etc. It also mentions a Bank; it might be Wells Fargo, HSBC, Citi, Chase or many others. It may be some sort of premium card: Gold, Platinum, Black. It may be a personal card or a company card. It may be a credit card or a debit card.

In a company I did some work for these different attributes were called:

- card.card_type
- card.card_product_type
- card.card_level
- card.card_category
- card.card_scheme_code

We can guess card_scheme_code but how do we match up the other names with what the attributes mean. I would use names like:

- card.scheme

- card.bank

- card.premium (which could take values: 'Gold', 'Standard', etc.)

- card.personal_or_company (with values: 'Personal' or 'Company')

- card.credit_or_debit (with values: 'Credit' or 'Debit')

Wouldn't you rather work on my database?

No Gratuitous Abbreviations

Abbreviations are bad. They cause confusion at best, and at worst are used to intimidate those who are not familiar with them.

Unfortunately, some of the leading vendors in our industry are serial offenders in this area. IBM, for example invented the term DASD (pronounced *daz-dee*). DASD stands for Direct Access Storage Device, or *disk* to normal people. *Disk* is clearly a better name for such devices. It is the same number of letters, half as many syllables and we know what it means. This is history, going back to the days of mainframes, but they are still doing it. In the industry data models provided by IBM, the party table is called IP. IP stands for *involved party*. By definition a party is some person or organization that is *involved* with the organization being modeled. A much better name for this table is party. If the parties can only be people and not organizations then the table should be called person.

IBM is by no means the only culprit. An abbreviation that has recently rattled my cage is SerDe. SerDe means *Serialize and Deserialize*, and these both mean *copy*. Typically the data is copied from one environment to another with some change in format, but no change in content. The terms come from object-oriented programming where the properties of the instance of an object may be copied (*serialized*) to some more permanent storage from which the object can later be restored (*deserialized*). The term SerDe is used in Hive (one of the Big Data tools) for copying files into database tables. *Serialize* and *deserialize* seem to be rather grand terms for the simple and universal operation of copying data. `SerDe` is unforgivable; say *copy* instead.

You will find very few abbreviations in this book. I do use `ID` to name the primary key in every table. `ID` is a very widely used abbreviation, not only when talking about data. I think this is a good use of an abbreviation. I also use `varchar`. This isn't pretty and there is often some doubt about how to pronounce it. The alternative is `character varying` which is worse in my opinion.

So there are some exceptions, but I still say, "do not use abbreviations where they are not absolutely necessary." In almost all cases, what you may save in typing will be lost many times over by you and other developers who work on your code. Use copy and paste for long names - it is quicker and there is less chance of error.

Do Not Use Clever Compression

We see lots of this in text messaging, for example *2EZ* ("too easy"), *un4tun8* ("unfortunate"), and many more. This kind of cryptic abbreviation has no place in our naming conventions. The purpose of naming things is to communicate clearly and unambiguously, not to show others how witty we are.

There are many other examples of compression. For example `Postgres SQL` is compressed to `PostgreSQL` (using the last letter of `Postgres` as the first letter of `SQL`). I like the `PostgreSQL` database a lot, but I do not like its name: it is difficult to say and confusing for everyone who has to deal with it.

Use Names That Accurately Describe What They Mean

Surprisingly often, objects are named in a way that is actually misleading. An example from a railway system is in a file called `track_category` where `level` is actually a record type defining whether the record contains data which reflects the current location, proposed values, budget or next year's data.

Be Economical

Do Not Use Prefixes

Many published naming conventions advocate prefixes for names to indicate context or data-type. This is usually unnecessary. It makes the names longer, harder to remember and it often means that you have to scroll to the right to see the part that you really need to know.

Database systems, object-oriented programming languages, ETL (Extract, Transform and Load) tools, reporting tools and other development tools store metadata that tells you the context and type of the object you are naming, so do not repeat the context or the type in the name.

We have seen databases where every table name was prefixed with TBL_, every view name with VW_, even every column with COL_. The database can tell you what the object is (and it is usually obvious from the context) so do not waste valuable characters at the start of the name to repeat this information.

A slightly different use of prefixes is to identify groups of columns in a database table. For example, we might have a table called party, like this:

party
id
title
family_name
first_name
date_of_birth
address_line_1
address_line_2
address_city
address_state
address_zip_code
credit_limit
customer_since

In this case, the five columns prefixed with `address_` suggest that perhaps we should consider having a separate `address` table.

Use the Shortest Word That Expresses the Meaning Accurately

For example:

- *use* rather than *utilize*
- *now* rather than *current_time*
- *clean* rather than *cleanse*
- *start* rather than *commence*
- *end* rather than *terminate*
- *copy* rather than *serialize/deserialize*

There is a very comprehensive list at the Plain English Campaign[30].

Do Not State the Obvious

Do not include words like *number, no, data, code, flag, indicator, ind* in the name. Some examples we have seen are:

- `wc_no`, which should have been `work_center`
- `tt_code`, which should have been `technical_type`
- `sc_data`, which should have been `switch_and_crossing` (a railway term)
- `bu_flag`, which should have been `business_unit`
- `tran_ind`, what were they thinking of?

Note the bizarre tendency to abbreviate the part that we need to know and to spell out in full the redundant part. This does not apply only to computer systems. Why would a company call itself "S&C Corporation"? This tells us that it is a legal entity trading as a corporation but gives no clue as to what it does. It could be "Sand and Cement," "Software and Consultancy," "Saxophones and Clarinets," "Switches and Crossings," "Sailing and Cruising." Whatever the appropriate name is, it would be better than "S&C".

---

30. http://www.plainenglish.co.uk/files/alternative.pdf

Use Names in the Singular

If some names are singular and some are plural, users will forget which is which, and therefore make mistakes. Since the singular is usually shorter, this is the better name to use.

For example have a table called `supplier`, not `suppliers`.

Unfortunately, this rule conflicts with the standard for database table names used in Ruby on Rails, which in other respects has very good naming standards. If you are using Ruby on Rails then I suggest that you compromise on this rule for table names only.

Do Not Make Names Too Long

Just as it is easy to make mistakes with short, cryptic names, it is also easy to get one character wrong in a name that is 60 characters long. The optimum name is between one and four short meaningful words linked together with word separators (underscores).

Be Easy to Read

Use a Single Underscore Between Words in a Name

Examples: `customer_account_number`, `value_excluding_tax`.

There are other standard ways of separating words. For example, programmers writing in languages such as C, C++ and Java often use uppercase letters to mark the beginning of each word in a name. The examples given above would be `CustomerAccountNumber` and `ValueExcludingTax`. This is known as `CamelCase`.

In general, CamelCase is not so good for database systems, because they generally do not use case sensitive names, so when the name is stored in the database and then retrieved, the difference between upper and lowercase is lost and it is no longer easy to see the start of each word. For example, using the Oracle database system in its usual default state, the names would appear as `CUSTOMERACCOUNTNUMBER` and `VALUEEXCLUDINGTAX` after they have been stored in the database and retrieved again. The loss of separation between the words makes it much harder to read these names.

With Oracle, and other database systems, you can use case-sensitive names, but if you do, they have to be enclosed in quotation marks (or square brackets in Microsoft SQL Server). The extra noise introduced by large numbers of quotation marks is certainly not worth the saving of underscores to separate words. Do not use CamelCase for database objects; use underscores to separate the words.

If I'm writing an application in Java and using a PostgreSQL database, then I use CamelCase in the application and underscore-separated words in the database. The examples in this book follow this convention. It's a compromise but it's OK. [31].

Always use an underscore between words. Sometimes common terms, consisting of two or three words, are stuck together. Examples are `filename, policynumber, zipcode`. Do not do this; use `file_name, policy_number, zip_code` instead.

If we always separate the words with underscores then we don't get into the annoying situation of typing a query with the column name shown properly and then finding that the query fails because the words have been stuck together.

COBOL programmers conventionally used the hyphen as a word separator, and their legacy lingers on. Using hyphens is a problem for languages that do not insist on white space between names and operators because these languages interpret the separator as a minus sign. SQL is such a language in most of its implementations, so don't use hyphens.

Use Lowercase

Use lowercase unless there is a good reason for using uppercase. In printed text, lowercase is more readable than uppercase. (Why are newspapers and books written mostly in lowercase?)

Use lowercase for key words and for reserved words too; it is not helpful to put key words and reserved words in uppercase. Most database

---

31. You might want to use a tool to keep the names consistent. An example of such a tool is http://wiki.geany.org/howtos/convert_camelcase

documentation is written this way, but that is because they are trying to teach you the SQL language; you do not have to write your code like that and it is better if you don't.

Beware *Type* and *Status*

These two words must be the most common component of field, column, attribute and property names. At best they need qualification, and if the qualifier describes the meaning accurately enough then the word *type* or *status* may be redundant.

For example, an insurance policy, in a system we encountered, could have a *status* of:

- Canceled
- Cloned
- Exception
- Expired
- Live
- Merged
- Referred

Cloned, Merged, Exception and *Referred* normally happened to *Live* policies, so when policies had these status values, they were probably *Live*, but the *Live* status was masked because the status field was being used to record the progress through another process. If the field name had been qualified sensibly, then it would have become apparent that it needed to be several different fields.

Also, consider a table recording the details of bank loans. If there is a field called `loan_type`, does this describe whether the loan is fixed-rate or variable-rate, or does it describe whether the loan is secured or unsecured, or some other attribute? It would be better to have a field called `fixed_or_variable_rate` and another one called `secured`, and not have a `loan_type` field at all.

Be Consistent

Use Existing Names Unless They Break the Other Rules

Use names that exactly (or as closely as possible) match the names of the same objects in other applications or databases, unless doing so would break too many other rules. If the existing names are meaningless (like `TRAN_IND`) or misleading, or break other rules listed here, use a meaningful name and document the match between them; otherwise use the original name.

Never Re-use a Field with a Name That Conflicts with What the Field Contains

There is a system, in a leading telecommunications company, which has a field called `bank_sort_code` and this field contains the renewal date of the customer's contract. This was done because the company is using a large packaged software product. In this product it is unjustifiably difficult to change the data model. A date, like a bank sort code, can be represented in six digits. The bank sort code field was not being used so they used it for the date. The cost of mistakes caused by this misleading name has been very significant; it would have been far less costly to create a new field with the correct name.

You might say that users should look up every name in the data dictionary. But you probably don't have a data dictionary. If you do have one it is almost certainly not up-to-date. If you have an up-to-date, accurate data dictionary you must be working for a very special organization. I'd be willing to bet, though, that the users are more likely to guess the meaning than they are to look it up.

Make the name accurate. This is your best chance of having the data used correctly.

Be Consistent

When you have designed a good name for some object in your system, always use that name for that object. Do not, for example, use `zip_code` in the database and `postal_code` in the application.

Chapter 6 - Data Types

Relational databases traditionally emphasize `strong data-types`. Strong data-types restrict the data that can be held in a column. If the column has the data-type `date`, then it can only hold a valid date, so `date` is a strong data-type. If a column has the data-type `varchar` (meaning a character string) it can hold any string of characters: a date, a number, a timestamp, or some words. `varchar` is therefore a weak data-type because it imposes very few restrictions on the data stored in it.

Strong data-types are a very good thing for the kinds of data that are best stored in a relational database. We are looking at data that needs to be managed with discipline. These are the systems where data quality matters, where we are keeping accurate, highly structured records.

There are several reasons why we use strong data-types:

- The most important reason for choosing strong data-types is to use the database to enforce a level of data quality. For example you might need to sum the values in a column. If that column is stored as a number you can guarantee that the sum will work. If it is stored as a character string, then at best you have to convert the data to numbers, and it may not work because someone may have entered something other than a number in that column.

- The second reason is that with strong data-types you will be able to use the database functions to manipulate the data and compare it with other data efficiently. In an annual subscription service you would store each member's renewal date. You could use the built-in date functions to easily pick out those members whose subscriptions are due for renewal in the coming month. This sort of date processing is needed very frequently in commercial and government systems.

- The third reason is that the database will be able to store and process the data most efficiently if it knows what kind of data it is dealing with. Matching values between tables works most accurately and most efficiently when the things being matched are both stored in the same data-type and follow the same rules. The database can also manage compression, indexing and data distribution most efficiently if it knows the data-type.

- If you want to return data ordered properly then the database needs to know the data type. The same applies if you want to compare two values to see which is bigger. If you store numbers as strings then "100" will be less than "90"; if you store dates as strings then "19-Dec-2015" will be less than "20-Jan 2013".

- Also, it will be easier to move your data to another database if you restrict yourself to the most widely used data-types. It is very rare, in practice, to move a live application from one database to another. The cost of doing so is almost never worthwhile. But there is no point in erecting unnecessary barriers to migration.

In some systems we find every data field stored as a long string. This does mean that you are unlikely to have any data load failures, but you will pay for it many times over. Often people do this through lack of experience or poor advice, but sometimes it looks more like a deliberate technique to hide errors in the system.

All relational databases have a range of data-types available. There is a standard for relational databases defined by the American National Standards Institute (**ANSI**) and the International Organization for Standardization (**ISO**). No database vendor sticks to the standard completely but the core data-types are reasonably consistent.

The data-types which are available in relational databases fall into several categories.

- Simple building blocks of computer systems: numbers, strings and booleans.

- Complex data-types that can be regarded as a single object with very specialized processing specific to the object type. These include dates, timestamps, *spatial* or *geometric* objects, network addresses and **UUID**s (Universally Unique Identifiers). The support for these types includes validation of input, so that the content of columns with these types is always valid. The database also supplies functions and operators that support useful manipulation of these types.

- Large *black box* types, often known as **blobs** (binary large objects).

Chapter 6 - Data Types

These are actually files which may contain an image, a sound clip or a video. The database does not provide any functions to manipulate `blobs`. There is no point in storing such objects in the database.

- Data-types which contain their own internal structure for holding traditional data, and have different tools for navigating and manipulating the data inside the data-type. You should never use these data-types.

Let's look at these in more detail.

Simple Data-Types

This is a nice short list. Most of the columns in your database should have data-types from this list (plus dates and timestamps from the complex data-types list). Use these and your database will run better for it.

- Integer
- Exact decimal numbers
- Floating point numbers
- Boolean
- Character strings

Integer

Integers are whole numbers, useful for identifiers (surrogate keys), whole number arithmetic and many other purposes. In most databases there are various sizes of integers: `smallint`, `integer` and `bigint`. In most cases:

- `integer` is stored in a 4-byte number, giving a range from about -2 billion to +2 billion
- `smallint` is stored in a 2-byte number, giving a range from about -32,000 to +32,000
- `bigint` is stored in an 8-byte number, giving a range from about 10^{-18} to 10^{+18}. That's about 10 billion billion.

Some databases, notably Oracle, store numbers in their own proprietary formats. I consider that to be a design error.

Normally, you should use `integer`, especially for identifiers.

If you have a very big table which may become larger than two billion rows, then use `bigint` for the identifier. This happens quite frequently with machine-generated data or with transaction data for large organizations.

The main benefit of using `smallint` is when you know that the values must always be less than about 32,000. In these cases, `smallint` gives a back-stop on data quality to prevent larger numbers being stored in the column by mistake.

Exact Decimal Numbers

Exact decimal numbers are used mostly to hold amounts of money.

A typical definition of a monetary amount would be:

```
decimal(9,2)
```

This means that there is a maximum of nine digits in total (the `precision`) and two digits to the right of the decimal place (the `scale`). So that's seven digits before the decimal point and two after.

Most currencies in the world have two places after the decimal point. Dollars and cents, euros and cents, pounds and pennies, rubles and kopeks, and so on. If you have a currency with no sub-division, or with three decimal places, you can specify that too.

For money, the result of any calculation involving multiplication or division (such as calculating interest amounts) must be rounded to the smallest unit (cent, penny, kopek, etc.) and the rounding must be done by a defined process. One reason for this is to avoid possible fraud in which a rogue application collects very many tiny rounding adjustments and pays them to somebody else. A more innocent reason is that we expect our bank statements to be precise and consistent. We do not expect to see amounts changing by the odd penny or varying between different reports. In accounting systems for banks, and for the financial processing of all organizations, the amounts of money are required to be exact.

Money must *always* be stored in an exact numeric type. If you store money in a `floating point number` (described below) you end up with tiny fractions of the monetary unit. With floating point it is far too easy to be inconsistent about rounding. You will find that totals that are supposed to match, do not. You also increase your exposure to rounding error fraud. Never, never, store money in floating point data-types.

There are corresponding data-types (data classes) in programming languages, such as `BigDecimal` in Java and `BigDecimal` in Ruby. These classes behave in ways which are compatible with the exact numeric data-types in relational databases. They have been created explicitly for handling money. The `BigDecimal` classes are completely compatible with the ANSI standard exact numeric types.

Floating Point Numbers

Floating point numbers have a very high level of precision, but are not necessarily exact. This may sound like a contradiction, but this happens because some numbers cannot be represented exactly by decimal numbers. This table shows the results of storing various fractions in a database column defined with data-type `float`.

Value inserted	Value stored in a column of data-type float
1/3	0.333333333333333
1/4	0.25
1/5	0.2
1/6	0.166666666666667
1/7	0.142857142857143

A quarter can be represented by a decimal number as 0.25 exactly. A fifth can be represented as 0.2 exactly. But a third cannot be represented exactly by a decimal fraction. We would need an infinite number of decimal places. 0.333333333333333 is a very precise representation of one third. It is accurate to less than one part in 1,000,000,000,000,000. So that is pretty good but it is not exactly correct.

A good use of floating point numbers is the storage of latitude and longitude coordinates in a mapping system, such as the GPS satellite navigation system in your car. These coordinates would typically be stored in floating point numbers representing decimal degrees with six decimal places. Your SatNav will, on a good day, record the position of your car to within about five meters of its actual position. This is certainly accurate enough to tell you exactly which road you are on, and generally it is accurate enough to show which lane you are in.

If we store latitude and longitude with six decimal places, for example (51.041353, 0.698843) this specifies the position to within about 11 centimeters, which is significantly better than the SatNav can do. So, for this kind of data, floating point is ideal.

Because floating point numbers are approximate, two floating point numbers are often not equal when you expect them to be. The two numbers may be very, very close but different only in the least significant decimal place. You might reasonably expect that:

```
5/6 - (1/2 + 1/3) = 0
```

If you try doing this with floating point arithmetic, you will get a different answer. The following SQL statement[32]:

```
select
    (cast(5 as float) / 6) -
    ((cast(1 as float) / 2) + (cast(1 as float) / 3));
```

returns:

```
0.0000000000000001110223302462516
```

It doesn't make sense to test for equality between floating point numbers, and you must never use floating point numbers as keys, because joins between floating point numbers will very rarely work.

Floating point numbers are useful for mathematical purposes. More and more of these applications are coming along now with the Internet of Things.

Consider the case of recording the position of a car on a series of days. You might want to know how often the car is driving to a particular place. Let's suppose you are a private investigator and you suspect that the car is visiting the home of some sleazy gangster. You have planted a tracking device on the gangster's car (assuming that this is a legal thing to do where you live). Even if the car is parking on the gangster's driveway, it

---

32. The example is written for PostgreSQL. If you want a version that illustrates the point in Oracle, you should write it like this: select to_char ((cast(5 as binary_float) / 6) - ((cast(1 as binary_float) / 2) + (cast(1 as binary_float) / 3)), '9.9999999999999999999') from dual;

will not be in exactly the same place every time.

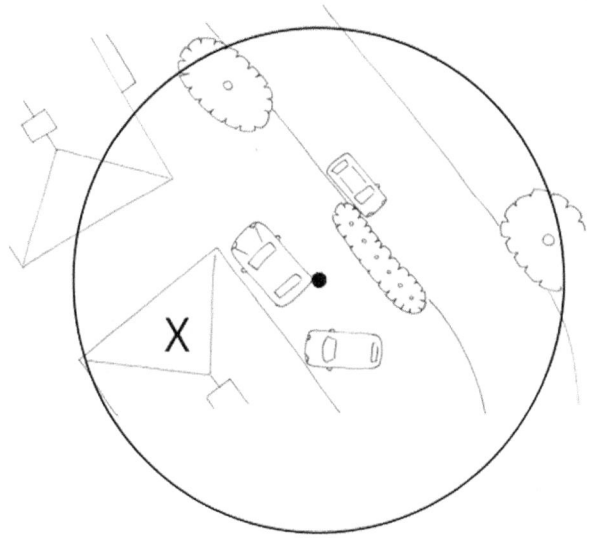

The car might be considered to have visited the property marked with an X if the car has stopped within the black circle for at least 15 minutes. Let's consider that the center of the circle is given by latitude and longitude coordinates: 52.656251, -0.623904, then the circle will extend from -0.623963 on the west to -0.623845 on the east, and from 52.656310 on the north to 52.656192 on the south. The car will never match the exact position it had before, but it may be in the range defined by the black circle, and then we've caught the driver **bang-to-rights** [33].

If you do need to match two floating point numbers, then the **equals** operator will probably not give you an exact match. Instead you must decide how close the two numbers must be to be considered as equal for your purposes. For example, if you determine that within one ten-millionth is close enough to consider that you have a match, then you could get the result you expect like this:

---

33. "Bang-to-rights" is a charming English expression, of mysterious etymology, meaning "caught red-handed".

download: close_enough.sql

```
select
  case
    when
        abs
        (
            (cast(5 as float)/6) -
            ((cast(1 as float)/2) + (cast(1 as float)/3))
        ) < 0.0000001
    then 'match'
    else 'no match'
  end;
```

- Do not test floating point numbers to see if they are exactly equal
- Do not try to join tables on floating point numbers
- Do not use floating point numbers to store money

Let's look at precision and the size of storage of floating point numbers.

A 4-byte floating point number may have the data-type: `float`, `real`, `binary_float`, or `float(6)` depending on which brand of database you are using. A 4-byte floating point number can hold values between 10^{-37} and 10^{+37}. That is a big range of numbers which will very rarely constrain what you want to achieve. You are more likely to be concerned about the precision. For a 4-byte floating point number the precision is at least six digits. This means that the first six digits of the number can be considered to be accurate, no matter where the decimal point is.

An 8-byte floating point number may have the data-type: `double precision`, `double`, `binary_double`, `real` or `float(p)`. Let's call an 8-byte floating point number a `double` for now. Usually `float(p)` means a `double` if p is 15 or greater. A `double` can hold values between 10^{-307} and 10^{+308}. I can't imagine a commercial application that would require such a range of numbers. I think you would have to be working on cosmology to care about a range beyond that. Precision is in the realms of reality though. A `double` has at least 15 decimal digits of precision and there are plenty of applications which need that.

Remember that `precision` is the number of digits, starting from the left, that can be considered to be accurate. Precision is not affected by the position of the decimal point. Again, longitude helps us to illustrate this.

A place in Norwich in the UK might have a longitude of +1.30573273. If we stored this value in a 4-byte floating point number we could assume that 1.30573 (the first six decimal digits) was accurate and any further decimal places were not reliable.

A place in Canberra, Australia could have a latitude of 149.06727537. If we stored this value in a 4-byte floating point number we could assume that 149.067 (also the first six decimal digits) was accurate and any further decimal places were not.

So, just because of the range of latitude numbers, we can store accuracy to the nearest 1.1 meters in Norwich, but only to the nearest 111 meters in Canberra. If we are concerned to have the same degree of accuracy around the world, then we have to allow for the biggest number of digits we need. To store the Canberra latitude numbers to five decimal places, to give us accuracy to the nearest meter, we would need eight decimal digits. We must therefore store all latitude values as `double precision` floating point numbers, to get enough precision.

If floating point numbers are appropriate for particular columns in your database, then it is worth thinking about whether a 4-byte float is precise enough for your use, or whether you need to use `double`. The choice will not make a lot of difference to storage space or performance unless you have very large numbers of measurements. If, for example you have one billion floating point numbers then you can save four gigabytes by storing them as 4-byte `float` rather than 8-byte `double`. It is not going to be a huge saving, and you would be hard-pressed to measure the performance difference between 4-byte and 8-byte floating point numbers. You can safely ignore the performance difference in this case.

Boolean

`Booleans` are not supported in most leading databases. In fact, PostgreSQL and the databases based on the PostgreSQL code are the only ones that support booleans effectively. I find `booleans` useful, but there are other ways to achieve the same result.

`Booleans` are just simple two-value fields. The values may be represented as Yes/No or true/false. There are various other possible representations including y/n, t/f and 0/1. In general, to avoid confusion, it is best not to use 0/1. (Does 0 mean true or does 1 mean true? Certain programmers would know, for their favorite languages, but most normal human beings do not.)

For clarity, we prefer to use a text value in files being transferred between systems. Yes/No is the simplest and most unambiguous form, provided the field is named sensibly.

You must name Boolean columns so that the value of the `boolean` tells you obviously and unambiguously what the meaning is.

For example, if you have a column that is called `security_flag` in an `employee` table, then does "true" mean that this person is considered a security risk, or does it mean that the person is approved for work requiring security clearance? If you name the column `security_approved` then it will be much more obvious what "true" and "false" mean.

Character String

Character strings are the `SQL` types: `varchar`, `char`, `varchar2` (Oracle), `character`, `character varying`, `nchar`, `nvarchar`, `vargraphic`, `text`, `string`, and maybe some others. They can hold any sequence of letters, numbers or special characters. They are appropriate for names, addresses, descriptions, etc.

Do not use strings to hold data that has one of the other strong data-types.

This is probably the most common cause of data quality errors, so use character strings only when the field is not a number, not a date, not a time and not a boolean. You can be pretty sure that if you define a date (for example) as a string then you will get multiple date formats in that column and you will get some values that don't even pretend to be dates.

You might think that character strings are simple, but they can be quite complicated. The `SQL` Standard defines variable-length strings with an upper limit, and fixed-length strings which are padded to the defined limit with spaces on the right. The official standard data-types are: `character(n)` (fixed length) and `character varying(n)`, abbreviated to `char(n)` and `varchar(n)` respectively.

Chapter 6 - Data Types

The lengths are in characters, not bytes, so if you have a multi-byte character encoding (such as UTF-8, in which each character is one or more bytes) the string may contain more bytes than characters.

The SQL Standard specifies some behavior around truncation and comparison which might not be what you expect. The various relational database vendors have come up with some non-standard solutions. Make sure you check your database documentation so that you know how it is behaving in these areas.

Fixed-length space-padded strings were more efficient a few decades ago, when relational databases first started being used. These days it makes no difference that you could detect.

So, to keep everyone's life simple, I always store character strings as variable-length, even for 1-byte strings. In most databases I define character strings as varchar(n) where n is the maximum length. In Oracle it has to be varchar2(n). If you are new to Oracle that may seem odd, but they renamed their varchar data-type to varchar2 early on with the intention of changing the behavior of varchar at sometime in the future.

Databases products generally support multiple character encoding schemes. In some schemes each character is represented by a single byte; in others a single character can be represented by multiple bytes.

The Web has now settled on UTF-8 with over 90% of all web pages being encoded in UTF-8. Commercial systems are following this trend but more slowly.

Some databases allow only one character set per database. Some allow different character sets for different columns. Whatever character set is being used it can be converted (usually automatically) into the character set of the client application.

The different character encodings can be quite confusing and I have seen time wasted in several projects on this issue[34].

I can see very little advantage in having multiple character encodings in the same database. My conclusion is to use UTF-8 for everything unless there is an overwhelming reason to use a different character set. Since

---

34. See: http://www.thedatastudio.net/dodgy_characters.htm for help if you are in this situation

UTF-8 has become established, I have never worked on a system where there was a better solution than UTF-8.

If you use UTF-8 for all character columns in your database you can use the varchar data-type for all your character data, unless you are using Microsoft SQL Server or SAP Sybase SQL Server in which case you must use nvarchar.

Complex Data-Types

Dates

If you have a column that is a date, without a timestamp, such as date of birth, then do define it as data-type date.

I have seen cases where dates are stored as character strings, and that is just asking for trouble. Someone, somewhere, will get a non-date value into a string through accident or design. Use the strong data-type and save everyone a lot of hassle.

When I started programming there were no tools to handle dates. We wrote partial date handling over and over again. We created the millennium bug, as well as many crimes against leap years and other idiosyncrasies of dates.

Today, most good development languages handle dates very thoroughly, and so do relational databases. They take into account complex aspects of dates, such as lost days[35] and different date numbering systems. They give you everything you need and more, so grab this free giveaway with both hands. Use the date data-type. (Did I say that already?)

Dates are the most useful complex type. They are usually stored as a simple integer, where zero is 1-Jan-1970. This is called the UNIX Epoch. Positive numbers record days after the UNIX Epoch and negative numbers record days before the UNIX Epoch. There is a mass of intelligence around the date data-types in relational databases and the Date classes in programming languages. These classes and data-types know how to get the actual date from the number stored, with the day of the week, the month of the year, the week number, and many other useful

---

35. See https://en.wikipedia.org/wiki/Old_Style_and_New_Style_dates

values. Don't even think about trying to do the conversion yourself.

Just make sure you use an unambiguous format when inserting a date value into your database.

Remember that Americans spell dates as MM/DD/YYYY, Brits spell dates as DD/MM/YYYY and Scandinavians spell them as YYYY-MM-DD. Scandinavians put the most significant part first and the least significant part last, which is the most logical.

I work across national boundaries as many of us do. The standard which I first saw on the `DEC VAX` systems (now defunct) specified dates as DD-Mmm-YYYY, for example 24-Dec-1950. That is unambiguous, so a step forward. I use this format for communication with other human beings.

For communicating with computer systems, especially databases, I usually use the Scandinavian style (and extend that to timestamps, which we will talk about next). So my favorite date format is YYYY-MM-DD, which has the advantage that it loads into `PostgreSQL` and some other databases without any conversion. The default behavior with Oracle is different, so we just have to be aware of the conventions in each database we use.

And one more thing. You don't save anything by specifying only the last two digits of the year. Always specify all four digits. I'm still embarrassed about the millennium bug. Many of us were born in the last century, so let's specify all four digits of the year and make sure our birthdays are recorded properly.

Timestamp

`Timestamps` include date and time. These are widely used to record, say, the date and time of a telephone call, the start of cover under a car insurance policy, and many other points in time.

`Microsoft SQL Server`, and `SAP Sybase SQL Server` used `timestamp` to mean an incrementing number on a row, not a date/time field at all. For what we refer to as `timestamp` here you should use `datetime2` in `Microsoft SQL Server` and `datetime` or `bigdatetime` in `SAP Sybase SQL Server`. `Microsoft` has now deprecated `timestamp` as a data-type in `SQL Server` and encourages the use of `rowversion` instead [36].

Everyone else calls a `timestamp` a `timestamp`, and that is what we do in the rest of this book.

As with dates, the `timestamp` data-type gives us a lot of support in doing calculations between timestamps, and in presenting them to the users. If your data is a timestamp, then store it using the `timestamp` data-type.

You might need `timezone`, which is an option on standard timestamps. It can all get quite confusing, so ideally keep all the timestamps in your database in the same timezone. You can always present the timestamp in any timezone, so long as you know what timezone it is recorded in.

It's hard enough keeping date formats straight, so if you have timestamps in your system, please choose a standard format and enforce it rigorously throughout your organization.

I strongly recommend the format "YYYY-MM-DD hh:mm:ss." "hh" in this format is the hour in 24-hour format. "MM" is the month as a 2-digit number, "mm" represents minutes. Hyphens, spaces and colons must be exactly as shown.

An example: "2014-06-03 20:52:41" (3rd June 2014 at 8:52pm and 41 seconds).

If you allow no flexibility, you will save yourself a lot of bother. It isn't a huge loss of freedom, so just use your freedom of expression in other areas and be absolutely rigid about your one and only timestamp format.

Spatial or Geometric Types

These types include: `point`, `linestring`, `polygon`, `circle`, `rectangle` and other shapes. They are most useful for geographic mapping applications. All the `GPS` applications for navigation and tracking of vehicles and people, on land, on sea and in the air, use these data-types.

As with other useful data-types these ensure that what is stored in each type is actually what it is supposed to be. In the databases that support these types there are very useful functions for querying spatial data. For

---

36. https://docs.microsoft.com/en-us/sql/t-sql/data-types/rowversion-transact-sql/

example, if you know the location (latitude and longitude) where a car is parked, you can easily find out the ZIP Code. The location of the car would be a point and the ZIP Code would be represented as a polygon that shows the boundary of the ZIP Code area.

There are spatial functions to find whether one object is contained in another, if they overlap, the area of a closed shape, the length of a line, the distance from one object to another and many other functions.

All processing of spatial objects must be done only by using the spatial functions.

A `linestring` is an array of pairs of numbers. I say, very firmly, that we should make all fields atomic and we should not have structures (such as arrays) inside a single field. The `linestring` data-type breaks both of these rules. The reason I think that linestrings and the other spatial data-types are good is that, like dates, their internal components are very tightly bound together and they are always accessed using the specific functions that are bundled with them. There is never a need to process anything inside a linestring. For example, you should never need to extract a location from within a linestring.

There are very few complex data-types that are worthwhile. Dates, timestamps and spatial data-types are the only ones that I have ever seen. All others, including the many specific objects in your applications, and mine, are much better handled using the simple data-types.

`PostgreSQL` has a few other useful data-types: `UUID`, `inet`, `cidr` and `macaddr`. These are all identifiers which have a particular format. Microsoft SQL Server provides an implementation of `UUID`s and does provide a function to generate new `UUID`s. None of the other leading relational databases provide any of these.

UUID

A `UUID` is a `Universally Unique Identifier` as defined by RFC 4122, ISO/IEC 9834-8:2005, and related standards. (Some systems refer to this data-type as a `globally unique identifier`, or `GUID`[37]). `UUID`s are used frequently in distributed systems where it is not feasible to have a single source for each unique key value. `UUID`s are designed to make it

---

37. https://www.postgresql.org/docs/10/static/datatype-uuid.html

extremely unlikely that the same key will be generated more than once.

UUIDs are actually hexadecimal numbers representing 128 bits, so that is 32 hexadecimal digits. They are normally presented with some hyphens, like this:

```
xxxxxxxx-xxxx-xxxx-xxxx-xxxxxxxxxxxx
```

Where each x is a hexadecimal digit (0-1, a-f) and each hyphen is a hyphen, for example:

```
fd44ac58-8801-27ac-59bd-523d3993408f
```

If you need to store UUIDs, and you are using PostgreSQL or Microsoft SQL Server, then use the UUID data-type because this will ensure that only valid UUIDs can be stored in this column. PostgreSQL does allow a few other input formats and always outputs in the standard format, so that may be helpful.

inet, cidr and macaddr

PostgreSQL also provides some network address formats: inet, cidr and macaddr.

inet and cidr hold an *IPv4* or *IPv6* host address. macaddr holds MAC addresses. All of these have standard formats.

If you need to store these kinds of hardware addresses and you are using PostgreSQL then the database will help to ensure the data quality in these columns, so use them.

Large Black Box Types (blobs)

There are many names for these data-types, including: lob, blob, clob, nclob, raw(n), long raw, raw binary, bytea, bfile, media types (audio, image, video, etc.) and others.

There is absolutely no benefit in storing these data-types in a relational database. There are less complex and less expensive solutions.

For many of these, the best solution is to store each blob in a separate file and to reference that file from the database, possibly with some metadata. In other cases, the Big Data tools may be a better way of managing these types of data.

I worked on a Call Center application, which kept a recording of each telephone call as a sound file in MP3 format. These files were very rarely accessed, but sometimes it would be necessary to find the calls with a particular customer, to verify what was actually said. The files were stored in a UNIX file system, in a directory structure something like this:

```
/<call_base>/<year>/<month>/<day>/<call_id>.mp3
```

for example:

```
/voicecalls/2003/12/15/83659271.mp3
```

The Call Center application passed some metadata about each call to a reporting application. The metadata included: start_of_call (timestamp), end_of_call (timestamp), call_id, agent, number_called_from, number_called_to. We stored all this metadata in a simple database table and wrote some reports for the Call Center supervisor. One report allowed the supervisor to search for calls based on a date range, the agent involved, or the telephone number, or any combination. Having identified a small number of calls that were interesting, the reporting application could construct, for each call, a URL to access the file containing the call. Having got the report on the screen the supervisor could click on the link containing the URL to listen to the call.

The calls took up a lot of space, but they could be stored on comparatively cheap storage, with minimal overheads. Individual calls could still be accessed in a couple of seconds. The metadata about the call was tiny by comparison, so access to the database was instantaneous.

This is a far less costly and more efficient solution than storing the voice call files in the database. This is the way to handle any large files of text, sound, images or other similar media. Do not store them in your database. It would be like using your nice shiny sports car to transport sacks of sand. Use a truck for that.

Sadly, some of these blob data-types have even found their way into the SQL standard. This is a very bad mistake, but you do not have to use these features.

To reiterate, relational databases are good at storing, searching and manipulating traditional data-types. I call these *traditional* because they were the types of data for which computers were developed. The applications which manipulate these data-types are accounting and record keeping. There are many modern applications which still need this kind of processing. All the online shopping systems will have to keep records of exact amounts of data, exact product identifiers, tracking deliveries by date, and so on. Modern systems may also have kinds of data which are better stored in non-relational systems. The important thing is to choose the right tool for the job.

Data-Types That Contain Their Own Internal Structure

There are some data-types which are incompatible with relational databases and these should never be used. That's right, I do mean *never*. These data-types hold traditional data, but have different tools for navigating and manipulating the data inside the data-type.

Data-types which actually conflict with the relational database concepts are:

- XML
- JSON
- arrays
- objects
- composite (or compound) data-types

All of these break the first rule of normalization, that data items should be atomic. They allow a single cell (a column value in one row) to contain multiple values packed into a structure. This is incredibly misguided.

To be clear: there is nothing wrong with these data-types outside the database; they are very useful when used appropriately. All I am saying is that none of them should be imported into the database in one big lump.

Let's take them one at a time.

XML

W3C[38] describes XML as:

> *"Extensible Markup Language (XML) is a simple, very flexible text format derived from SGML (ISO 8879). Originally designed to meet the challenges of large-scale electronic publishing, XML is also playing an increasingly important role in the exchange of a wide variety of data on the Web and elsewhere."*

Since XML carries its metadata with it, it is very useful for documents which have some structure, and for short variable messages. As XHTML, XML is the backbone of the world-wide web. XHTML is also what I use to format this book. Other file types (pdf, ePub and MOBI) are then generated automatically from the XHTML. This is an appropriate use of XML.

But I cannot understand why many people seem to think that XML is the ideal format to store *all* kinds of data. I have seen many cases where millions of records, all in exactly the same format, are stored in XML, and this is not a good use of XML.

Suppose we have some data structured like this:

policy_number	inception_date	expiry_date	premium	voucher_number
XYZ/00149204	17-Nov-2011	16-Nov-2012	544.87	2308388
XYZ/00063742	11-Apr-2011	10-Apr-2012	665.12	2129304
XYZ/00025348	20-Nov-2010	19-Nov-2012	275.27	2334157
XYZ/00025348	20-Nov-2010	19-Nov-2012	644.93	2334064
XYZ/00126466	29-Sep-2011	28-Sep-2012	309.56	2266203
XYZ/00007196	3-Jul-2010	2-Jul-2012	235.8	2005019

This looks normal and is easy to read. Suppose I now save this data as a csv file (comma-separated values) which looks like this:

---

38. http://www.w3.org/XML/

```
policy_number,inception_date,expiry_date,premium,voucher_number
XYZ/00149204,17-Nov-2011,16-Nov-2012,544.87,2308388
XYZ/00063742,11-Apr-2011,10-Apr-2012,665.12,2129304
XYZ/00025348,20-Nov-2010,19-Nov-2012,275.27,2334157
XYZ/00025348,20-Nov-2010,19-Nov-2012,644.93,2334064
XYZ/00126466,29-Sep-2011,28-Sep-2012,309.56,2266203
XYZ/00007196,3-Jul-2010,2-Jul-2012,235.8,2005019
```

That is not quite so easy for a human being to read because the columns are not aligned, but it is very easy for a computer to read, and most database systems will load this file very easily.

Now suppose that I feel the need to label every column in every row, like this:

policy_number	inception_date	expiry_date	premium	voucher_number
XYZ/00149204	17-Nov-2011	16-Nov-2012	544.87	2308388
policy_number	inception_date	expiry_date	premium	voucher_number
XYZ/00063742	11-Apr-2011	10-Apr-2012	665.12	2129304
policy_number	inception_date	expiry_date	premium	voucher_number
XYZ/00025348	20-Nov-2010	19-Nov-2012	275.27	2334157
policy_number	inception_date	expiry_date	premium	voucher_number
XYZ/00025348	20-Nov-2010	19-Nov-2012	644.93	2334064
policy_number	inception_date	expiry_date	premium	voucher_number
XYZ/00126466	29-Sep-2011	28-Sep-2012	309.56	2266203
policy_number	inception_date	expiry_date	premium	voucher_number
XYZ/00007196	3-Jul-2010	2-Jul-2012	235.8	2005019

If I gave you a spreadsheet looking like this, I think it would be fair enough if you asked whether I had lost my mind. Why would I repeat the headings on every row?

XML repeats the headings *twice* on every *field*, as shown below.

download: bordereau.xml

```
<?xml version="1.0" encoding="UTF-8"?>
<bordereau>
  <policy>
    <policy_number>XYZ/00149204</policy_number>
    <inception_date>17-Nov-2011</inception_date>
    <expiry_date>16-Nov-2012</expiry_date>
    <premium>544.87</premium>
    <voucher_number>2308388</voucher_number>
  </policy>
```

Chapter 6 - Data Types

```
    <policy>
      <policy_number>XYZ/00063742</policy_number>
      <inception_date>11-Apr-2011</inception_date>
      <expiry_date>10-Apr-2012</expiry_date>
      <premium>665.12</premium>
      <voucher_number>2129304</voucher_number>
    </policy>
    <policy>
      <policy_number>XYZ/00025348</policy_number>
      <inception_date>20-Nov-2010</inception_date>
      <expiry_date>19-Nov-2012</expiry_date>
      <premium>275.27</premium>
      <voucher_number>2334157</voucher_number>
    </policy>
    <policy>
      <policy_number>XYZ/00025348</policy_number>
      <inception_date>20-Nov-2010</inception_date>
      <expiry_date>19-Nov-2012</expiry_date>
      <premium>644.93</premium>
      <voucher_number>2334064</voucher_number>
    </policy>
    <policy>
      <policy_number>XYZ/00126466</policy_number>
      <inception_date>29-Sep-2011</inception_date>
      <expiry_date>28-Sep-2012</expiry_date>
      <premium>309.56</premium>
      <voucher_number>2266203</voucher_number>
    </policy>
    <policy>
      <policy_number>XYZ/00007196</policy_number>
      <inception_date>3-Jul-2010</inception_date>
      <expiry_date>2-Jul-2012</expiry_date>
      <premium>235.8</premium>
      <voucher_number>2005019</voucher_number>
    </policy>
  </bordereau>
```

These four examples all contain exactly the same data. The `csv` file contains 372 characters; the XML file contains 1,489 characters. This file contains only six records. Suppose we have a file with 20 million such records. The `csv` file will then be about 1.2GB. The equivalent XML file will be 5.5GB. At this level, the XML imposes a significant overhead. Suppose we have to send several of these files across our network every hour. That will take a significant amount of bandwidth. Suppose we have to archive these files. We would compress the files, of course. That does reduce the ratio between the XML file and the `csv` file. An uncompressed XML file of this type is normally over four times the size of an equivalent uncompressed `csv` file. If we compress them both then the ratio comes down to something over three times. A compressed XML file of this type is normally over three times the size of an equivalent compressed csv file. Just imagine telling your IT services people that you need to pay for three times as much disk space for archiving as you actually need.

And suppose you actually want to do something with the data in this XML file. If so, you'll have to parse it to extract the fields that you want. When you are dealing with high volumes, the processing power required can be very significant.

The point is that XML should not be used for large files in which the records have a consistent format. Simple. XML is good for documents, web pages, and for very variable data in files or messages which are small, say up to a few megabytes. XML was never intended for large fixed-format files.

So how does this affect the database? Most modern relational databases have been persuaded to support XML, so that you can store a whole XML file in one cell in the database. The vendors then supply functions which let you parse the XML data in the database. This is tedious to write and slow to run. The XML hides its metadata inside the XML file so the database can join from one element in an XML column to some other data in the database *only* by applying the XML parsing function to extract the element to join on. It is possible but it is horribly inefficient.

Remember our first rule: data cells must be atomic. An XML file is not atomic.

Here are some better options:

- Do not use XML for large files
- Do not use XML for files where the records all have the same fields
- If the number of characters taken up by tags in your XML file is bigger than the number of characters taken up by data, that is a good indication that the file should not be stored as XML.
- If you need to load XML into the database to process individual elements, parse the data, just once, into its elements before you load it into the database, and then load it into proper tables with atomic columns.
- Otherwise, store the XML files in a file system and store a reference to the XML file in the database.

JSON

JSON (JavaScript Object Notation) performs a similar function to XML. As with XML it is good for small documents with variable format. JSON is also wasteful for files with large numbers of consistently structured records. JSON is less inefficient than XML, but there is no need to incur the inefficiency at all.

Arrays

Array data-types enable you to store a list of things in one cell. In First Normal Form we split data into atomic units for a reason, actually a number of reasons. Read *Chapter 1 - Learning to Drive Your Database on page 32* again if you are not convinced. Relational databases have a simple consistent way of handling all data structures. It is a great mistake to introduce a different way of doing the same thing.

The PostgreSQL[39] documentation describes the array processing possibilities in meticulous detail, and then includes the following tip:

> *"Arrays are not sets; searching for specific array elements can be a sign of database misdesign. Consider using a separate table with a row for each item that would be an array element. This will be easier to search, and is likely to scale better for a large number of elements."*

I wonder why PostgreSQL felt compelled to support this data-type. I would rephrase the tip in a less diplomatic way. My version would be:

> *"Arrays are a sign of seriously bad database design. Do not use arrays. Design your database using a separate table with a row for each item that would be an array element."*

Objects

Oh dear. What an appalling misunderstanding. Finally, after years of confusion between *object-oriented* people and *relational database* people, David Heinemeier Hansson had the clarity of vision to see that there is no conflict. People had been looking for the keys to the universe

---

39. https://www.postgresql.org/docs/10/static/arrays.html

and, all along, it wasn't locked. A well-designed relational database table maps to a well-designed object. In an object-oriented program, each object will have its properties and a number of methods associated with them; in the database the object (that is, the table) will just have its properties (that is, the columns). Many objects may be things which will never be stored in a database; that's OK.

The very worst thing to do is to come up with a data-type which can store an object. This is a complete mismatch of ideas.

Just have a look at the way Ruby on Rails works with relational databases. This is the right way, so do it like this and stop fretting.

Composite Data-Types

Dates, timestamps and spatial data-types are composite types. These make sense because they are very widely used and their sub-components are really tightly bound together. It is very hard to think of new cases for useful composite types. If you think you have found one, think very carefully. Either you're a genius, or you are mistaken. It's much less embarrassing to question yourself than to promote something which really is not a great boon to mankind.

There has been pressure to make relational databases more flexible and to incorporate features that belong in development languages rather than databases. The pressure has come to some extent from customers, assuming that more flexibility and more features must be better. This is a mistake. Vendors have seen the opportunity to make incremental revenue and to lock customers in to their products by complying with these requests. Perhaps this is why some of the open source products actually have more of what Brooks calls *conceptual integrity*:

> "I will contend that conceptual integrity is the most important consideration in system design. It is better to have a system omit certain anomalous features and improvements, but to reflect one set of design ideas, than to have one that contains many good but independent and uncoordinated ideas." [40]

Sadly, Gartner[41] does not use conceptual integrity as one of the axes of

---

40. See Bibliography [Brooks]

its `magic quadrant`. Rather, it champions *completeness of vision* which is far more likely to encourage overweight and overpriced products with too many features. If your company has looked at the Gartner magic quadrant and bought a database from the top right hand corner, you can quietly mitigate the problem by using only the features that make sense for the role that the database must fulfill.

Back in 2005, at the Open Source Convention[42], David Heinemeier Hansson gave a talk entitled "Secrets Behind Ruby on Rails." He finished his talk with these wise words:

> *"Flexibility is over-rated.*
>
> *Too many technologies are chasing flexibility as [if it were] free. It is not. [...]*
> *Rails trades flexibility and gets a whole lot in return [...]*
> *Constraints are liberating.*
> *When you don't need to worry about all those small things and can just follow a path, you get to worry about your business logic, the stuff that your application is actually supposed to do."*

The more obscure or proprietary features you use in a particular database, the less well your database will work and the more you will become tied into that vendor. Your applications will take longer to develop and will be more difficult to maintain and enhance. The best way to use a relational database is to focus on the core features which are well established and robust. For processing that is outside the scope of the core relational database functionality, it is much better to use development languages that are independent of any particular database or application supplier. These are languages such as Java, Ruby (with or without Rails), Python and many others.

---

41. http://www.gartner.com
42. See Bibliography [Heinemeier Hansson]

Chapter 7 - Nulls

This is a whole chapter about nothing. It has to be done.

In the early days of relational databases I was working for Ingres (the forerunner of PostgreSQL and other fine databases). At that time Ingres did not support `nulls`. Oracle did support `nulls`. There were many academic and commercial arguments about whether `nulls` were a good thing or not, but eventually `nulls` won the commercial argument and all relational databases (including Ingres and PostgreSQL) support them today.

The main argument against `nulls` was that people don't understand them and that is as true today as it ever was.

However, `nulls` are useful and if we are going to use relational databases then we must understand them.

`Null` is the absence of a value. Maybe we don't know the value - the customer refused to reveal his date of birth, for example. Maybe the value is not applicable in this case. If we have a cancellation date on our policy record then unless the policy is canceled the cancellation date is not applicable.

The first thing to understand is that `null` is not a value. It is not minus one, not infinity, not zero, not blank. Think of each cell of a relational database, each intersection of a row and a column, as being an object. That object has a value (possibly) and some other attributes. It has a datatype, it has a name, it possibly has a relationship to another attribute in another table, it may have a default value. It also has an attribute that tells you whether it is `null` or not. If this instance is `null` then the cell does not have a value. If this instance is `not null` then the cell does have a value.

The data definition says whether a column is allowed to be `null` or not. If the column is defined as `not null` then all instances of it must have a value. If a column is allowed to be `null` then some instances may have values and some may not.

The second thing to understand is that `null` does not equal `null`. If two cells are both `null` then neither of them has a value. They have no values to compare. They cannot be equal. One cannot be bigger than the other, nor can it be smaller than the other.

I realize that I am using a sledgehammer to crack a nut here. I am doing so because this is so widely misunderstood. The examples should make this clearer. So let's look at what actually happens.

If, in our `person` table in the Claims system, we have a row with both `first_name` and `family_name` missing then we need to try to find out who this person is. We'll look up the contact details using this query:

download: missing_name.sql
```
select
  telephone_number,
  email_address,
  address_line_1,
  city,
  state,
  zip_code
from
  person
where
  first_name is null and
  family_name is null;
```

Notice that we write `is null` (not `= null`, which would be wrong). SQL insists on this to reinforce the point that `null` is not equal to anything, not even `null`.

In this table there is only one row with both names missing, and this is shown below. At least we have an address so we can write and ask for the details. (Or we could if it were real data.)

telephone_number	email_address	address_line_1	city	state	zip_code
434-982-0929		25 Lexann Lane			27669

(1 row)

Since we now know that there is one row where `first_name` is null and `family_name` is null, we can write a rather silly query to emphasize this point one more time.

download: null_never_equals_anything.sql

```
select
  telephone_number,
  email_address,
  address_line_1,
  city,
  state,
  zip_code
from
  person
where
  first_name is null and
  first_name = family_name;
```

```
 telephone_number | email_address | address_line_1 | city | state | zip_code
------------------+---------------+----------------+------+-------+----------
(0 rows)
```

This query, as expected, returns no rows. It will never return any rows because if `first_name` is `null` it can never be equal to `family_name`.

Arithmetic

Any arithmetic expression using a `null` value returns `null`. This table will let us demonstrate this.

download: show_table_nulls_in_arithmetic.sql

```
select * from nulls_in_arithmetic;
```

```
 id | value |     comment
----+-------+------------------
 53 |     5 | Value is not null
 74 |       | Value is null
(2 rows)
```

We can run a query on this table to demonstrate the behavior of `null` in arithmetic expressions.

Chapter 7 - Nulls

download: nulls_in_arithmetic.sql

```
select
    id,
    10 + value as ten_plus_value,
    10 - value as ten_minus_value,
    10 * value as ten_times_value,
    10 / value as ten_divided_by_value,
    comment
  from
    nulls_in_arithmetic;
```

The query returns the following:

```
 id | ten_plus_value | ten_minus_value | ten_times_value | ten_divided_by_value |    comment
----+----------------+-----------------+-----------------+----------------------+------------------
 53 |             15 |               5 |              50 |                    2 | Value is not null
 74 |                |                 |                 |                      | Value is null
(2 rows)
```

Notice that the query does not fail. You just do not get an answer. The users will be quick to spot missing figures in their reports. One unexpected null in the data is all it takes to cause this.

However, aggregation functions behave differently. We'll look at those next.

Aggregates

Now, it just so happens (because I arranged it that way) that we have some dodgy data in the transaction table. There is a row that has a null amount and we can find it, with some of its neighbors, as shown in the following query and resulting data set.

download: find_null.sql

```
select
  id,
  amount,
  created_at
from
  transaction
where
  (created_at between '2015-03-01 12:00:00' and '2015-03-01 17:00:00') and
  actual_or_reserve = 'Actual' and
  payment_or_recovery = 'Recovery'
order by
  created_at;
```

```
    id   | amount  |     created_at
---------+---------+--------------------
   92874 |   73.25 | 2015-03-01 13:57:24
   28589 |   87.15 | 2015-03-01 14:30:11
  153494 | 8128.05 | 2015-03-01 14:38:57
   17999 |         | 2015-03-01 15:02:53
   81604 | 8445.70 | 2015-03-01 15:38:16
(5 rows)
```

The next example uses these rows to show what happens when we apply aggregate functions to a set of values that include a null.

download: aggregate_null.sql

```
select
    count(*)       as count_rows,
    count(amount)  as count_amount,
    sum(amount)    as sum_amount,
    min(amount)    as min_amount,
    max(amount)    as max_amount,
    avg(amount)    as avg_amount
from
    transaction
where
    (created_at between '2015-03-01 12:00:00' and '2015-03-01 17:00:00') and
    actual_or_reserve = 'Actual' and
    payment_or_recovery = 'Recovery';


count_rows | count_amount | sum_amount | min_amount | max_amount |     avg_amount
-----------+--------------+------------+------------+------------+----------------------
         5 |            4 |   16734.15 |      73.25 |    8445.70 | 4183.5375000000000000
(1 row)
```

Is that what you expected? There is a logic to this, but it isn't always what you might expect. You just have to learn how it works. Here are the rules:

- `count(*)` gives the number of rows, whether any of the column values are `null` or not.
- `count(amount)` gives the number of `non-null` values.
- `sum(amount)` gives the sum of the `non-null` values.
- `min(amount)` gives the minimum of the `non-null` values. (Not only is `null` not equal to anything; `null` is also not less than anything. Try saying that with fewer negatives!)
- `max(amount)` gives the maximum of the `non-null` values. (Not only is `null` not equal to anything; `null` is also not greater than anything.)
- `avg(amount)` gives the average of the `non-null` values. This is the sum of the `non-null` values divided by the number of `non-null` values.

Chapter 7 - Nulls

In all cases, this is what you normally want, but you really do need to know what these expressions will deliver and how they are calculated.

Joins ...

If we enforce Primary Key constraints, and allow Foreign Keys to be `null` only if the relationship is optional, our joins will work properly. We do still need to be aware of optional relationships and we will need to use outer joins sometimes, as described in *Chapter 10 - Select From Many Tables on page 193*.

Here's a case where it might not be so obvious. Suppose we want to know which drivers in our Claims system are also named as passengers in a claim. This type of query could be used to detect possible claims fraud, where a ring of criminals make multiple claims (usually whiplash claims).

We will take a few steps to get there. It is useful to understand what is happening over the next few queries. You will run into the situations that are being described here and, hopefully, this will save you a lot of puzzling over the results when you see them in the real world.

The first query is a first attempt to assess the scale of the situation. Putting a query in parentheses and then running a count on the results is cheaper than selecting all the data, so we can see if we have a reasonably sized data set to start with.

download: join_null.sql
```
select
  count(*)
from
  (
    select
      b.first_name as driver_first_name,
      b.family_name as driver_family_name
    from
      driver a
      join
      person b
      on a.person_id = b.id
  ) x
  join
  (
    select
      d.first_name as passenger_first_name,
      d.family_name as passenger_family_name
```

```
        from
          passenger c
          join
          person d
          on c.person_id = d.id
      ) y
      on
        x.driver_first_name = y.passenger_first_name and
        x.driver_family_name = y.passenger_family_name;
```

The result is 280 rows.

```
 count
-------
   280
(1 row)
```

This query is not joining the result sets on Primary and Foreign Keys; it is matching on `first_name` and `family_name`.

...and Set Operators

Let's cross-check our results by running another query, which uses the set operator `intersect` to find the names that are in both result sets.

download: intersect_null.sql
```
select
  count(*)
from
  (
    select
      b.first_name as driver_first_name,
      b.family_name as driver_family_name
    from
      driver a
      join
      person b
      on a.person_id = b.id
    intersect
    select
      d.first_name as passenger_first_name,
      d.family_name as passenger_family_name
    from
      passenger c
      join
      person d
      on c.person_id = d.id
  ) x;
```

This time we get 286 rows.

```
count
-------
  286
(1 row)
```

What is going on?

We can find the rows that are in one result set and not the other by using the set operator **except**, as shown in the next query. It is quite long, but I simply copied and pasted the two queries I had before and put **except** in between them.

download: except_null.sql

```sql
select
  z.driver_first_name,
  z.driver_family_name
from
  (
    select
      b.first_name as driver_first_name,
      b.family_name as driver_family_name
    from
      driver a
      join
      person b
      on a.person_id = b.id
    intersect
    select
      d.first_name as passenger_first_name,
      d.family_name as passenger_family_name
    from
      passenger c
      join
      person d
      on c.person_id = d.id
  ) z
except
select
  x.driver_first_name,
  x.driver_family_name
from
  (
    select
      b.first_name as driver_first_name,
      b.family_name as driver_family_name
    from
      driver a
      join
      person b
      on a.person_id = b.id
```

```
    ) x
    join
    (
      select
        d.first_name as passenger_first_name,
        d.family_name as passenger_family_name
      from
        passenger c
        join
        person d
        on c.person_id = d.id
    ) y
    on
      x.driver_first_name = y.passenger_first_name and
      x.driver_family_name = y.passenger_family_name;
```

Here are the results:

```
driver_first_name | driver_family_name
------------------+-------------------
Marina            |
                  | Toder
                  | Wedgbury
Nathanael         |
                  | Fielder
Kelan             |
(6 rows)
```

In all cases, either the `first_name` or the `family_name` is null. These are not returned by our initial query because the `driver_family_name` found via the `passenger` relationship is null and this is not equal to the `driver_family_name` found via the `driver` relationship, which is also null. Null does not equal null.

However, when we run the set functions, a row with ("Marina", null) does match another one with ("Marina", null). The queries look equivalent, but they are not.

It is important to remember that the set operators will match rows containing nulls. In fact, the set operators also match rows where all the columns are null in both sets. Depending on the problem you are trying to solve, the join might work better for you or the set operators might be the right one to use. Once you understand the differences in behavior, you can choose the query that is best for your situation.

Another way to match nulls is to convert them to some arbitrary string as shown in the next example.

Chapter 7 - Nulls

Coalesce returns the first of its arguments that is not **null**. The usual way of using **coalesce** is to provide two arguments, the first of which is a column that may be **null**, and the second of which is a literal, as in this example.

```
select
    coalesce(first_name, 'UNKNOWN') as first_name,
    family_name
from
    person
where
    first_name is null;

 first_name | family_name
------------+-------------
 UNKNOWN    | Toder
 UNKNOWN    | Wedgbury
 UNKNOWN    | Fielder
(3 rows)
```

Coalesce is very useful, but be aware that the value you convert nulls to may exist already in the data. If there were a value of, literally, "UNKNOWN" in the first_name column in the example above, then we would not be able to see from this query whether the original value was null or "UNKNOWN".

The next query shows the use of **coalesce** to convert any nulls to strings and we can match the strings. It returns names where they have a value, and the string "<null>" in any names that are **null**. This query returns 286 rows, including the six rows that have **null** names.

download: coalesce_null.sql

```
select
  count(*)
from
  (
    select
      b.first_name as driver_first_name,
      b.family_name as driver_family_name
    from
      driver a
      join
      person b
      on a.person_id = b.id
  ) x
  join
  (
    select
      d.first_name as passenger_first_name,
```

```
              d.family_name as passenger_family_name
        from
            passenger c
            join
            person d
            on c.person_id = d.id
    ) y
    on
        coalesce(x.driver_first_name, '<null>') =
            coalesce(y.passenger_first_name, '<null>') and
        coalesce(x.driver_family_name, '<null>') =
            coalesce(y.passenger_family_name, '<null>');
```

Strings

In most databases, an empty string is not the same as a `null` string. Oracle is different, treating the empty string as a `null` string. Either way it is confusing. You cannot tell whether a string is empty or `null` just by looking at it, but, with `PostgreSQL` and most other databases you can distinguish them in the `where` clause. The example below sets up some data in `PostgreSQL` and shows how different queries handle the `null` field.

download: null_vs_empty_postgres.sql

```
    create table string (id integer, color varchar(8));

    insert into string (id, color) values(1, 'Green');
    insert into string (id, color) values(2, '');
    insert into string (id, color) values(3, 'Orange');
    insert into string (id, color) values(4, null);
    insert into string (id, color) values(5, 'Purple');
```

```
# select id, color from string;
 id | color
----+--------
  1 | Green
  2 |
  3 | Orange
  4 |
  5 | Purple
(5 rows)

# select id, color from string where color = '';
 id | color
----+--------
  2 |
(1 row)
```

```
# select id, color from string where color is null;
 id | color
----+--------
  4 |
(1 row)
```

Let's compare that with the set up for Oracle. The only difference in the set-up is that we use `varchar2` instead of `varchar`, as advised by Oracle. But the results of the queries are different, as the results show; Oracle treats the empty string as `null`.

download: null_vs_empty_oracle.sql

```
create table string (id integer, color varchar2(8));

insert into string (id, color) values(1, 'Green');
insert into string (id, color) values(2, '');
insert into string (id, color) values(3, 'Orange');
insert into string (id, color) values(4, null);
insert into string (id, color) values(5, 'Purple');


SQL> select id, color from string;

        ID COLOR
---------- --------
         1 Green
         2
         3 Orange
         4
         5 Purple

SQL> select id, color from string where color = '';

no rows selected

SQL> select id, color from string where color is null;

        ID COLOR
---------- --------
         2
         4

SQL>
```

`Oracle` is the only database that behaves this way, as far as I am aware. I have tested all of the following databases and they all distinguish between `null` strings and empty strings:

- PostgreSQL
- IBM DB2 for Linux

- MySQL
- SQLite
- Microsoft SQL Server
- Netezza
- NuoDB

This is a pain, because it means that our applications must behave differently depending on which database brand we are using. It is possible to build applications so that they behave the same way with both systems, by avoiding creating empty strings in the database for example, but this adds some work too.

There are, of course, many subtle differences between the databases, but this treatment of empty and null strings is particularly subtle and when it does appear it can waste a lot of time until the developer works out what is happening or finds someone who has seen this before.

Inserts and Updates

We will talk about inserts, updates and deletes in detail in *Chapter 11 - Populating Your Database on page 227*.

Inserts and updates provide ways to set columns as null in the database, of course. With inserts, if you do not mention a column then it is set to null (unless you have defined a default value). With updates, columns that you do not mention are not changed.

With insert you can use the keyword null to set a column to null, like this.

```
insert into string
    (id, color)
values
    (5, null);
```

The syntax for update uses "=" as an assignment operator in the set part as well as using "=" as a comparison operator in the where part. The example is straightforward:

download: update_null.sql

```
update string
  set color = null
where
  id = 5;
```

Java

Handling **nulls** in **JDBC** seems a bit awkward to me, and I can understand why **Java** developers complain about it. It is one of several features in **Java** that are a bit long-winded.

Given that I have to use several different development languages, **Java** is still one of my favorites and I don't get too upset about a few extra words in my source code. Many languages commit far worse crimes.

The code below shows how to check for null in **Java/JDBC**. What seems odd to me is that you have to get the value first, and then ask if it was null, which tells you whether your previous statement worked as expected or not. If you don't do the `wasNull` check, your `amount` object will be null (**Java**'s null) and you will get an exception if you try to use it.

download: null_java.sql

```
while (resultSet.next())
{
  id = resultSet.getInt("id");
  amount = resultSet.getBigDecimal("amount");
  if (resultSet.wasNull())
    System.out.println("id: " + id + ", amount is null");
  else
    System.out.println("id: " + id + ", amount: " + amount);
}
```

Bite the bullet - you just have to do it for every column that could be null, otherwise you will get exceptions. It is tedious, but not exactly difficult.

Chapter 8 - Keys

Relational databases depend on keys to identify every record and to link records together. This chapter explains how they work and gives you the pros and cons for different ways of allocating key values. This may be similar to what you know in other contexts but it is important to understand the particular requirements for your relational database.

A key must uniquely identify one object, must not be null and should be unchanging for the life of the object.

In the examples in this book we have used *surrogate keys* everywhere. Some explanation is overdue.

Natural and Surrogate Keys

A key is some field whose value can be used to identify a row in a database or an object in an application. For this purpose we can use *natural keys* or *surrogate* keys.

Natural keys are fields that exist in the real world, outside the database. In most normal situations, at work or at the sailing club that I belong to, for example, my name is a perfectly good key. I don't meet many other Ballards and never another Ron Ballard, so, in these environments my name identifies me uniquely and distinguishes me from everyone else.

However, if I Google my name then I find many other Ron Ballards, in my country and around the world. This means that for my dealings with big companies, like my bank, my mobile phone company or any online retailer, my name is not suitable as a key. If these organizations used my name as a key for my account then the transactions would get tangled up with those belonging to other Ron Ballards.

There are other natural keys that are better, as identifiers, than the names that we are given.

In the USA every citizen and every resident has a Social Security Number. In the UK every person who has ever had a job has a National Insurance number. There are equivalents in other countries. The authorities go to considerable trouble to make sure that these numbers

Chapter 8 - Keys

identify each individual person uniquely, so they are potentially good keys. However, some people do not have these numbers.

The same characteristics apply for Driving License Numbers. For people who drive this is a good unique key, but many people do not drive.

Many countries give each person a unique number at birth. This is probably pretty reliable.

Often, natural keys have information coded into them. My driving license number has my date of birth embedded in it, for example. This may help to ensure that you have a unique key, but if you actually need the embedded information as a value in its own right, you should capture it in a field of its own.

Other things, apart from people, have natural keys. For example cars have identification numbers (Vehicle Identification Numbers and license plates). The authorities again go to great efforts to ensure that these numbers are unique, so that each car can be identified precisely, to record ownership and to find the owner in case they break the laws on driving or parking. However, car identification numbers can change during the life of the car. People get attached to particular sequences of letters and numbers and they want to keep the same number when they buy a new car. In these cases, the natural key is not reliable over time.

Mobile phone numbers look like pretty good keys, but they do get recycled over time, so the same number will get you to a different phone and often a different owner a few years later.

If we want a primary key then this must be unique, not null, and (as far as I'm concerned) unchanging for the life of the object. *Unique* means that each key identifies exactly one object, or exactly one row in each table. *Not null* is obviously important because if the key is null then we cannot use it to identify anything.

I want keys to be unchanging, so that each key takes the same value for the life of the object. If the key changes this gives us a lot more work. We would have to change the key and everything that is related to it. Since other systems, not using our database, may have the old key, then changing it is going to have effects that we cannot possibly control. There will be confusion and errors.

Natural keys are appealing precisely because they have meaning outside the database. A human being can look at a natural key and relate it to some other records, maybe paper records. It may also be possible to tell what the key means just by looking at it. Several of the natural keys we have mentioned above have recognizable formats. Unfortunately, though, natural keys do not always prevent duplicates, there may be some missing values and the key may change over time. Natural keys are often very long, with a mixture of letters, numbers and punctuation. All keys are at risk of transcription errors and the longer the key, the higher the risk.

Data-types for Surrogate Keys

Surrogate keys are keys made up by the system (the application or the database). They have no meaning outside the database. Surrogate keys are usually positive integers, stored in four bytes with a range from one to just over two billion. This gives more than enough unique values for most tables. For very large tables, such as transaction tables in retail or banking systems, or machine-generated data, such as telematics, you will often need larger numbers. In these cases you can use a `big integer`, an 8-byte number that can hold over 9,000,000,000,000,000,000. I had to look up what that is called; it's nine quintillion. It doesn't really matter; it should be big enough. Of course, if you are using Oracle, then the default is a 38-digit number. I never understood why, but it seems to work.

It is not unusual now to use UUIDs for primary keys. A UUID is a 36-character string that uses a complex combination of factors that may include the machine address, the current timestamp, random numbers and hashes of locally stored values. This is all to try to ensure unique keys in distributed systems where it is not feasible to go to a single source to get the next unused value. In fact only 32 of the characters are significant, but there are four hyphens, which are always the same and always in the same positions. A well-generated UUID is probably unique, but uniqueness cannot be guaranteed.

If you don't have a distributed database, and if the chances are vanishingly small of it ever being a distributed database, with a very, very large number of records, I would suggest that you use integers instead of UUIDs.

Allocating Surrogate Key Values

One great advantage of surrogate keys is that you can change the natural keys without any drama. So, in a database of cars, when the owner gets a new license number that almost spells her name, she can change it and all we have to do in the database is to change the license number. All the relationships will use the surrogate key, none of them are affected by the change in the license number.

One potential difficulty with surrogate keys is that they don't have any meaning to human beings, so we have to do thorough testing to make sure that the key does not get changed inadvertently. Just scanning a few records to see if the data looks sensible will not be an acceptable test.

Some people feel very uncomfortable with the knowledge that the same numbers can be keys for different objects in different tables. 527 could be my person `ID`, someone else's claim `ID`, an unrelated vehicle `ID` and so on. It doesn't matter, because you always look for a key within one specific table, but again, it is necessary to be careful and test properly to avoid confusion. One solution to this is to draw all the keys in the whole database from one single source. This will work if you use integer keys and have less than two billion rows in your database in total. Or you could use `big integers` everywhere, which will be fine in almost all systems. Then you only ever have one object with each key value.

The primary key in one table must match the foreign key in another table which is related to it. With a single sequence, then you can't join the wrong things together. With overlapping key sequences, suppose each table has its own sequence, starting from one and allocating the next number for each record in each table, then you could do some silly joins, which would not fail, but would be wrong. For example, in our claims database, it would be possible to do a join on passengers and transactions, even though there is no actual logical link between them. If you have people joining tables on the wrong keys, then you have a bigger problem and you should deal with that. People do guess at what the database means and they can produce plausible results that are completely wrong.

In high volume transaction systems, the single source of the key values would be a bottleneck and would be likely to have some effect on transaction performance.

Once again, the Ruby on Rails defaults are best for most systems: use integers for keys and start the sequence at one for each table.

We should mention the allocation of keys. In the early days of relational databases, it was usual to create a `last_used_key` table to hold a single row with a single column. Whenever we inserted a new row, and a new key was needed, we started a transaction, read the `last_used_key` record, updated it by adding one to the value, wrote it back to the database and committed the transaction. Then we used the new value as the key for the record we wanted to insert. This worked, but when we got into high transaction volumes with lots of users hitting the database at the same time, the `last_used_key` table did slow things down.

The database vendors responded with special tables called **sequences**. These perform only one purpose, and that is to deliver the next unique key value. The vendors were able to streamline the process of getting the next key safely and quickly. Sequence tables are used in most systems today and they work well. Most databases make this even easier by letting you define that you want a column populated with the next unique key value automatically when you insert a new row. You define this when you create the table. The syntax varies from one database to another as shown in the following table:

Database	Automatic key generation syntax
PostgreSQL	serial or bigserial
Oracle	generated always as identity
DB2	generated always as identity
MySQL	auto_increment
Microsoft SQL Server	identity
Sybase	identity
Teradata	identity

Under the covers these databases use sequences to implement automatic key generation.

If you do a complicated migration and you unload the table, then recreate it (with some extra columns, for example) and reload it again, bear in mind that the sequence used for the automatic key generation will start from one again by default. You usually want to override the default with the starting number for the next key, because you don't want new keys to clash with those already in the table.

Chapter 12 - Database Migrations That Preserve Data on page 244 shows one way of dealing with sequences being reset.

Compound Keys

A key can be a combination of columns. For a primary key, this combination must be unique and none of the columns may be `null`. You will find that you need compound keys if you are using natural keys rather than surrogate keys. For example a natural key for a vehicle in the USA could be state and license_number. Since vehicles are licensed by state, the license number should be unique within a state.

Let's create a table in our `PostgreSQL` database to illustrate what happens:

```
create table vehicle
(
    state                         varchar(2),
    license_number                varchar(8),
    make                          varchar(32),
    model                         varchar(64),
    constraint primary_key_vehicle primary key (state, license_number)
);
```

Now if we ask `PostgreSQL` what the table looks like, this is what we get:

```
# \d vehicle
             Table "public.vehicle"
     Column     |         Type          | Modifiers
----------------+-----------------------+-----------
 state          | character varying(2)  | not null
 license_number | character varying(8)  | not null
 make           | character varying(32) |
 model          | character varying(64) |
Indexes:
    "primary_key_vehicle" PRIMARY KEY, btree (state, license_number)
```

We can see that `PostgreSQL` has made the state and license_number not null because that is the rule for primary keys. It has also given us an index on the combination of these two fields. Again that is useful because we will often access the table on the primary key. Having an index will make accessing the table by its key quicker and helps `PostgreSQL` to make sure that the key stays unique.

If this table `Has_many` drivers (for example) then we will have to store the state and license_number in the driver table as the foreign key linking back to the vehicle. When we join the two tables we will have to match both columns like this.

```
driver.state = vehicle.state and
driver.license_number = vehicle.license_number
```

This all works fine, but it does make more code than using surrogate keys.

The Bottom Line

You have some choices with keys. We've talked about the pros and cons. In most cases, the best choice is to use surrogate keys that are generated by the database from a sequence. These will usually be integers.

Once again, these are the default settings for Ruby on Rails. You can see why I like Rails, although I don't often get a chance to use it in big corporates.

Part C - Getting Data From Your Database

To get data out of your database you use the `SQL select` statement. Here we build up your expertise, starting with the simplest possible `select` statement and progressing to sophisticated analytics.

Chapter 9 - Select From One Table

You may want to grab one existing record to show it to the user and maybe allow her to edit it. You may be writing a report to give the sales team daily tracking of sales by territory. You may have worked out a way to carry out some innovative analytics to tell your boss something he didn't know about the operation of your company. You may be preparing the data for some fancy visualization for a presentation to your customers. For any of these you will use the `SQL select` statement.

So let's make a start.

Your First Select Statement

For most of the examples in this book, we use a database representing an imaginary car insurance claims system. This database includes a table called `vehicle`. Let's see what it contains by typing this query:

```
select * from vehicle;
```

Here are the first few rows returned by this query:

```
 id | policy_id | license_number | state_where_licensed |      created_at       |      updated_at       |     make      |        model         | year_first_licensed
----+-----------+----------------+----------------------+-----------------------+-----------------------+---------------+----------------------+---------------------
  1 |         2 | EUKOUU         | OH                   | 2016-02-06 21:49:15.052014 | 2016-02-06 21:49:15.052014 | GMC           | Sierra               | 2007
  2 |         3 | P279SHK        | MO                   | 2016-02-06 21:49:15.052014 | 2016-02-06 21:49:15.052014 | Cadillac      | ELR                  | 2015
  3 |         4 | IWD NOV        | GA                   | 2016-02-06 21:49:15.052014 | 2016-02-06 21:49:15.052014 | Cadillac      | Escalade             | 2009
  4 |         8 | JBR OJR        | AL                   | 2016-02-06 21:49:15.052014 | 2016-02-06 21:49:15.052014 | Ram           | ProMaster City       | 2007
  5 |         9 | C480TOW        | DE                   | 2016-02-06 21:49:15.052014 | 2016-02-06 21:49:15.052014 | Lexus         | RX                   | 2006
  6 |        10 | 288 103        | OH                   | 2016-02-06 21:49:15.052014 | 2016-02-06 21:49:15.052014 | Land Rover    | Range Rover Evoque   | 2013
  7 |        11 | F14DIL         | RI                   | 2016-02-06 21:49:15.052014 | 2016-02-06 21:49:15.052014 | Nissan        | Cube                 | 2011
  8 |        12 | 959 KYP        | MS                   | 2016-02-06 21:49:15.052014 | 2016-02-06 21:49:15.052014 | Mini          | Cooper Convertible   | 2012
  9 |        13 | UQBZLA         | WI                   | 2016-02-06 21:49:15.052014 | 2016-02-06 21:49:15.052014 | Nissan        | Armada               | 2006
 10 |        15 | EEF 212        | ID                   | 2016-02-06 21:49:15.052014 | 2016-02-06 21:49:15.052014 | Jeep          | Renegade             | 2011
 11 |        18 | 4V645MO        | MI                   | 2016-02-06 21:49:15.052014 | 2016-02-06 21:49:15.052014 | Infiniti      | QX80                 | 2006
 12 |        20 | KLK 4          | DC                   | 2016-02-06 21:49:15.052014 | 2016-02-06 21:49:15.052014 | Chevrolet     | Sonic                | 2007
 13 |        22 | 836346         | OR                   | 2016-02-06 21:49:15.052014 | 2016-02-06 21:49:15.052014 | Dodge         | Challenger           | 2010
 14 |        24 | C776LQY        | NY                   | 2016-02-06 21:49:15.052014 | 2016-02-06 21:49:15.052014 | Volkswagen    | Touareg              | 2007
 15 |        26 | G743LUE        | LA                   | 2016-02-06 21:49:15.052014 | 2016-02-06 21:49:15.052014 | Subaru        | Impreza              | 2010
 16 |        27 | 0212PEL        | ID                   | 2016-02-06 21:49:15.052014 | 2016-02-06 21:49:15.052014 | Cadillac      | Escalade EXT         | 2015
 17 |        30 | USSLHF         | AK                   | 2016-02-06 21:49:15.052014 | 2016-02-06 21:49:15.052014 | Mini          | Cooper Coupe         | 2012
 18 |        31 | 322774         | DE                   | 2016-02-06 21:49:15.052014 | 2016-02-06 21:49:15.052014 | Mercedes-Benz | GLK-Class            | 2007
```

This statement gave us the answers we asked for, but we had to print the result set in a *very* small font to fit it on the page, and this is quite a narrow table.

`Select *` ... says "select all the columns." This often gives you a very wide table to look at, and you usually are not interested in all the columns. So, usually we list only the columns that we are interested in, like this:

Chapter 9 - Select From One Table

download: select_vehicle_columns.sql

```
select
    make,
    model,
    state_where_licensed,
    license_number
from
    vehicle;
```

The results are:

```
    make      |        model        | state_where_licensed | license_number
--------------+---------------------+----------------------+----------------
 GMC          | Sierra              | OH                   | EUKOUU
 Cadillac     | ELR                 | MO                   | P279SHK
 Cadillac     | Escalade            | GA                   | IWD NOV
 Ram          | ProMaster City      | AL                   | JBR QJR
 Lexus        | RX                  | DE                   | C480TOW
 Land Rover   | Range Rover Evoque  | OH                   | 288 103
 Nissan       | Cube                | RI                   | F14DIL
 Mini         | Cooper Convertible  | MS                   | 959 KYP
 Nissan       | Armada              | WI                   | UQBZLA
 Jeep         | Renegade            | ID                   | EEF 212
 Infiniti     | QX80                | MI                   | 4V645WO
 Chevrolet    | Sonic               | DC                   | KLK 4
 Dodge        | Challenger          | OR                   | 836346
 Volkswagen   | Touareg             | NY                   | C776LQY
 Subaru       | Impreza             | LA                   | G743LUE
 Cadillac     | Escalade EXT        | ID                   | 0212PEL
 Mini         | Cooper Coupe        | AK                   | USSLHF
 Mercedes-Benz| GLK-Class           | DE                   | 322774
```

Selecting specified columns lets us focus on the values we are interested in.

We usually want to choose the number of *rows* we see, too, rather than seeing the first few that the database happens to return to us.

Most databases have large numbers of rows, and you can't read them all. Just as you can't look at the two million people at the Mardi Gras Carnival and make a reliable estimate of how many have read *To Kill a Mockingbird*, you cannot browse all the rows from a two-million row table and derive any useful analysis from them. The interesting and valuable patterns in the database will not leap out at you, but you can use **SQL** to find them. The examples coming up show you many ways to find the treasure in the mass of data in your database.

So next, we will limit the rows we look at in a purposeful way by specifying some condition that we want the returned rows to satisfy.

There is a **person** table in our database. The person table has over 12,000 rows, so we don't want to see all of those. Let's suppose that we have been told that some people in our database, who live in the state of Arizona, have not told us which city they live in.

Here's the query. The where clause says that we want people with a **state** of 'AZ' and with a null **city** . **Null** (described in *Chapter 7 - Nulls on page 150*) is a special term meaning that the **city** has no value assigned to it.

download: select_person_where.sql

```
select
    city,
    state,
    family_name,
    first_name,
    email_address
from
    person
where
    state = 'AZ' and
    city is null;
```

And here are the results:

```
city | state | family_name | first_name |   email_address
-----+-------+-------------+------------+--------------------
     | AZ    | Bacon       | Sidra      |
     | AZ    | Sandifer    | Darnell    | Darnell@rura.com
     | AZ    | Springett   | Wrightson  | Wrightson@nati.com
(3 rows)
```

We can see that there are three people with no city entered on their records. For two of them we have email addresses so we can send them a message and ask them to update their profiles.

Let the database do the work.

Too often we see people selecting all the data out of the database and trying to manipulate it in a spreadsheet. It is much cheaper and more effective to do the analysis in the database and then, maybe, copy the limited, processed results into a spreadsheet or a presentation tool.

The database can handle billions of rows; the spreadsheet cannot. In the examples in this book we are working with small numbers of rows, but in real applications dealing with business data or data from public services, the numbers of records get large very quickly.

Notice that we are not stepping through the rows, no `loops`, no `list iterators`, no `if`, `then`, `else` branching. Relational databases manipulate *sets of records*.

Tell the database what to do, not how to do it.

Working this way makes your code simpler and a lot faster.

Let's look at the `where` clause in more detail. Suppose we want to contact people in the city of Minneapolis. We can look up their telephone numbers and email addresses in our next query.

download: select_minneapolis.sql

```
select
    first_name,
    family_name,
    telephone_number,
    email_address,
    city,
    state
from
    person
where
    city = 'Minneapolis';
```

And here are the results.

```
first_name | family_name | telephone_number |     email_address     |    city     | state
-----------+-------------+------------------+-----------------------+-------------+------
Leen       | Lyne        | 952-273-7850     |                       | Minneapolis | MN
Flynn      | Garnett     | 763-254-0029     |                       | Minneapolis | MN
Luka       | Mcgirr      | 320-294-8990     | Luka@refugitque.com   | Minneapolis | MN
Jaedan     | Yarwood     | 952-215-6192     |                       | Minneapolis |
Glynis     | Henty       | 507-255-7501     | Glynis@arisque.com    | Minneapolis | MN
(5 rows)
```

Note that the matching is case sensitive and that the literal value 'Minneapolis' is enclosed in single quotes. The *smart quotes* used in Microsoft Word are different. Don't try preparing your queries using Word; if you do you will get strange error messages. Use a plain text editor instead.

Pattern Matching

You can make the search case-insensitive as shown below. We use the **upper** function to convert all the letters in the city name to uppercase and then match against the uppercase version of the name.

download: select_any_case.sql
```
select
    first_name,
    family_name,
    telephone_number,
    email_address,
    city,
    state
from
    person
where
    upper(city) = 'MINNEAPOLIS';
```

The table below shows the results of the case-insensitive search and we can see that, as well as having a record with the city name in uppercase, someone has entered the city name with alternate letters in uppercase and lowercase. It's hard to imagine why someone would do that, but you do find all kinds of idiosyncrasies in real data.

first_name	family_name	telephone_number	email_address	city	state
Leen	Lyne	952-273-7850		Minneapolis	MN
Flynn	Garnett	763-254-0029		Minneapolis	MN
Luka	Mcgirr	320-294-8990	Luka@refugitque.com	Minneapolis	MN
Jaedan	Yarwood	952-215-6192		Minneapolis	
Glynis	Henty	507-255-7501	Glynis@arisque.com	Minneapolis	MN
Knikki	Loach	763-225-5704	Knikki@patriasque.com	MINNEAPOLIS	MN
Hamish	Frakes	218-275-4525	Hamish@altos.com	MiNnEaPoLiS	MN

(7 rows)

The **upper** function is one that is consistent across all the leading relational databases.

There are many functions that are built into **SQL** databases. Unfortunately, every database provides a slightly different set. There is a lot of overlap, but you need to check the actual implementation in the database you are using. Find the online documentation for the database you are using and check the built-in functions because this is an area that will not be completely standard.

One form of pattern matching that is standard across all relational databases is the `like` operator (as in "is X like Y?" rather than Facebook's meaning "do you like Z?"). The `SQL` `like` operator is used with patterns, which may include "%" meaning *match zero or more characters* and "_" (underscore) meaning *match exactly one character*.

So, if we're not sure whether the city is Minneapolis or Mineapolis or Minneapolus we can run this basic pattern-matching query.

download: select_like.sql

```
select
    first_name,
    family_name,
    telephone_number,
    email_address,
    city,
    state
from
    person
where
    upper(city) like 'MIN%EAPOL_S';
```

The table below shows the result of searching for the variants of Minneapolis.

```
first_name | family_name | telephone_number |      email_address      |    city     | state
-----------+-------------+------------------+-------------------------+-------------+------
 Leen      | Lyne        | 952-273-7850     |                         | Minneapolis | MN
 Judith    | Rickard     | 320-224-6910     | Judith@orsus.com        | Minneapolus | MN
 Flynn     | Garnett     | 763-254-0029     |                         | Minneapolis | MN
 Luka      | Mcgirr      | 320-294-8990     | Luka@refugitque.com     | Minneapolis | MN
 Felicity  | Futcher     | 507-284-9893     | Felicity@reditu.com     | Mineapolis  | MN
 Jaedan    | Yarwood     | 952-215-6192     |                         | Minneapolis |
 Glynis    | Henty       | 507-255-7501     | Glynis@arisque.com      | Minneapolis | MN
 Knikki    | Loach       | 763-225-5704     | Knikki@patriasque.com   | MINNEAPOLIS | MN
 Hamish    | Frakes      | 218-275-4525     | Hamish@altos.com        | MiNnEaPoLiS | MN
(9 rows)
```

With the simple pattern matching available in all relational databases, using `like` and `upper` it is possible to find the results you want in poor-quality data. It is much better to fix data quality at the point where the data enters the system, but this is often neglected, so the help that `SQL` offers is welcome.

Pattern matching is not only a tool for use with poor data quality. There are many uses for `like` queries. An example is ZIP Code analysis. The first digit of a ZIP Code represents a certain group of U.S. states, the second and third digits together represent a region in that group (or sometimes a large city) and the fourth and fifth digits represent a group of delivery addresses within that region. The next query shows how to match only the first three characters of the ZIP Code, and the following table shows the results.

download: select_like_zip_code.sql

```sql
select
    first_name,
    family_name,
    telephone_number,
    city,
    state,
    zip_code
from
    person
where
    zip_code like '412%';
```

```
first_name | family_name | telephone_number |     city     | state | zip_code
-----------+-------------+------------------+--------------+-------+----------
Sherlock   | Meyers      | 989-231-6479     | Ann Arbor    | MI    | 41294
Zara       | Mottram     | 313-233-8611     | Lansing      | MI    | 41223
Jalika     | Townsend    | 248-939-4185     | Grand Rapids | MI    | 41211
Leewan     | Dickeson    | 380-538-7093     |              |       | 41293
Tavish     | Pendrich    | 380-671-1417     |              |       | 41207
Mason      | Steed       | 260-882-7702     |              |       | 41253
Spencer    | Nurse       | 906-271-1398     |              |       | 41291
(7 rows)
```

Some databases provide more advanced pattern matching functions such as: **soundex, Levenshtein edit distance, metaphone** and **regular expressions**. If your database provides any of these, you will probably find them useful, depending on the searches you are asked to do.[43]

Sorting

Relational databases do not define the sequence of the rows in a table. You may even get the rows in a different sequence if you run the same query more than once. This is by design. A row in a table is an object, an instance of the class defined by the table. The state of each object is the set of values of its properties. The sequence in which the objects might be stored somewhere is irrelevant to the states of those objects. All the information about each row is in the values in that row. We do not use

---

43. You can find out more about this topic at:
    http://www.thedatastudio.net/standardize_for_searching.htm

some external variable, such as the ordinal position in a file, as a hidden attribute. The important thing to remember is that if you do not specify the order in which you want your rows to be presented, the order will be unpredictable.

To sort your result set you add an order by clause at the end of your SQL query. Logically, the result set is constructed by the database first, and only then sorted according to the order by clause as the last step before presenting the data to the user. It makes sense, therefore to have the order by clause as the last one. This also means that you can order by a calculated value, and that can be very useful.

You can order the records in any sequence you like based on the values in particular columns. You can sort the rows into ascending sequence based on one column, or descending sequence, or on multiple columns specifying whether each column is to be ascending or descending. The database knows the data-type and can sort properly depending on that data-type. If you use strong data-types such as dates and time stamps, instead of strings, the database will know how to sort the dates and times correctly.

The next query shows how we sort by zip_code_area (ascending) and within that by family_name (descending). You must use the abbreviations asc for ascending and desc for descending. If you do not say whether to sort ascending or descending then the default is ascending. Each column in the order by clause is labeled separately, so whatever you labeled any other column, an unlabeled column in the order by clause will be sorted ascending.

download: select_order_by.sql

```
select
    substring(zip_code for 3) as zip_code_area,
    family_name,
    email_address
from
    person
order by
    zip_code_area asc,
    family_name desc;
```

The next table shows part of the result set from this query. We can see that rows are shown in ascending order of zip_code_area, and within each zip_code_area the rows are in descending order by family_name.

```
zip_code_area  |    family_name    |        email_address
---------------+-------------------+-----------------------------
     010       |    Walsh          |    Jacinda@ueniamque.com
     010       |    Sidgwick       |    Suzanne@auxilium.com
     010       |    Imison         |    Tara@dirae.com
     010       |    Chafin         |    Adina@clarum.com
     011       |    Wheadon        |
     011       |    Wall           |    Bernadette@nullo.com
     011       |    Shaddick       |
     012       |    Varick         |    Knikki@digrediens.com
     012       |    Taft           |    Lachlan@futuris.com
     012       |    Frisbee        |    Jaryn@iuuant.com
     013       |    Hubbucks       |    Soloman@positum.com
```

In this query, we found the `zip_code_area` by using another SQL function, `substring`, which in this case is taking the first three characters of the `zip_code` and naming the result `zip_code_area`. The `substring` function is one that does vary from one database to another. Oracle, for example calls its similar function `substr` and the parameters are arranged differently. Always check the functions for your particular database.

We have specified multiple conditions in some of the `where` clauses. You can combine conditions using `and`, `or` and `not`. As with other languages, be careful to put parentheses in the right places to get what you want, especially when using mixtures of `and`, `or` and `not`.

Grouping and Aggregating

`Aggregating` means looking at the properties of groups of rows in our database. The properties might be the total value or the average value for example.

Let's suppose that we want to look at the payments we have made in our claims system, and see how much we have paid to each claimant.

The query below adds up all the payments that were actual payments (rather than reserves), for each claimant. We're sorting the results by the total amount paid, in descending order because the most costly claimants are the most interesting. The `where` clause is restricting the data we are considering to only those transactions that are `actuals` rather than `reserves` and are `payments` rather than money recovered from other people involved in the claim. So, for actual payments we are looking at the `claimant_id` and the `amount` paid. The `group by` says that we want to do something with all the actual payments for each claimant, and in this case we are calculating the sum of those payments for each claimant.

download: select_group_by_claimant.sql

```
select
    claimant_id,
    sum(amount) as total_paid_out
from
    transaction
where
    actual_or_reserve = 'Actual' and
    payment_or_recovery = 'Payment'
group by
    claimant_id
order by
    total_paid_out desc;
```

The first few results are shown below.

```
claimant_id | total_paid_out
-------------+----------------
       8458 |       280092.02
       7766 |       196180.25
       8489 |       189882.91
       5872 |       187030.76
       6090 |       178681.01
       6946 |       177757.59
      13096 |       177359.12
       9814 |       175420.11
      12688 |       172151.29
       1510 |       167212.71
```

Columns in the `select` list must either be columns by which we are grouping, or columns that we are aggregating. It does not make sense to list any other columns (say the `created_at`) column) because there could be many `created_at` values for each `claimant_id`. We are only returning one row for each `claimant_id`, so which `created_at` value would we want?.

Most databases do not allow you to include other columns, and that makes sense. `MySQL` does allow you to include other columns, but the value you get for each group is just one of the possible values; you don't know which one it will be, and it can be different every time you run the query, so it really is not useful. `MySQL` documentation explains very clearly what happens, but even if you are using `MySQL`, I suggest that you follow the normal rules to avoid confusion.

Every column in the select list should be either a grouping column or an aggregate. Do not include any other columns in aggregate queries.

The aggregate functions available are:

- count
- avg (meaning average)
- sum
- min (meaning minimum)
- max (meaning maximum)

You can see them all in the next query, followed by its result set.

download: select_all_aggregates.sql

```
select
    claimant_id,
    sum(amount) as total_paid_out,
    count(amount) as number_of_payments,
    avg(amount) as average_paid_out,
    min(amount) as minimum_payment,
    max(amount) as maximum_payment
from
    transaction
where
    actual_or_reserve = 'Actual' and
    payment_or_recovery = 'Payment'
group by
    claimant_id
order by
    total_paid_out desc;
```

claimant_id	total_paid_out	number_of_payments	average_paid_out	minimum_payment	maximum_payment
8458	280092.02	7	40013.145714285714	19.96	96780.21
7766	196180.25	4	49045.062500000000	2.30	98560.55
8489	189882.91	5	37976.582000000000	91.58	93219.30
5872	187030.76	5	37406.152000000000	44.54	95536.74
6090	178681.01	6	29780.168333333333	559.13	99215.43
6946	177757.59	9	19750.843333333333	2.05	87949.64
13096	177359.12	4	44339.780000000000	26.13	94133.62
9814	175420.11	9	19491.123333333333	57.89	96365.19
12688	172151.29	5	34430.258000000000	30.00	96667.46
1510	167212.71	5	33442.542000000000	1320.12	97793.40

There are some options with count. These are illustrated in the next query, followed by its result set.

download: select_count_options.sql

```
select
    count(*)                        as count_star,
    count(family_name)              as count_family_name,
    count(distinct family_name) as count_distinct_family_name
from
    person;


 count_star | count_family_name | count_distinct_family_name
------------+-------------------+----------------------------
      12538 |             12411 |                       4259
(1 row)
```

`count(*)` means count all the rows which qualified according to the `where` clause.

`count(family_name)` means count all the family_names that are not null. You could also say `count(all family_name)` which is the same as `count(family_name)`.

`count(distinct family_name)` means ignore duplicates. If the family_name `Wilson` is in 15 `person` records we only count it once.

You can use `distinct` on the other aggregate functions (`sum`, `min`, `max` and `avg`) but I cannot think of a sensible use for that.

Just as we can order by multiple columns, so we can group by multiple columns. The next query shows an example of this. We want to report payments by claimant and by month.

download: select_group_multiple.sql

```
select
    claimant_id,
    to_char(created_at, 'YYYY-MM') as payment_month,
    sum(amount) as total_paid_out
from
    transaction
where
    actual_or_reserve = 'Actual' and
    payment_or_recovery = 'Payment'
group by
    claimant_id,
    payment_month
order by
    claimant_id,
    payment_month;
```

There are several ways of converting the transaction timestamp (`transaction.created_at`) to a year and month. The method used here is actually a formatting function, and it returns a string. We have chosen this particular format because it will be easily understandable by the user and so that we can sort the months into chronological order.

In this case we are ordering by the same columns that we are grouping by. This is often what we want, but the two clauses are independent. We can order by any combination of columns in the result set. We have not specified whether we want the order to be ascending or descending, so we will get the default order which is always ascending.

Here are the first few rows of the result set.

```
claimant_id | payment_month | total_paid_out
------------+---------------+---------------
          1 | 2013-02       |          18.36
          1 | 2014-02       |        6163.58
          1 | 2014-03       |          68.43
          1 | 2015-05       |          52.37
          1 | 2015-10       |        2020.61
          2 | 2015-02       |         103.12
          2 | 2015-03       |          20.55
          2 | 2015-05       |          56.93
          3 | 2015-02       |          46.95
          3 | 2015-05       |           7.08
          3 | 2015-08       |        4744.96
          4 | 2013-07       |          60.85
          5 | 2013-03       |          33.20
          5 | 2013-04       |        3078.43
          5 | 2014-09       |          74.15
```

Suppose we want to see only those claimants who have been paid more than $100,000 in one month. There is a clause for that. The `having` clause selects only those *groups* that satisfy the `having` condition.

We have seen that the `where` clause is applied to select the data *before* we do any grouping. In contrast, the `having` clause is applied *after* the data is grouped together, and returns only the groups we want. So, `where` applies to individual rows, and `having` applies to the groups that result from the aggregate function.

A sample query using the `having` clause is shown below, followed by its result set. It is worth getting familiar with the `having` clause because it enables you to do a lot of useful data analysis with a construct that is quite simple, when you get used to it.

download: select_having.sql

```
select
    claimant_id,
    to_char(created_at, 'YYYY-MM') as payment_month,
    sum(amount) as total_paid_out
from
    transaction
where
    actual_or_reserve = 'Actual' and
    payment_or_recovery = 'Payment'
group by
    claimant_id,
    payment_month
    having sum(amount) > 100000
order by
    payment_month desc;


 claimant_id | payment_month | total_paid_out
-------------+---------------+----------------
        8987 | 2015-04       |      104214.76
        4246 | 2015-03       |      106747.39
       13781 | 2015-02       |      107314.64
       12261 | 2014-05       |      102221.02
(4 rows)
```

Window Functions

When we use SQL we try hard to think in terms of a set of records, rather than stepping through the records one at a time. This almost always gives better performance and avoids many common programming errors that occur in coding loops and conditions.

But there are some cases where we need to look at a sequence of rows and do some calculation between rows in the sequence. Window Functions enable us to do this efficiently and simply in the database server.

Window Functions are often used in statistical analysis, and so they are often known as "analytic functions".

To demonstrate how the window functions work we will use an example from the "Internet of Things", in this case vehicle tracking, as used by trucking companies and, increasingly, by private car insurance companies. The vehicle is fitted with a device that is a GPS tracker and that can send messages over the cellphone network. This device sends a message every few seconds giving the current position of the vehicle, and some other data. One interesting piece of information from such devices is how far the vehicle has travelled. The devices often present this as an odometer, like the one you have in your own car, showing the total distance travelled by the vehicle since it first left the factory where it was made. The messages are received and stored in a central database where the various data elements are processed into information that is useful to the user: the trucking company, the insurance company or the individual driver.

To hold this data, we have added another table, called track, to our database, like this:

download: track.sql

```
create table track
(
    id                                     serial not null,
    vehicle_id                             integer not null,
    location_timestamp                     timestamp not null,
    odometer_meters                        double precision,
    latitude                               double precision,
    longitude                              double precision,
    created_at                             timestamp not null default now(),
    updated_at                             timestamp,
    constraint track_primary_key           primary key(id),
    constraint foreign_key_track_vehicle   foreign key (vehicle_id)
                                           references vehicle(id)
);
```

Here is some of the data in the track table for a particular vehicle on a particular day:

```
 vehicle_id | location_timestamp  | odometer_meters |    latitude   |   longitude
------------+---------------------+-----------------+---------------+--------------
       3310 | 2015-08-06 10:02:50 |        19390077 |     51.3184103 |     1.1171609
       3310 | 2015-08-06 10:03:00 |        19390220 |      51.318396 |     0.9741752
       3310 | 2015-08-06 10:03:10 |        19390367 |      51.318396 |     1.1211752
       3310 | 2015-08-06 10:03:20 |        19390516 |     51.3197966 |     0.9735758
       3310 | 2015-08-06 10:03:30 |        19390656 |     51.3203986 |     1.1129738
       3310 | 2015-08-06 10:03:40 |        19390807 |     51.3213046 |     1.2630678
       3310 | 2015-08-06 10:03:50 |        19390950 |     51.3199032 |     1.4046664
       3310 | 2015-08-06 10:04:00 |        19391113 |     51.3205715 |     1.5669981
       3310 | 2015-08-06 10:04:10 |        19391280 |     51.3212228 |     1.4006494
       3310 | 2015-08-06 10:04:20 |        19391439 |      51.322145 |     1.5587272
       3310 | 2015-08-06 10:04:30 |        19391608 |     51.3227196 |     1.7271526
```

We want to use the odometer reading from each row and the odometer reading from the previous row to work out how far the car has traveled. We will use a window function to do this.

When we say "previous row" we are thinking of the rows in order of location_timestamp, so we need to put an order by clause in our SQL statement. We then imagine a window over two adjacent rows so that we can see the current and previous row at the same time. We can think of the window sliding through the result set showing us each row and the previous one, like this:

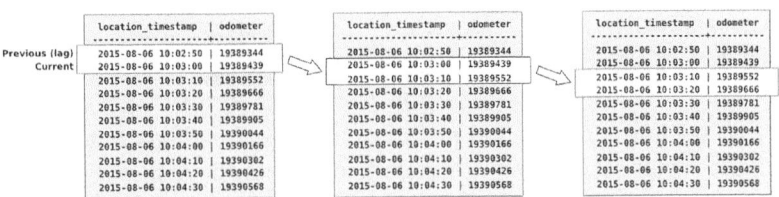

Here is the SQL we need:

download: current_and_previous_odometer.sql

```
select
    location_timestamp,
    lag(odometer_meters)
        over (partition by vehicle_id order by location_timestamp)
        as previous_odometer,
    odometer_meters as current_odometer
from
    track
where
    vehicle_id = 3310;
```

The over clause tells the database how to construct the window. We say partition by vehicle_id because we want each window to show only rows for one vehicle_id. We also say, order by location_timestamp because, within each window, we want the rows to be in location_timestamp sequence. Then looking at each row we want to get the odometer reading from the current row and the odometer reading from the previous row. We say lag(odometer_meters) to identify the odometer reading in the previous row. Obviously, in the first row of each window, there is no previous row, so previous_odometer will be null in this case.

Here are the first few rows from of our result set:

```
location_timestamp  | previous_odometer | current_odometer
--------------------+-------------------+------------------
2015-08-06 10:02:50 |                   | 19390077
2015-08-06 10:03:00 |          19390077 | 19390220
2015-08-06 10:03:10 |          19390220 | 19390367
2015-08-06 10:03:20 |          19390367 | 19390516
2015-08-06 10:03:30 |          19390516 | 19390656
2015-08-06 10:03:40 |          19390656 | 19390807
2015-08-06 10:03:50 |          19390807 | 19390950
2015-08-06 10:04:00 |          19390950 | 19391113
2015-08-06 10:04:10 |          19391113 | 19391280
2015-08-06 10:04:20 |          19391280 | 19391439
2015-08-06 10:04:30 |          19391439 | 19391608
```

Now that we have current and previous odometer readings in the same row in the result set, we can use them to calculate the distance traveled between messages. Here's the SQL:

download: distance_travelled.sql

```sql
select
    location_timestamp,
    previous_odometer,
    current_odometer,
    current_odometer - previous_odometer as meters_travelled
from
    (
        select
            location_timestamp,
            lag(odometer_meters)
                over (partition by vehicle_id order by location_timestamp)
                as previous_odometer,
            odometer_meters as current_odometer
        from
            track
        where
            vehicle_id = 3310
    ) x;
```

Note that the inner query is the one we used before.

Here are the first few results:

```
location_timestamp  | previous_odometer | current_odometer | meters_travelled
--------------------+-------------------+------------------+-----------------
2015-08-06 10:02:50 |                   | 19390077         |
2015-08-06 10:03:00 |          19390077 | 19390220         |              143
2015-08-06 10:03:10 |          19390220 | 19390367         |              147
2015-08-06 10:03:20 |          19390367 | 19390516         |              149
2015-08-06 10:03:30 |          19390516 | 19390656         |              140
```

```
2015-08-06 10:03:40 |     19390656 |     19390807 |          151
2015-08-06 10:03:50 |     19390807 |     19390950 |          143
2015-08-06 10:04:00 |     19390950 |     19391113 |          163
2015-08-06 10:04:10 |     19391113 |     19391280 |          167
2015-08-06 10:04:20 |     19391280 |     19391439 |          159
2015-08-06 10:04:30 |     19391439 |     19391608 |          169
```

By default, `lag` gives us the previous row, which is usually what we want. We could look back several rows: `lag(odometer_meters, 3)` would get the value from the row three before the current one. I have never found a use for that. We can also look ahead by saying, `lead` instead of `lag`. I usually find it is easier to think of the current row compared with the previous one, but it works looking forwards too.

Having found the distance travelled we could calculate the speed at each 10-second interval, and convert it to miles-per-hour (or kilometers-per-hour) if we wanted to.

There are other window functions including `row_number`, `rank`, `ntile` (as in quartile, percentile, etc.) and some other options. They are useful for many kinds of statistical analysis.

`row_number()` gives the ordinal position of each row within the partition, taking account of the order that has been specified using the over clause. `rank()` gives the ordinal position of the value. Values may be duplicated, so that different rows in the result set can be tied (as in: two runners crossing the finish line at the same time) on the value used to order the results. An example should make this clear:

download: row_count_and_rank.sql

```
select
    row_number() over (order by value),
    value,
    rank() over (order by value)
from
    test_row_count_and_rank
order by
    row_number;
```

```
row_number | value | rank
-----------+-------+-----
         1 |    13 |    1
         2 |    17 |    2
         3 |    17 |    2
         4 |    17 |    2
```

```
     5 |    29 |   5
     6 |    31 |   6
     7 |    31 |   6
     8 |    37 |   8
     9 |    41 |   9
(9 rows)
```

For tied values the rank is equal to the row_number of the first of the tied values. So the three occurrences of the value 17 have row_numbers 2, 3 and 4, but they all have rank = 2.

We'll use row_number() to calculate the median of a set of numbers. The median can be very different from the average, and is often an important measure in statistical analysis. The median is the middle value in an ordered set of numbers. In the table above the median value is 29 because there are four values that come before it in the list and four afterwards.

Here's another example:

row_number	value
1	13
2	17
3	17
4	17
5	29
6	31
7	31
8	37
9	41
10	43

Because there is an even number of rows here, there are two in the middle: row_numbers 5 and 6. Normally, in such cases, the median is calculated by taking the average of the two middle values, so in this case the median is (29 + 31) / 2 = 30.

So what is the easiest way of finding the middle value using SQL?

If we run two queries, one to give the row_number by ascending value and the other to give the row-number by descending value, we get this:

Chapter 9 - Select From One Table

row_number order by value ascending	value	value	row_number order by value descending
1	13	43	1
2	17	41	2
3	17	37	3
4	17	31	4
5	29	31	5
6	31	29	6
7	31	17	7
8	37	17	8
9	41	17	9
10	43	13	10

So now we just have to look for matching rows in the two result sets, where the value is the same and the row_number in one of the result sets is no more than one different from the row_number in the other.

- If the number of values is odd, and there are no duplicates around the median, we will get back exactly one value.
- If the number of values is even, and there are no duplicates around the median, we will get back exactly two values (as in this example).
- If there are many duplicates around the median then we will get back all the duplicated values, and they will all be the same.

So, whichever case describes our data, all we have to do is to take the average of the returned values and that will be the correct median value.

Here is the query:

download: median.sql

```
select
    avg(a.value) as median
from
    (
        select
            value,
            row_number() over (order by value asc)
        from
            test_row_count_and_rank
    ) a,
    (
        select
            value,
            row_number() over (order by value desc)
```

```
          from
               test_row_count_and_rank
     ) b
where
     a.value = b.value and
     abs(a.row_number - b.row_number) <= 1;
```

The answer is:

```
      median
--------------------
 30.0000000000000000
(1 row)
```

You should be able to adapt this easily to your own data

There are other approaches, but this is a particularly elegant one[44] and it performs well with small and large data sets in the cases we have tested.

Used in appropriate cases, the Window Functions can be very powerful. The alternative approach of selecting the data out into your application and looping through it is likely to have much worse performance and to be more error-prone.

---

44. Credit for this solution goes to Adam Machanic at http://sqlblog.com/blogs/adam_machanic/archive/2006/12/18/medians-row-numbers-and-performance.aspx. Adam Machanic credits Joe Celko (http://www.amazon.com/Celkos-Analytics-Kaufmann-Management-Systems/dp/0123695120/sr=8-1/qid=1166482464/ref=sr_1_1/105-6595410-7450029?ie=UTF8&s=books) as his source for this solution.

Chapter 10 - Select From Many Tables

Joining Data from Multiple Tables

In our database design, we went to some trouble to separate our data into tables that obey some strict rules. We now have to put the data back together.

I do hear complaints about relational databases parsing everything into tables, but I do not understand the complaint. When I write a Java program, even the most simple one will have the String object separated out. I will refer to Strings in my own classes but I will not re-implement the String functionality inline in my own class - that would be stupid. Also, I find that in building a class I may need to build a component of that class which is a List, complete with ListIterator. This is very useful, so I build my List as a separate class, which implements the List interface. I refer to the List class from other classes. How else would you do it?

Joining tables in relational databases is not any more difficult than using class hierarchies in an object-oriented programming language. Both are very useful paradigms.

Let's start with an easy example.

In our Insurance Claims system the person reporting the claim initially is usually the policy holder. If we have recorded policy_number FQE/67815 against a claim and we want to find the policy holder's contact details, then we can do so with a simple join command.

download: join_simple.sql

```
select
    a.policy_number,
    b.first_name,
    b.family_name,
    b.telephone_number,
    b.email_address
from
    policy a
```

```
    join
    person b
    on a.person_id = b.id
where
    a.policy_number = 'FQE/67815';
```

Here is our result.

```
policy_number | first_name | family_name | telephone_number |   email_address
--------------+------------+-------------+------------------+--------------------
FQE/67815     | Edna       | Barnsley    | 682-323-1117     | Edna@acerrimus.com
(1 row)
```

The `join` is specified in the `from` clause. Normally the `join` condition specifies a primary key to foreign key relationship, as it does here.

The default type of `join`, which we are using here, is an `inner join` that returns a row where there are matching rows in both tables. So, in this case, it returns a row for every case where `person_id` in the `policy` table has a matching `id` in the `person` table.

If there is a `person` row with an `id` that does not match any `person_id` in the `policy` table, then that `person` row will not appear in the result set.

If there is a row in the `policy` table with a `null person_id` then that `policy` row will not appear in the result set.

We have chosen to use `aliases` for the tables. In the `from` clause we label `policy` as "a" and `person` as "b." We then use "a" and "b" to show which tables we want to take each column from. In this case, it is important because both the `policy` and `person` tables have a column called `id` and a column called `policy_number`. We could do this without aliases, by qualifying columns with the table name in full, as shown in this version of the same query:

download: join_named_table.sql

```
select
    policy.policy_number,
    person.first_name,
    person.family_name,
    person.telephone_number,
    person.email_address
from
    policy
```

```
    join
    person
    on policy.person_id = person.id
where
    policy.policy_number = 'FQE/67815';
```

This is not too bad with short table names, but in real systems the table names may be longer as we create tables which model more and more detailed objects in the business. Some people use elaborate abbreviation schemes with short sequences of characters to represent each table. I prefer to use a single letter for each table and I do not even attempt to use a letter that is a mnemonic. These aliases are always used locally within each query, so it is easy to check which letter stands for which table. Trying to come up with short mnemonic abbreviations just leads to another set of alternative names for things that, hopefully, have meaningful and consistent names already. Using a single letter makes it clear that the alias is not another name for the object; it is just a local label. I find this to be the best scheme.

Columns that are unambiguous, that do not have the same name in another table being used in the query, do not need to be qualified. For single-table queries I do not use an alias and I do not qualify the columns with the table name because there is no ambiguity. For all `join` queries I use aliases to qualify every column. Using a single letter alias on every column is easy, and we have to know which table the column is coming from anyway. This saves us the decision about whether the column name is ambiguous or not and defends us against future changes where a column is added to a table making some of our queries ambiguous. Consistency saves us work.

For an inner `join`, it is possible to put the `join` condition in the `where` clause as shown below. This is not wrong, but I prefer to use the `join` syntax as shown in the first example above because it also works for the other types of `joins` that we will discuss very soon. I think it is preferable to code all `joins` the same way.

download: join_where.sql

```
select
    a.policy_number,
    b.first_name,
    b.family_name,
    b.telephone_number,
    b.email_address
from
```

```
    policy a,
    person b
where
    a.person_id = b.id and
    a.policy_number = 'FQE/67815';
```

We have discussed the simplest join, an inner join on two tables. Next we will look at joining three tables.

In *Grouping and Aggregating on page 180* we showed payments to each claimant and we identified each claimant by her id. Our users are not interested in claimant_ids, they are interested in the claimant's name, so let's rewrite our original query and find the names. The query we need is shown below.

download: join_three_tables.sql

```
select
    a.claimant_id,
    c.first_name,
    c.family_name,
    sum(a.amount) as total_paid_out
from
    transaction a
    join
    claimant b
    on a.claimant_id = b.id
    join
    person c
    on b.person_id = c.id
where
    a.actual_or_reserve = 'Actual' and
    a.payment_or_recovery = 'Payment'
group by
    a.claimant_id,
    c.first_name,
    c.family_name
order by
    total_paid_out desc;
```

The diagram below shows how we are navigating through the relationships we have built in the database using the primary and foreign keys.

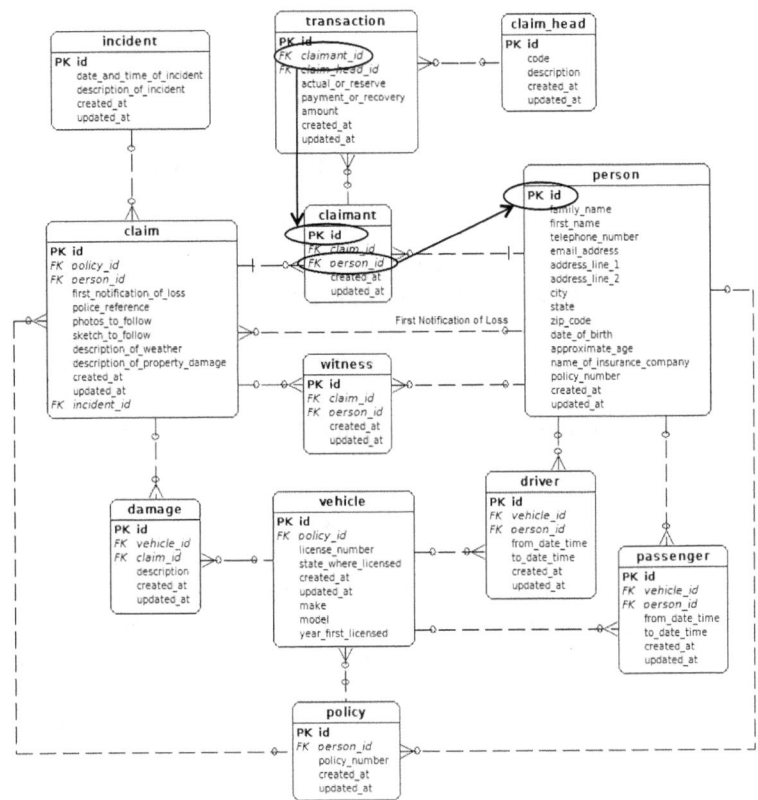

It is not difficult, but do make sure that you know what relationships you are using and what the properties of those relationships are. As you can see, there are several relationships shown between `claim` and `person`

- First Notification Of Loss (many-to-one)
- Claimant (many-to-many)
- Witness (many-to-many)
- Via Policy
- Via Damage, Vehicle and Driver
- Via Damage, Vehicle and Passenger

The relationship properties you have to think about are:

- Are you using the correct primary and foreign keys, and possibly an intermediate table to follow the relationship you are interested in?
- The **cardinality** of the relationship: is it one-to-one, one-to-many,

many-to-many?
- Is the relationship mandatory or optional, at both ends? Must every parent row have a child? Must every child row have a parent?

These academic-sounding properties reflect the way your organization works. When you look at these properties in terms of the actual business objects and processes in your organization, they become concrete and easier to understand. As a developer, you need to know if a policy can cover one car or many cars, one driver or many drivers. If the answers are "many", are there limits? Can a policy exist with no car at all? Maybe it is suspended while the policy holder's car is off the road, in storage for a few months perhaps. These are business rules that are reflected in the data model of your organization and you must understand them.

It is not unusual to have up to ten **joins** in one query in a real business system, and modern relational databases can handle these with no trouble. We will talk about tuning in *Chapter 14 - Tuning on page 273*, but usually in development you don't have to worry about this. If you find that you have many more than ten **joins** in one query then you should ask why. There are no hard-and-fast rules but you want to be sure that the level of complexity you are dealing with is really necessary. In practice, in my experience, very complex databases and very complex queries are usually signs of bad design.

Finally, never use one of the graphical query builders to construct these queries. Query builders are trying to guess how you built your database. People follow different database conventions and the query builder cannot always guess correctly how your database is structured. Think for yourself; you are more likely to get the right answer this way. You don't want to give your boss the wrong report because you let an "Evil Wizard" choose your **join** relationships for you. See *The Pragmatic Programmer*, Chapter 6. [45]

Joining Incomplete Sets

There are very many cases where we want to report on incomplete data. We'll explore some examples here.

---

45. See Bibliography [Hunt&Thomas]

Which Claims Have Witnesses?

For car insurance claims, ideally there would always be one or more witnesses, but very often there are none. In reporting on a claim, perhaps to put the information for a claim on a call center agent's screen, we want to show the details of witnesses if there are any. The inner join, which we described above, would be no good in this case because a claim without witnesses would not be found. What we need to use here is an outer join. The next code sample shows a query to do this, and followed by the first few results.

download: join_outer.sql

```
select
    a.id                          as claim_id,
    a.first_notification_of_loss,
    b.id                          as witness_id
from
    claim a
    left outer join
    witness b
    on a.id = b.claim_id
order by
    claim_id;
```

```
 claim_id | first_notification_of_loss | witness_id
----------+----------------------------+------------
        1 | 2014-01-15 19:54:35        |
        2 | 2013-08-05 10:44:44        |       2396
        3 | 2014-11-28 05:43:48        |       2839
        4 | 2013-04-16 03:15:22        |
        5 | 2014-09-01 22:04:31        |       2403
        6 | 2014-09-06 15:17:44        |
        7 | 2014-08-13 17:19:27        |       2724
        8 | 2013-01-29 07:25:21        |        176
        8 | 2013-01-29 07:25:21        |       1681
        8 | 2013-01-29 07:25:21        |       2406
        9 | 2014-05-30 01:03:18        |
       10 | 2014-11-19 04:54:28        |        779
       10 | 2014-11-19 04:54:28        |        692
       11 | 2014-12-02 05:09:20        |
```

From these results we can see that several claims do not have witnesses (claim_id: 1, 4, 6, 9, 11); some claims have one witness (2, 3, 5, 7); some have two witnesses (10), and some have three witnesses (8). We will look at how to analyze this properly in the section *Analyzing Numbers of Witnesses on page 218*.

The important part of the query is the `left outer join`. If we lay this piece out in a single line, like this:

```
claim left outer join witness
```

then `claim` is on the left and `witness` is on the right. `Left outer join` means return all the rows from the left table that satisfy the `where` clause, if there is one. (There isn't a `where` clause here, so all rows are returned.) If there is a matching row in the right table then return any values from that. If there is no matching row in the right table set any columns in the result set that are drawn from the right table to `null`. In other words, we are using the `join` condition to find matching rows, but we want to report on all of the claims whether or not they have a matching witness.

Claims with Witness Names Where There Are Any

We can use the `witness_id` values that are returned to find the names and contact details of those witnesses, as shown below, followed by the first few results.

download: join_outer_three_tables.sql

```
select
    a.id                           as claim_id,
    a.first_notification_of_loss,
    c.first_name                   as witness_first_name,
    c.family_name                  as witness_family_name
from
    claim a
    left outer join
    witness b
    on a.id = b.claim_id
    left outer join
    person c
    on b.person_id = c.id
order by
    claim_id;
```

```
 claim_id | first_notification_of_loss | witness_first_name | witness_family_name
----------+----------------------------+--------------------+--------------------
        1 | 2014-01-15 19:54:35        |                    |
        2 | 2013-08-05 10:44:44        | Aoife              | Petz
        3 | 2014-11-28 05:43:48        | Sydney             | Hawkesworth
        4 | 2013-04-16 03:15:22        |                    |
        5 | 2014-09-01 22:04:31        | Jamilah            | Unglesby
        6 | 2014-09-06 15:17:44        |                    |
        7 | 2014-08-13 17:19:27        | Olwen              | Varick
        8 | 2013-01-29 07:25:21        |                    | Nash
```

```
     8 | 2013-01-29 07:25:21     | Eve         | Bettison
     8 | 2013-01-29 07:25:21     | Eoin        | Foster
     9 | 2014-05-30 01:03:18     |             |
    10 | 2014-11-19 04:54:28     | Clayton     | Matson
    10 | 2014-11-19 04:54:28     | Joshua      | Alcock
    11 | 2014-12-02 05:09:20     |             |
```

Notice that we have to use an `outer join` between `witness` and `person` because the rows returned from the first `join` include those that did not match `witness`. If we used a plain `inner join` to `person`, then we would not get data for those that did not have witnesses and the `inner join` would restrict the result set. There are other ways of dealing with this, as we will see in *Nested Outer Join on page 219*

There is a `right outer join` command. This takes the table on the right (the second mentioned in the pair) as the main table and adds data from the table on the left (the first mentioned) where it exists.

I find it easier to think of the table on the left as being the main table, so I always write `left outer joins` and never use `right outer join`. A `right outer join` can always be written as a `left outer join` by switching the order of the tables in the statement. If there are two ways to do the same thing, I prefer to choose one way and always use that (unless there are significant performance implications, and there are not in this case).

Sailors and Musicians

Very occasionally, we need to `join` two tables so that the result set contains every row from each table, with data from the other, where it exists. This is a `full outer join`. To find an example of this, we need to look outside our Insurance Claims system. Here's one from my sailing club. Quite a few of the sailors are also musicians and when they want to put a band together for a party they often call in musicians from outside the club. So we have two lists that we'll implement as two tables, as shown below.

```
# select * from sailor;
 id | name  | boat
----+-------+----------
  1 | John  | Merlin
  2 | Donna | Wanderer
  3 | Ali   | Tasar
  4 | Ruth  | Topper
  5 | Robin | Topaz
  6 | Clare | Laser
```

```
(6 rows)
# select * from musician;
 id | name  | instrument
----+-------+------------
  1 | Ali   | Guitar
  2 | Ruth  | Vocal
  3 | Robin | Bass
  4 | Jill  | Drums
  5 | Mark  | Keyboard
(5 rows)
```

We then use a `full outer join` between `sailor` and `musician`. The results are shown below the query.

download: join_full_outer.sql

```
select
    a.name,
    b.name,
    a.boat,
    b.instrument
from
    sailor a
    full outer join
    musician b
    on a.name = b.name;


 name  | name  |   boat   | instrument
-------+-------+----------+------------
 John  |       | Merlin   |
 Donna |       | Wanderer |
 Ali   | Ali   | Tasar    | Guitar
 Ruth  | Ruth  | Topper   | Vocal
 Robin | Robin | Topaz    | Bass
 Clare |       | Laser    |
       | Mark  |          | Keyboard
       | Jill  |          | Drums
(8 rows)
```

As you can see, Ali, Robin and Ruth are sailors and musicians; Clare, Donna and John are only sailors; and Jill and Mark are only musicians. The first `name` column comes from the `sailor` table and the second `name` column comes from the `musician` table. When they are both present then they must be the same because that is how the `join` is specified. But we don't want to see the name in two columns. We can tidy this up as shown below.

download: join_coalesce.sql

```
select
    coalesce(a.name, b.name) as name,
    a.boat,
    b.instrument
from
    sailor a
    full outer join
    musician b
    on a.name = b.name;
```

The `coalesce(first, second)` function says: if `first` is not null, return `first`, otherwise return `second`. Other databases have other names for this function. Oracle does provide it, but most Oracle developers use `nvl` instead. The `coalesce` function goes well with the `full outer join`, to find a value that is in either of the tables but possibly not both. It has many other uses too.

```
 name  |   boat    | instrument
-------+-----------+------------
 John  | Merlin    |
 Donna | Wanderer  |
 Ali   | Tasar     | Guitar
 Ruth  | Topper    | Vocal
 Robin | Topaz     | Bass
 Clare | Laser     |
 Mark  |           | Keyboard
 Jill  |           | Drums
(8 rows)
```

The Cartesian Product

If we `join` two tables without specifying any `join` conditions then we get a `Cartesian Product` (also known as a `cross join`). This is usually a mistake and can use a lot of resources. What happens is that every row in the first table is joined to every row in the second table. So if you have 10,000 rows in the first table and 100,000 rows in the second table then your result set has 10,000 * 100,000 rows - that is one billion rows.

Your database may run out of memory, or disk space. This is usually embarrassing, at best.

You get the same result with a multi-table query if you do not have enough `join` conditions in your query to link all the tables properly.

There are some genuine cases for using a Cartesian Product. One case is where you know, absolutely, that all the tables have only one row each. Another is where you want to generate a large volume of data for testing. You will test every case in your application, using very small volumes, but at some time you need to test that the application still works with the volumes you will get in the real world. The Cartesian Product can be useful to help you generate a lot of test data very easily.

Set Operators

`Joins` construct a result set by taking columns from several tables to populate each row, as we have seen.

In contrast, the `set operators` work on compatible rows in different tables, so each row in the result set is taken entirely from one table, but different rows come from different tables.

Suppose I say:

```
select name from sailor;
```

then the result set is a one-column table of `first_names`.

If I then say:

```
select name from musician;
```

then the result set is also a one-column table of `first_names`.

So these two result sets are compatible tables and I can apply the set operators to them.

The most commonly used set operator is `union`. An example is shown below with its result set.

download: union.sql

```
select name from sailor
union
select name from musician;
```

```
name
-------
John
Robin
Donna
Ruth
Ali
Jill
Clare
Mark
(8 rows)
```

Looking at this result set we can see that all the names from both `sailor` table and `musician` table are included, so the two result sets have been combined. Each name is present only once. The default is to remove duplicates, which is usually what we want.

If we do want to see all the results, including the duplicates, we can say `union all` instead of `union`, which looks like this:

download: union_all.sql

```
select name from sailor
union all
select name from musician
order by name;
```

```
name
-------
Ali
Ali
Clare
Donna
Jill
John
Mark
Robin
Robin
Ruth
Ruth
(11 rows)
```

I added the `order by` clause so that it is easier to see the duplicates.

`Union all` is quicker for larger data volumes because the database does not need to deduplicate the results.

There are cases where you want to see rows that are in one data set but not in another. The `except` operator does this. Some databases have `minus` as a synonym for `except`. Looking at our sailors and musicians we can find the sailors who are not musicians, as shown below.

download: except.sql

```
select name from sailor
except
select name from musician;
```

```
name
-------
John
Clare
Donna
(3 rows)
```

Finally, if we want to find the people who are both sailors and musicians then we can use the `intersect` operator, as shown in our next query and result set.

download: intersect.sql

```
select name from sailor
intersect
select name from musician;
```

```
name
-------
Ruth
Ali
Robin
(3 rows)
```

The Venn Diagram is a useful tool to represent the way these operators are used. The diagrams and the use of the set operators can be extended to many sets, although both get difficult before the number of sets gets anywhere near double figures.

Chapter 10 - Select From Many Tables

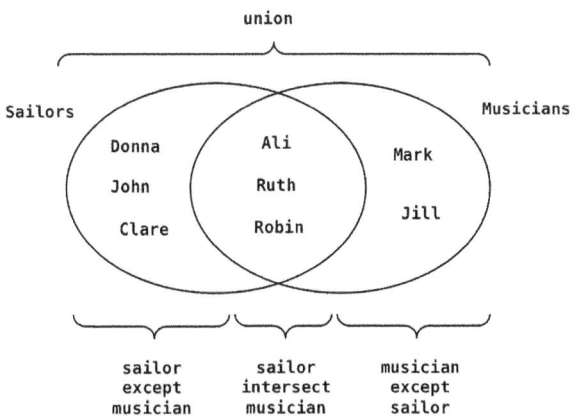

We said that the data sets being processed with the set operators must be *compatible*. Since a result set is a table, we can engineer the things to which we are applying the set operators to make them compatible. *Compatible* means that each row has the same columns, with the same meaning. In practice, the relational database can only check that the data-types are compatible; you have to take responsibility for making sure that the columns actually mean the same thing. You can give two different columns the same name. It would be sensible to do this only if they are compatible. You rename the columns using **as**. Let's look at an example of how to do that. With our sailors and musicians we could say (as a neglected partner might) that sailing dinghies and musical instruments are all *toys*. Since we have defined both **boat** and **instrument** as character strings we can rename them as toy and then treat them as being compatible, as shown below. In fact the names do not have to match, so long as the data-types do, but I find it helps to show what we are doing if we do rename them.

download: union_as.sql

```
select
    name,
    boat as toy
from
    sailor
union
select
    name,
```

```
        instrument as toy
from
    musician
order by
    name;

name   |   toy
-------+----------
Ali    | Tasar
Ali    | Guitar
Clare  | Laser
Donna  | Wanderer
Jill   | Drums
John   | Merlin
Mark   | Keyboard
Robin  | Topaz
Robin  | Bass
Ruth   | Topper
Ruth   | Vocal
(11 rows)
```

Another use of the set operators is in checking referential integrity, that is, looking for broken or missing links in the database. If the database designer has failed to define the Primary Key to Foreign Key relationships, these relationships will not be enforced. You can then use the set operators to check for any broken relationships.

Going back to our Insurance Claims database, if we had failed to define the constraints between the vehicle and driver tables, we could use the except operator, as shown below, to select all drivers that do not have a related vehicle. Of course, we expect to get zero rows because we have the Foreign Key constraint enforced on this table.

download: find_broken_link.sql

```
select vehicle_id from driver
except
select id from vehicle;

vehicle_id
------------
(0 rows)
```

Let's look at some of the data we have about drivers and vehicles. Here is a query to do this, followed by a small sample of the results.

download: join_cars_drivers.sql

```
select
    a.first_name,
    a.family_name,
    c.id            as vehicle_id,
    c.make,
    c.model,
    c.license_number
from
    person a
    join
    driver b
    on a.id = b.person_id
    join
    vehicle c
    on b.vehicle_id = c.id;
```

```
 first_name |  family_name  | vehicle_id |     make      |       model        | license_number
------------+---------------+------------+---------------+--------------------+----------------
 Nadimah    | Flynn         |       6627 | Buick         | Verano             | EGC SOA
 Bianca     | Back          |       6628 | Land Rover    | Range Rover Evoque | 9COI609
 Adam       | Chandler      |       6629 | Cadillac      | Escalade           | 918 203
 Elaine     | Mcfadden      |       6630 | Toyota        | Venza              | 419ABT5
 Kristin    | Weltch        |       6631 | Audi          | A4 Allroad         | GIO 337
 Kore       | Hainge        |       6633 | Mercedes-Benz | Sprinter           | UWG GJG
 Gilchrist  | Cooper        |       6634 | Land Rover    | Range Rover Evoque | D348TMC
 Irvin      | Fison         |       6635 | Honda         | HR-V               | 507T50R
 Shelda     | Tansell       |       6636 | Mercedes-Benz | CLS-Class          | 522228
 Bricen     | Milligan      |       6637 | Lexus         | GS                 | SUG 350
 Brandon    | Treadway      |       8406 | Hyundai       | Santa Fe           | F530WAQ
```

If we try to delete a vehicle when we have a driver recorded as driving it, then the database protects us from breaking the link. We'll try to delete the fifth vehicle in the above table, the Audi A4 Allroad. The database prevents us from damaging our data like this.

download: delete_vehicle.sql

```
delete from vehicle
where id = 6631;
```

```
ERROR:  update or delete on table "vehicle" violates foreign key constraint
        "foreign_key_driver_vehicle" on table "driver"
DETAIL:  Key (id)=(6631) is still referenced from table "driver".
```

We can, of course remove the constraint, like this:

download: drop_foreign_key_constraint.sql

```
alter table driver drop constraint foreign_key_driver_vehicle;
```

```
ALTER TABLE
```

Like undoing your seat belt when you are driving, this is very easy and is also a very bad idea.

We can now repeat the command to delete the vehicle, and this time, as shown below, the database dutifully reports that we have deleted one row.

download: delete_vehicle.sql

```
delete from vehicle
where id = 6631;
```

```
DELETE 1
```

You can be quite sure that, if referential integrity constraints are not specified, or are switched off, then you will find broken links in your database. So let us now look at how you find the failures. We'll run the same query that we ran above, and this time we find the broken link that we just caused.

download: find_broken_link.sql

```
select vehicle_id from driver
except
select id from vehicle;
```

```
vehicle_id
------------
       6631
(1 row)
```

It is worth doing this for every relationship in your database if referential integrity constraints are not in place. As a developer you may not have control over the enforcement of constraints. In some organizations this may be the responsibility of a separate database administration team who are the only people allowed to define or enforce constraints, and often they choose not to. If you are developing an application in this type of environment, you can still use the set operators to ensure that your data links are robust and your application will run properly.

Another use of the set operators is in building a Changed Data Capture system. These are frequently used in Data Warehousing applications where there is a lot of data to load every day and we can save time by loading only the data that has changed since the previous load[46].

---

46. If you are interested you can learn more at *http://www.datamgmt.com/detecting-changed-data*

Case Expressions

One more feature before we move on to nested queries: `case` statements.

Suppose our users want to see the individual payments made to claimants in bands. They define these bands as:

- Small: Less than $1,000
- Medium: At least $1,000 and less than $10,000
- Significant: At least $10,000 and less than $100,000
- Large: At least $100,000 and less than $1,000,000
- Exceptional: At least $1,000,000

If these bands are fairly stable, then we could create a new table, like this:

Band	From (inclusive)	To (exclusive)
Small	$0	$1,000
Medium	$1,000	$10,000
Significant	$10,000	$100,000
Large	$100,000	$1,000,000
Exceptional	$1,000,000	$999,999,999

We could then `join` this table to the claim transactions and pick out the appropriate band label. This would be a good way to solve this particular problem. A second way to solve the same problem would be to use the `case` expression, as shown below.

download: case_expression.sql
```
select
    id as transaction_id,
    case
        when amount < 1000      then 'Small'
        when amount < 10000     then 'Medium'
        when amount < 100000    then 'Significant'
        when amount < 1000000   then 'Large'
        else                         'Exceptional'
    end as payment_band,
    amount
from
    transaction
where
    actual_or_reserve = 'Actual' and
```

```
        payment_or_recovery = 'Payment' and
        amount >= 0 and
        created_at between '2015-05-01 14:00:00' and '2015-05-01 18:00:00'
order by
        amount desc;
```

I have restricted the query to just a few hour's transactions to be able to show a range of results in one small result set. Looking at the `case` statement itself, we can see that it starts with `case` and ends with `end`. I have given the result a name: `payment_band`. The lines between `case` and `end` each have a test and a result. They are tested in order and the first one that is found to be true gives the answer; no further `when` or `else` clauses are checked once we have found one true result. In this case it was easy to order the clauses to give the correct answer. I also put an overall condition in the `where` clause to eliminate any negative amounts before we even consider them in the `case` expression. Finally, I have asked for descending order so that the largest amounts are shown first. Remember that if you do not include an `order by` clause at all then the results come out in any order. If you include `order by` but don't include `desc` then you will get the results in ascending order.

Here are our results

```
 transaction_id | payment_band |  amount
----------------+--------------+----------
          59324 | Significant  | 62852.80
         163047 | Significant  | 62560.39
         138569 | Medium       |  6736.11
         131273 | Medium       |  5464.65
          41061 | Medium       |  4218.07
          53776 | Medium       |  3075.26
         134618 | Medium       |  2183.60
         153634 | Small        |   868.57
          56800 | Small        |   775.03
          70337 | Small        |   300.74
          10992 | Small        |    99.34
          61073 | Small        |    77.10
          83092 | Small        |    67.84
          97442 | Small        |    58.93
         150885 | Small        |    58.76
          80269 | Small        |    46.70
          57442 | Small        |    38.83
          59495 | Small        |    31.24
(18 rows)
```

So this was a simple example that could have been implemented with a band table. It is also not very useful (except for illustration, I hope) because in practice we would be more likely to be interested in the sum of payments to a particular claimant, or for a particular claim.

The `case` expression is useful for quick queries, especially if you don't have permission to set up a new band table in the live database at a moment's notice. In these cases though you should consider the `case` expression as a candidate for `refactoring` if it becomes part of the production suite of queries. Refactoring means improving programming code without changing its interface, so it still does the same as before, but now does it more efficiently, or in a way that will be easier to change in the future, or is better in some other way. For a more detailed discussion, see *Refactoring: Improving the Design of Existing Code* [47].

Another good use of `case` expressions is for multi-factor analysis.

An example of this technique is shown below as a decision table for costing a house-building project. (Of course the numbers in this table are fictitious, so do not use it for costing your house-building project! Most multi-factor decision tables are highly valuable and jealously guarded tools that will give your business a competitive edge, so real examples are not readily available.)

Design	Complex	Complex	Complex	Complex	Simple	Simple	Simple	Simple	Simple	Simple	Simple
Accessible	N	N	Y	Y	N	N	Y	Y	Y	Y	Y
Site Slope	>=10%	<10%	>=10%	<10%	>=10%	<10%	>=10%	<10%	<10%	<10%	<10%
Material	-	-	-	-	-	-	Other	Brick	Brick	Wood Frame	Wood Frame
Trees	-	-	-	-	-	-	-	Y	N	-	-
Windows	-	-	-	-	-	-	-	-	-	Hardwood	UPVC or Softwood
Cost Multiplier	3.50	3.20	2.90	2.70	2.10	2.05	1.90	1.70	1.40	1.30	1.15	1.00

The design of the house to be built is classified as *Simple*, which means that your house is a rectangular box, or *Complex*, meaning any other shape. *Accessible* means that you can get a big truck with building materials (roof trusses, for example) right up to your site. And so on.

You usually find that a small number of factors have the greatest impact and as you work your way down, you have to take more things into account.

To use the decision table, you work your way down the first column. If all the conditions are satisfied then you use the value from the bottom row to weight your building cost. In this case, if the design is complex, the site is not easily accessible and the site slopes by at least 10%, then

47. See Bibliography [Fowler&others]

it is going to be an expensive build. You may get a great view, but these things don't come cheap.

In the general case, conditions are listed at the top of the table, and actions are listed in the lower rows. In this case we have only one action, but it is possible to have many.

You can implement a decision table in a spreadsheet, using nested `if` statements, and many people do, but the number of nested parenthetical statements makes it difficult to ensure that the table works correctly.

The `case` statement is a more elegant way to present the solution, as shown below. Each `when` ... `then` ... block implements one column in the decision table.

download: case_multi_factor.sql

```
select
    id,
    case
        when
            design = 'Complex' and
            not accessible and
            site_slope_percentage >= 10
        then
            3.50
        when
            design = 'Complex' and
            not accessible and
            site_slope_percentage < 10
        then
            3.20
        when
            design = 'Complex' and
            accessible and
            site_slope_percentage >= 10
        then
            2.90
        when
            design = 'Complex' and
            accessible and
            site_slope_percentage < 10
        then
            2.70
        when
            design = 'Simple' and
            not accessible and
            site_slope_percentage >= 10
        then
            2.10
        when
```

```
            design = 'Simple' and
            not accessible and
            site_slope_percentage < 10
        then
            2.05
        when
            design = 'Simple' and
            accessible and
            site_slope_percentage >= 10
        then
            1.90
        when
            design = 'Simple' and
            accessible and
            site_slope_percentage < 10 and
            material not in ('Wood Frame', 'Brick')
        then
            1.70
        when
            design = 'Simple' and
            accessible and
            site_slope_percentage < 10 and
            material = 'Brick' and
            trees
        then
            1.40
        when
            design = 'Simple' and
            accessible and
            site_slope_percentage < 10 and
            material = 'Brick' and
            not trees
        then
            1.30
        when
            design = 'Simple' and
            accessible and
            site_slope_percentage < 10 and
            material = 'Wood Frame' and
            windows = 'Hardwood'
        then
            1.15
        when
            design = 'Simple' and
            accessible and
            site_slope_percentage < 10 and
            material = 'Wood Frame' and
            windows in ('UPVC', 'Softwood')
        then
            1.15
    end as cost_multiplier
from
    house_proposal;
```

You could argue that the whole decision table should be implemented entirely in data because data is easier to change than code. There are many cases where this is true, but for problems like this one you can bet that the next weird set of conditions that the analyst comes up with will not be handled by the code you wrote to process the decision table and you'll have to change code anyway. Some problems are best expressed in code, and this is one of them.

If you are working in an Oracle environment you will see lots of decode statements. Oracle introduced decode well before case expressions were available. Decode statements are a bit easier to read than spreadsheet if statements, especially if they are formatted nicely, but they do suffer from having a potentially long list of arguments, and the meaning of each argument is determined by its position, so they can be hard to read. Every decode statement can be written as a case expression and you should do that, as a kindness to the person maintaining the code after you. Oracle also suggests that case statements are more efficient than decode statements, so there's no excuse for using decode really.

Nested Queries

I have been looking forward to this section, but it was important to get through the most useful variants of an individual SQL statement first. As we have mentioned several times, the results of a SQL statement are in the form of a table. These result sets can be used immediately in a SQL statement, without having to formally create a table to hold them. This is a very powerful feature of SQL.

I'll give some examples that tidy up some of our earlier queries that were a bit unsatisfactory without nesting.

Missing Data as Percentages

Way back in *Chapter 9 - Selecting Data From One Table At A Time: null city on page 174* we said that it would be nicer to see the amount of data missing as percentages. The next query and result set shows how to do this.

download: nested_percentage.sql

```
select
    a.total_rows,
    ((b.missing_city * 100) / a.total_rows) || '%'
        as missing_city,
    ((c.missing_family_name * 100) / a.total_rows) || '%'
        as missing_family_name,
    ((d.missing_date_of_birth * 100) / a.total_rows) || '%'
        as missing_date_of_birth
from
    (
        select count(*) as total_rows
        from person
    ) a
    cross join
    (
        select count(*) as missing_city
        from person where city is null
    ) b
    cross join
    (
        select count(*) as missing_family_name
        from person where family_name is null
    ) c
    cross join
    (
        select count(*) as missing_date_of_birth
        from person where date_of_birth is null
    ) d;

 total_rows | missing_city | missing_family_name | missing_date_of_birth
------------+--------------+---------------------+-----------------------
      12538 | 12%          | 1%                  | 69%
(1 row)
```

In the `from` clause of the above query we see four SQL statements, each enclosed in parentheses and each given a label (a, b, c and d). These are used in the outer query just as if they were tables.

In the outer query we `join` these four tables together using a Cartesian Product. We do not specify any `join` conditions. Since we know that each of the four sub-queries will return exactly one row, this is OK.

The operator `||` is `string concatenation`. We are simply adding the "%" sign to the end of each number. String concatenation works if at least one of the things being concatenated is a string. The "%" sign is a string, so the database converts the number into a string too.

The `/` operator means `integer divide`. Integer divide always rounds down, so if we wrote:

```
b.missing_city / a.total_rows * 100
```

we would get 0% instead of 15% because the expression is evaluated from left to right.

```
1965 / 12537 = 0
0 * 100 = 0
```

whereas

```
b.missing_city * 100 / a.total_rows
```

evaluates as

```
1965 * 100 = 196500
196500 / 12537 = 15
```

We can force floating point arithmetic, by casting the first argument to float, like this:

```
select cast(1965 as float) * 100 / 12537;
```

The result is 15.6736061258674

If we want it rounded to the nearest whole number then we do this:

```
select round(cast(1965 as float) * 100 / 12537);
```

and the answer is 16.

Analyzing Numbers of Witnesses

When we were looking at claims and witnesses (*Which Claims Have Witnesses? on page 199*) we said that we would analyze the number of witnesses per claim properly. We want to know:

- how many claims have a witness?
- do some have more than one witness?
- how many have two, three or more witnesses?

The query to do this is shown below, followed by its result set.

download: nested_count.sql

```
select
    number_of_witnesses,
    count(*) as number_of_claims
from
    (
        select
            a.id         as claim_id,
            count(b.id)  as number_of_witnesses
        from
            claim a
            left outer join
            witness b
            on a.id = b.claim_id
        group by
            a.id
    ) x
group by
    number_of_witnesses
order by
    number_of_witnesses;

 number_of_witnesses | number_of_claims
---------------------+------------------
                   0 |             4029
                   1 |             2039
                   2 |              535
                   3 |              105
                   4 |               15
                   5 |                3
(6 rows)
```

The query in parentheses `joins` the `claim` table and `witness` table, and for each claim, counts the number of witnesses. We then have a virtual table, which we have labeled x, where each row contains a `claim_id` and the number of witnesses for that claim. From that virtual table, for each value of `number_of_witnesses`, we count the total number of claims.

Nested Outer Join

We can rewrite the query from *Claims with Witness Names Where There Are Any on page 200*, as shown below. This puts the `join` between `witness` and `person` in a `sub-query` in parentheses, and because sub-queries are executed first, we will get a virtual table that `joins witness` and `person`. This table is then joined with `claim`, using a `left outer join` because not all claims have witnesses and we want to return both claims that have witnesses and those that do not.

download: nested_sub_query.sql

```
select
    a.id            as claim_id,
    a.first_notification_of_loss,
    b.witness_first_name,
    b.witness_family_name
from
    claim a
    left outer join
    (
        select
            x.claim_id,
            y.first_name    as witness_first_name,
            y.family_name   as witness_family_name
        from
            witness x
            left outer join
            person y
            on x.person_id = y.id
    ) b
    on a.id = b.claim_id;
```

This query returns exactly the same results as our original `left outer join` query. The nested sub-query version is a little bit longer. If the meaning is clearer this way then it is a better implementation. That's debatable in this case, but it does show another use of sub-queries.

Sub-Queries in the Where Clause

Sub-queries are not only used in the `from` clause; they are also often used in the `where` clause.

Suppose we want to find out the names of people who have been paid compensation for bodily injury. Here is a possible query to do this, with its result set.

download: nested_sub_query_where.sql

```
select
    first_name,
    family_name
from
    person
where
    id in
    (
        select
            a.person_id
        from
```

```
                claimant a
                join
                transaction b
                on a.id = b.claimant_id
                join
                claim_head c
                on b.claim_head_id = c.id
           where
                c.description like '%Bodily Injury%' and
                b.payment_or_recovery = 'Payment' and
                b.actual_or_reserve = 'Actual'
        );

 first_name     |     family_name
----------------+----------------------
 Elaine         | Mcfadden
 Kristin        | Weltch
 Brandon        | Treadway
 Georgina       | Solomon
 Bathsheba      | Warmsley
 Barry          | Sunderland
 Deidre         | Sneyd
 Gethin         | Harrisson
```

The sub-query in the **where** clause finds all the claimants who have transactions for bodily injury claims. The sub-query returns a result set of **person_ids**. We are not interested in counting how many transactions each claimant has; we just want to know their names, if they have any bodily injury claims. The top-level query returns the name of the person if that person is in the result set returned by the sub-query. Using this query, each person is returned only once. If we wrote the query as a **join** between the four tables, we would get some names repeated where one person had several qualifying transactions.

Notice that we did not give a name to the query in the **where** clause, but we have always given names to the queries in the **from** clause. Often we have to name the queries in the **from** clause because we have the same column name in more than one query and we need to be clear about which one we are referring to. The **SQL** standard says that we must always name queries in the **from** clause, even if there is only one of them. Some databases (such as **PostgreSQL**) enforce this standard and others do not. To make your **SQL** portable, and to avoid annoying error messages, it is good to get into the habit of always naming queries in the **from** clause and never naming them in the **where** clause.

Also note that the sub-query returns **person_id**, which is an integer, and we compare it with `person.id` which is also an integer. (They are also both person IDs, which is good, but SQL does not check that.)

You can compare multiple columns, as shown in the next example.

download: nested_compare_many.sql

```
select
    telephone_number,
    email_address,
    zip_code
from
    person
where
    (first_name, family_name, date_of_birth) in
    (
        select
            first_name,
            family_name,
            date_of_birth
        from
            person
        where
            approximate_age is null
    );
```

```
telephone_number  |       email_address         | zip_code
------------------+-----------------------------+---------
442-289-9352      | Bianca@ultrices.com         | 99643
424-299-8228      | Adam@uentris.com            | 94631
415-300-9546      | Elzear@captiuaque.com       | 94910
408-310-5772      | Tanner@excussit.com         | 94089
949-370-3514      |                             | 94429
818-341-9575      |                             | 92243
714-381-7193      | Hiram@quaeque.com           | 98353
650-332-9767      |                             | 93039
415-333-4122      | Arthur@iungam.com           | 92928
```

When comparing multiple columns in a `where` clause with a sub-query, the number of columns returned must be the same as the number of columns being compared. Also, the data-types must be comparable.

Cross-Tab Reports

I frequently get asked how to do `cross-tab` or `pivot-table` reports in SQL.

Here's the challenge. We have a table that was created like this:

download: create_for_pivot.sql

```
create table transaction
(
    id                   integer,
    claimant_id          integer,
    claim_head_id        integer,
    actual_or_reserve    varchar(7),
    payment_or_recovery  varchar(8),
    amount               numeric(8,2),
    created_at           timestamp,
    updated_at           timestamp
);
```

and we want a report like this:

Actual or Reserve	Payment or Recovery	2015Q2	2015Q3	2015Q4	2016Q1
Actual	Payment	25,593,120.54	25,724,698.40	26,028,240.14	9,202,088.05
Actual	Recovery	9,340,889.44	8,555,264.57	8,680,410.63	3,584,824.21
Reserve	Payment	25,806,542.44	25,699,383.72	25,411,909.79	7,814,403.72
Reserve	Recovery	9,034,181.32	8,695,679.11	8,810,539.61	2,591,892.73

What makes this tricky is that some of the headings (the quarters) are derived from data values, not from column names. We want each quarter to show as a separate column, so we want to pivot the result set to make rows into columns.

The quarters are derived from the `created_at` date, so to select the data for our table we write a query like this:

download: select_for_pivot.sql

```
select
    extract(year from created_at) ||
    'Q' ||
    extract(quarter from created_at) as quarter,
    actual_or_reserve,
    payment_or_recovery,
    sum(amount) as total_amount
from
    transaction
where
    created_at >= '2015-04-01'
group by
    quarter,
    actual_or_reserve,
    payment_or_recovery;
```

and the results come out like this:

```
 quarter | actual_or_reserve | payment_or_recovery | total_amount
---------+-------------------+---------------------+--------------
 2015Q2  | Actual            | Payment             |   25593120.54
 2015Q2  | Actual            | Recovery            |    9340889.44
 2015Q2  | Reserve           | Payment             |   25806542.44
 2015Q2  | Reserve           | Recovery            |    9034181.32
 2015Q3  | Actual            | Payment             |   25724698.40
 2015Q3  | Actual            | Recovery            |    8555264.57
 2015Q3  | Reserve           | Payment             |   25699383.72
 2015Q3  | Reserve           | Recovery            |    8695679.11
 2015Q4  | Actual            | Payment             |   26028240.14
 2015Q4  | Actual            | Recovery            |    8680410.63
 2015Q4  | Reserve           | Payment             |   25411909.79
 2015Q4  | Reserve           | Recovery            |    8810539.61
 2016Q1  | Actual            | Payment             |    9202088.05
 2016Q1  | Actual            | Recovery            |    3584824.21
 2016Q1  | Reserve           | Payment             |    7814403.72
 2016Q1  | Reserve           | Recovery            |    2591892.73
(16 rows)
```

I suggest that you run this nice simple query and then use a spreadsheet tool or a visualization tool (such as Tableau[48] or QlikView[49]) to present the results as a cross-tab.

If you really want to use `SQL` to format it, this is possible. I am not including the solution here because I think it is much better to use a spreadsheet or other visualization tool for this[50]

Stick to the Knitting

Consistency

If you have read the previous chapter and this one all the way through then you have covered most of the `SQL` constructs you will ever need to write `select` statements. There are other variations and many more functions that you can apply, and sometimes those will be useful. The product documentation is the ultimate source for obscure features, but really you gain by using a consistent set, and certainly by not using alternative forms to write the same thing. If you, and the rest of your team, prefer an alternative form, then use it instead of the one I have shown, but do not use both.

---

48. http://www.tableau.com

49. http://www.qlik.com/us/

50. The solution is available on my website. If you really want to see how it can be done look at http://thedatastudio.net/ugly_cross_tab.htm. But please don't do it this way, it is so ugly!

Think in Sets; Not in Individual Records

Now that you can run queries across complete data sets, this is something you should often do. You must be sensitive to performance issues in your environment, of course. In a telephone company, for example, you probably will not run a query across all the call data records for the last year unless you have a seriously expensive data warehouse appliance that can handle the volume. However, when investigating issues or when advising the boss on the impact of changing a business policy, you should check whole sets of data.

If you are working with a Business Analyst on fixing some problem with one of your organization's systems, and the Business Analyst says that he has looked at half a dozen examples and he can see what is wrong, you can test his hypothesis by checking the entire set of records. Use SQL to look at all the cases, not just half a dozen. With a few select statements you can not only test the Business Analyst's hypothesis, but also extract all the problematic examples, analyzed into the different variants of the problem. SQL enables you to understand and solve the whole problem rather than picking off individual symptoms.

With SQL, you say what to do, not how to do it. If you think in terms of iterating through nested structures you will miss a lot of opportunities for simple and powerful analysis. But if you get used to thinking in sets of data, rather than individual records, you will be able to use the relational database to perform very much more.

Part D -
Populating And Tuning Your Database

Having learned how to get data from a database, we now look at the ways of populating a database. This will normally be a large part of what your application does.

We then look at migrating your database as you develop your application, iteration by iteration, so that the database always has a clean model of the data that the application is processing. This is very manageable and very important to save your database from the confused state that so many databases end up in.

We then look at how to deal with exceptions, and how to avoid or overcome performance issues.

Finally we look at metadata, the way that relational databases manage their own description and make it available to us, always up-to-date and accurate.

Chapter 11 - Populating Your Database

Data gets into our relational database mostly through the applications we write. Our Claims application will interact with the claims handlers in the call center to help them collect accurate data from the customers who are making claims. The application will then `insert` the collected data into the database. The other way data gets into the database is through bulk uploads, such as when we load all the `claim head` reference values in our insurance claims system.

We use `update` and `delete` less frequently in interactive applications. Usually if we need to correct or delete a previous entry in accounting data, we do not update or delete the old record. Instead we create a new record that cancels out, or corrects the old one. This enables the auditors to see how we got to a particular point. There will also be information on each entry to say who made it, when and why, especially when we are changing or deleting anything to do with money.

But `updates` and `deletes` are used sometimes in interactive applications, and they are used a lot in migrating the database from one release to another without losing information.

`insert`, `update` and `delete` can be applied to a single record or to whole sets of records. Interactive applications usually process one record at a time. Other processes, like database migration, process whole sets of records.

Insert

Here is a sample `insert` statement, as I would write it.

download: insert_person.sql

```
insert into person
(
    family_name,
    first_name,
    telephone_number,
    email_address,
    address_line_1,
    address_line_2,
    city,
    state,
```

```
        zip_code,
        date_of_birth,
        approximate_age,
        name_of_insurance_company,
        policy_number
)
values
(
        'Flynn',                    -- family_name
        'Adam',                     -- first_name
        '423-749-2946',             -- telephone_number
        'adam@enceladus.org',       -- email_address
        '90 Windemere Lane',        -- address_line_1
        null,                       -- address_line_2
        'Kimbolton',                -- city
        'TN',                       -- state
        '37002',                    -- zip_code
        '1973-12-15',               -- date_of_birth
        42,                         -- approximate_age
        null,                       -- name_of_insurance_company
        null                        -- policy_number
);
```

The basic form is:

```
insert into <table_name> (<column names>) values (<column values>);
```

<table_name> is the name of the table that we are inserting into. No problem there.

<column names> is the list of columns that we want to insert data into. <column values> is the list of values in the same order as the list of <column names>.

You can leave out the (<column names>) part. If you do this then the values must start with the first column in the table, as the table is currently defined, and you must specify values for each column in sequence. The SQL standard says that you must provide a value for every column if you do not list the columns explicitly.

I always specify the list of column names. I do this to protect my application, or my script, against someone recreating the table with the columns in a different sequence. If you specify the column names, your application will run correctly even if the order of columns in your insert statement does not match the order of the columns in the database.

I find the way SQL requires two separate lists of column names and column values awkward, especially when there is more than just a handfull of columns. It would be nicer if we could list each column name, paired with its correct value, but that is not the way `SQL` works so we have to live with it. If there are more than two or three columns (and often there are a hundred or more), I label each value by adding a comment after it, which identifies the column name. The "`--`" (two hyphens) signals to `SQL` that the rest of the line is a comment, so this is an easy way to label each value. When you come back to edit this next time, you will be grateful.

This does, of course, mean that there is one column name per line and one value per line. I know many developers who feel physical pain at the thought of putting a `newline` after every element. It is OK, really! You are allowed to do this. We rarely print out our code now, so we don't even have to be concerned about wasting paper. I want to make my `SQL` statements as easy to read as possible, and I think this approach helps to do that and to avoid mistakes.

Any columns that you do not mention in the `insert` statement are set to their default values if they have them, and `null` if they do not. In the example above, I did not specify the value of `id` or `created_at`. In this case `id` is a PostgreSQL `serial` column so it automatically gets the next available value. `created_at` has a default of `now()` so it gets the current timestamp.

As you can see it is also possible to set columns to `null` explicitly.

You can also take the data to be inserted from an existing table. This changes the basic form of the `insert` statement to:

```
insert into <table_name> (<column names>) select <column values>) from …
```

Suppose we want to populate a table[51] of all the people whose last name is Dinsdale; the `insert` statement would look like this:

download: insert_dinsdale.sql

```
insert into dinsdale
(
    family_name,
    first_name,
    telephone_number,
    email_address,
```

---

51. I already created the table; as I will explain in *Chapter 18 - Database Features To Be Wary Of* on *page 318*, I never use `create table ... as select ...`

```
    zip_code
)
select
    'Dinsdale',    -- family_name
    first_name,
    telephone_number,
    email_address,
    zip_code
from
    person
where
    family_name = 'Dinsdale';
```

This example is rather contrived but it does show that the values list can be the result set from a select statement.

I could have taken the family_name from the person table. I set it as a constant to show that option. The end result is the same in this case. I labeled the constant, but there was no need to label the other columns since their names were staying the same.

In this case seven people with the family name "Dinsdale" get inserted into the table dinsdale as shown below.

```
family_name | first_name | telephone_number |      email_address      | zip_code
------------+------------+------------------+-------------------------+---------
Dinsdale    | Emrys      | 442-486-9622     |                         | 95520
Dinsdale    | Heron      | 936-796-7349     |                         | 75984
Dinsdale    | Adelaide   | 213-985-1431     | Adelaide@sistam.com     | 99637
Dinsdale    | Pascal     | 817-353-9070     | Pascal@omnino.com       | 72968
Dinsdale    | Maliha     | 938-215-3505     |                         | 34136
Dinsdale    | Noel       | 707-468-5088     | Noel@fremet.com         | 90770
Dinsdale    | Zahrah     | 561-368-6919     |                         | 37840
(7 rows)
```

This form of the insert statement is not likely to be used in an application, but it is very useful for database migrations and when transforming data, for loading into a data warehouse for example.

Bulk inserts are handled differently by different databases, as shown in the next table. Once again, PostgreSQL has a very straightforward method using the copy statement. Copy transfers data between a file and a table, in either direction. The file can be a comma-separated values (csv) file, which is the best way to load large volumes of data[52].

---

52. Have a look at *Chapter 6 - Data Types on page 125* for the reasons I say that.

Chapter 11 - Populating Your Database

Database	Bulk insert tools
PostgreSQL	copy
Oracle	SQL*Loader
MySQL	mysqlimport load data ... infile ...
IBM DB2 UNIX	import load ingest
IBM DB2 z/OS	High Performance Unload
Microsoft SQL Server	bcp bulk insert
SAP Sybase	input load table
Teradata	FastLoad
The appliance formerly known as Netezza	nzload

Other database vendors also have bulk data loaders. These are all so different that my only advice is to go to your database documentation. Hopefully this table will at least help you find the tool you need. The complexity and usability of the tools varies significantly between products. It seems to me that there is some correlation between the marketing input to the tool name and its complexity, and an inverse correlation with usability. It's hard to beat **copy** from PostgreSQL, which does what it says with minimum fuss[53].

Update

Sometimes we want to change an existing record, rather than creating a new current copy and marking the old version in some way to show that it is not current. It is possible that, in a `customer` table, we never want to keep old addresses; when the customer moves to a new address; we simply want to replace the old address with the new one and never see the old address again.

We'll start by looking at the data in one row of the `person` table.

```
id                : 27681
family_name       : Flynn
first_name        : Adam
telephone_number  : 423-749-2946
email_address     : adam@enceladus.org
address_line_1    : 90 Windemere Lane
```

[53]. For an example of just how complex some vendors make this, see http://www.thedatastudio.net/hive_csv_serde_changes_table_definitions.htm.

```
address_line_2           :
city                     : Kimbolton
state                    : TN
zip_code                 : 37002
date_of_birth            : 1973-12-15
approximate_age          : 42
name_of_insurance_company :
policy_number            :
created_at               : 2016-02-20 10:14:54.776266
updated_at               :
```

Here is the SQL statement to update Adam Flynn's address in the person table.

download: update_flynn.sql

```
update person
set
    address_line_1 = '47 King Street',
    address_line_2 = 'Shepway',
    city           = 'Tunbridge Wells',
    state          = 'TN',
    zip_code       = '37002',
    updated_at     = now()
where
    id             = 27681;
```

The most important part of this update statement is the where clause. We use the primary key (id) because this is guaranteed to be unique, so we update Adam Flynn's data and nobody else's. If, instead, we said: where family_name = 'Flynn' we would change the address in every row in the table where the family_name is "Flynn." Since there are two Flynns in our person table, this would be wrong. There was a case in a leading educational establishment, when relational databases were new, that someone changed every student's name to Carruthers by forgetting to include the where clause.

This also illustrates why it is important not to run ad-hoc SQL statements on live databases. We test everything thoroughly and only run tested scripts on live data. We do not type in commands that change the live database on the SQL command line, or in our fancy SQL graphical user interface tool. We don't like making mistakes.

Anyway, our update statement is correct, and after running it we see that exactly one row has been changed (because the response from PostgreSQL is "UPDATE 1" and the record for Adam Flynn now looks like this:

Chapter 11 - Populating Your Database

```
id                         : 27681
family_name                : Flynn
first_name                 : Adam
telephone_number           : 423-749-2946
email_address              : adam@enceladus.org
address_line_1             : 47 King Street
address_line_2             : Shepway
city                       : Tunbridge Wells
state                      : TN
zip_code                   : 37002
date_of_birth              : 1973-12-15
approximate_age            : 42
name_of_insurance_company  :
policy_number              :
created_at                 : 2016-02-20 10:14:54.776266
updated_at                 : 2016-02-20 10:22:41.865958
```

There are a few other things to notice about the **update** statement.

Columns to be changed are specified in a list of name/value pairs (for example `zip_code = '37002'`). This is different from the way column values are specified in **insert** statements.

Columns that are in the table, but not mentioned in your **update** statement, remain unchanged.

We can specify values as literal values or as functions. We use the function `now()` to set **updated_at**.

SQL does not require the `created_at` or `updated_at` columns, but including them in most tables is a good standard to follow and is the default behavior in Ruby on Rails.

In a live application the values to be applied would probably be parameters derived from a web form, rather than literal values. As usual our example is a simple case.

Using interactive tools, such as the **SQL** command line, the database responds to an **update** with the number of rows updated. In **JDBC**, we can easily find the number of rows updated as shown below.

download: update_jdbc.sql

```
rowsUpdated = statement.executeUpdate
(
  "update person " +
  "set " +
    "address_line_1 = '47 King Street', " +
    "address_line_2 = 'Shepway', " +
```

```
            "city"         = 'Tunbridge Wells', " +
            "state"        = 'TN', " +
            "zip_code      = '37002', " +
            "updated_at    = now() " +
        "where " +
            "id            = 27681;"
    );
    System.out.println("Rows updated: " + rowsUpdated);
```

The `Java/JDBC statement.executeUpdate` method returns the number of rows affected by the `update`. So does the Ruby on Rails `ActiveRecord update` method. In this example we are simply printing the number of rows affected. In a real application we would test the number of rows affected and raise an exception if it was not as expected.

It would also be wise to `rollback the transaction` if the number of rows updated is not what you expect. (See the section *Transactions on page 238*.) The application should also raise an exception to trigger the investigation of this unexpected behavior (see *Chapter 13 - When Things Go Wrong on page 264*).

`Updates` are quite rare in applications, for the reasons we described above, mainly that we usually need to keep an audit trail. However, `updates` are much more common in migrations and in data transformations for populating data warehouses and other systems.

It is possible in most databases to `update` one table using the contents of another table. In the example below, we assume that someone has identified some data errors in addresses and ZIP Codes in the `person` table. The rows with errors are shown the following table.

```
  id    | family_name |      address_line_1       | zip_code
--------+-------------+---------------------------+----------
 15708  | Abrahamson  |                           |  92719
 17447  | Purl        |                           |  47486
 19186  | Balkunas    | 38 Keystone Avenue        |  93947
 20925  | Taucher     | 8 Ludbury Lane            |  95230
 22664  | Hampson     |                           |  14554
 24403  | Fortescue   | 22 Draper Cemetery Road   |  94346
 26142  | Bourton     |                           |  99140
(7 rows)
```

And someone has created a table of corrections like this:

```
person_id | family_name |  address_line_1   | zip_code
----------+-------------+-------------------+---------
    15708 | Abrahamson  | 15 Creek Road     | 92719
    17447 | Purl        | 3 The Bothy       | 47486
    19186 | Balkunas    | 38 Keystone Lane  | 93947
    20925 | Taucher     | 30 Ludbury Lane   | 95230
    22664 | Hampson     | 125 Glossop Road  | 32845
    24403 | Fortescue   | 22 Draper Road    | 54348
    26142 | Bourton     | 3 Beach Alley     | 99140
```

So now we want to update the **person** table, using our table of corrections. We do not want to type them in again because we have carefully checked these. OK, so with seven corrections it wouldn't be a big deal anyway, but in cases I have worked on there are often hundreds or even thousands of corrections, and in these cases preparing a separate table and checking it carefully before applying the changes is definitely a good strategy.

Using **PostgreSQL** it is very easy to do what we want, as shown in the next code sample.

download: update_from_table.sql

```
update person a
set
    address_line_1 = b.address_line_1,
    zip_code       = b.zip_code
from
    person_address_corrections b
where
    a.id = b.person_id;
```

Although there are ways to update multiple tables in one **update** statement, in **PostgreSQL** and in other databases, it is a complex and error-prone operation. If you are updating your live database, then you want the updates to be as simple and easy to test as possible. Don't make your life more complicated than it has to be. If you need to update several tables, write a separate **update** statement for each one.

We can take data from any number of other tables and join those to the table being updated. Having multiple input tables is fine, but always have only one output table.

I think it is easy to see what is happening from the **update** syntax used in **PostgreSQL**. Other databases allow us to **update** one table from another, but some databases use different syntax. With **Oracle**, for example, we have to write the **update** statement like this:

download: update_from_table_oracle.sql

```
update person a
set
    (address_line_1, zip_code) =
    (
      select address_line_1, zip_code
      from person_address_corrections b
      where a.id = b.person_id
    )
where
    a.id in (select person_id from person_address_corrections);
```

So let's look at what is happening in the **Oracle** version. In Oracle the value given to a column can be the result of a **select** statement. In this case we are setting two columns, and the **select** statement that provides the values must provide exactly one value for each column being updated. Within the **select** statement, we refer to the table being updated so that we can match the changes to the row they apply to. So a.id is the **id** of the row in the **person** table that we want to update, and b.person_id is the matching **id** in the **person_address_corrections** table.

So far so good, but now we have to refer to the table **person_address_corrections** in the overall **where** clause for the **update** statement. If we do not do this, then **Oracle** sets **address_line_1** and **zip_code** to **null** in all the rows in **person** that do not have a matching row in **person_address_corrections**. This is not what we want, so we must state again, in the outer query, that we want to update the person only for those rows in **person** that have a matching row in **person_address_corrections**.

As is often the case, **Oracle** makes a meal of the job compared with the clean solution offered by **PostgreSQL**. Often we have to use **Oracle**, but when I have a choice, I use **PostgreSQL** or one of the products derived from **PostgreSQL**.

In fact, **Oracle**'s more difficult syntax is part of the **SQL** standard, and **PostgreSQL** does support it partially. To be fair, the standard is open to some interpretation in this area. **Oracle** and **IBM**'s **DB2** (z/OS and **UNIX**) only support the difficult way. **Microsoft SQL Server** and **Sybase** support the easy way. **MySQL** (and **PostgreSQL**, as noted above) support both. If you have the choice, take the easy way.

Whatever database you are using, these bulk update scripts need to be tested thoroughly. Make sure the updates that you want to apply are applied, and make sure that nothing else is changed.

Delete

Sometimes we really want to delete a row so that it is gone for ever. This might be because the row was a duplicate of another one and we have carefully chosen which of the two to delete. It might be because the row was entered by mistake and should never have been in the database in the first place. It might be because regulation (or just honest good practice) says that we must not keep data about people who are no longer our customers.

Suppose we decide (before we run the corrections update shown above) that we have some doubts about the update and we should remove the row for `person.id` 17447 (Purl, 3 The Bothy, 47486). The next example shows how to do this.

download: delete.sql
```
delete from person_address_corrections
where
    person_id = 17447;
```

We are deleting a whole row, so we do not mention any columns until we get to the `where` clause. The `where` clause, in this case, specifies the primary key (`person_id`) with the precise value that this statement must delete. The primary key is defined to be unique in any table. In this case, the `delete` statement returns the count of rows deleted and it is 1, so all is well.

The `where` clause on a `delete` can specify anything that identifies the rows to be deleted, and any number of rows can be deleted. This means that you have to be careful that you are deleting only the rows you want to delete. If you do not supply a `where` clause, all the rows in the table will be deleted.

In most cases it is best to identify the row to be deleted using its primary key. Your application may have presented the row to the user and asked for confirmation that she wants to delete this data completely. Then, when you have confirmation you can use the primary key to delete the data you presented.

Bulk deletions are appropriate for some migrations, and for removing data that has expired. Obviously, bulk deletions, like all deletions. must be scripted and tested. Never type a `delete` statement into a command line or graphical user interface SQL tool, on your live database or any database containing data that you might want to keep. You may get it right this time, but you will regret it one day.

Deletions are often comparatively inefficient in most databases, especially bulk deletions. If you do want to clear a whole table you can usually use `truncate table` instead, which is much faster. In some databases, notably Oracle, a `truncate table` statement is not under transaction control, so if you include a `truncate table` statement in a transaction and then roll back, the table will still be truncated. This is another case where you need to check the documentation for the database product you are using.

Transactions

Suppose you want to pay some money into my account from yours. Perhaps you are buying a vintage saxophone from me for $6,000. The system that manages the payment must make sure that both:

- the money leaves your account, and
- the money arrives in my account.

Each of these is an `insert` into a database (actually, a number of inserts) and if one of them happens then the others *must* happen. If the money leaves your account and then the application crashes, or the disk fills up, or the data center catches fire, before the money arrives in my account, then we expect the bank to sort out the mess.

These two actions form part of one transaction. The database must guarantee that a transaction is done successfully in total, or not at all.

If your bank returns a message to say that it cannot complete the transaction at this time, that will be irritating, but not a big problem so long as the money is still in your account. You can try again later, or use PayPal, or meet me and give me the cash. But if the money leaves your account and does not arrive in mine then we will both be very unhappy.

I don't like acronyms, but this is an important one: `ACID`. `ACID` stands for *Atomic, Consistent, Isolated, Durable*.

- *Atomic* means that a transaction cannot be subdivided. Either its components are all done successfully or none are. If the database crashes for any reason, it can be restored to its state at the end of the last completed transaction.

- *Consistent* means that, at the end of the transaction, the database will still obey all the constraints defined for it. The constraints include `primary key`, `foreign key`, `not null`, and so on. If the transaction tries to break any constraint, it will fail, and the transaction will have changed nothing in the database.

- *Isolated* means that the transaction is isolated from any other actions taking place in the database. This means that however many transactions are running at once, the end result will be the same as if the database had run one transaction after another. A lot of work has gone into relational databases to ensure that, as much as possible, other tasks can continue while not breaking the isolation rule.

- *Durable* means that once a transaction is done it cannot be undone. Once you have sent me the money for my saxophone you cannot change your mind. If you do decide that you don't want the saxophone after all, I may agree to another transaction to refund your money, but we cannot undo the original transaction.

All serious relational databases provide `ACID` compliance with complete reliability. At the time of writing, Big Data tools do not.

With `PostgreSQL` and `Microsoft SQL Server`, if you do nothing then each `insert`, `update` or `delete` statement is treated as a transaction. Either the whole statement works, or none of it does. If, in one statement you update 25 rows, then 25 rows, exactly, will be updated. This is known as `autocommit`.

If the statement cannot update all 25 rows, then it will put back the values to what they were before and give you an error response, which you must check and act upon.

With `MySQL` you can set `autocommit` on as an option.

`Autocommit` is sufficient for some applications, but not for those, such as banking applications, that need multi-statement transactions.

So how do you apply multi-statement transactions? Unfortunately, it depends on which database you are using. The syntax varies between products, and so does the behavior. If you need multi-statement transactions, and many applications do need them, then you must read the documentation of the product you are using and make sure that your applications do what is necessary. You must also devise multi-user tests to ensure that the transactions are being handled as you intend them to be. These are not the easiest tests to build, but it must be done.

In some databases, you start each multi-statement transaction explicitly, by issuing the following commands:

- `start transaction;` or `begin;` (PostgreSQL, MySQL)
- `begin transaction;` (Microsoft SQL Server, PostgreSQL)

In other databases, the start of a transaction is indicated by any of a number of different events:

- `commit` or `rollback`. The end of the previous transaction also starts the next one (Oracle, IBM DB2)
- the start of the session
- issuing a valid data definition language (DDL) statement, even if it fails
- completing any data definition language (DDL) statement successfully

I prefer the explicit transaction start, as used in `PostgreSQL`, `MySQL` and `Microsoft SQL Server`. If your code explicitly commands the start of the transaction, that is much easier to get right, and to debug, than having any of a number of events at various other places in your code that may have caused this transaction to start. Well-engineered applications have minimal and well-defined interactions between different parts of the code. We must define the start and end of transactions explicitly to be able to follow this principle. Not all database products support this. Those that do not support the explicit start of a transaction impose bad engineering on the developers of systems that use them.

Chapter 11 - Populating Your Database

Fortunately, the command for the end of a transaction is consistent across all the databases, or to be more precise, we can make it consistent.

To finish a transaction successfully the command is:

- `commit;`
  or
- `commit work;`
  or
- `commit transaction;`

Since `commit;` works with all relational databases, always say simply `commit;`. The words `work` and `transaction` have no effect on this command so do not ever use them.

To abandon a transaction, and remove all traces of what this transaction was doing, the command is:

- `rollback;`
  or
- `rollback work;`
  or
- `rollback transaction;`

Again, `rollback;` works in all databases, so do not use the noise words `work` or `transaction`.

Some databases support `savepoints` within transactions and `named transactions`. If you find yourself wanting to use these, have a very careful think about the design of your application and talk about it with the brightest person you know. You should be able to avoid these complexities.

A very important consideration is the use of `connection pools`. Large multi-user programs often use connection pools. The application is making changes to the database on behalf of the users and does not keep one connection per user. However, each connection handles one database session and each transaction belongs to one database session. The application must not switch connections in the middle of a transaction. Everything from `start transaction` to `commit` or `rollback` for one user must be done on the same connection.

To implement transactions, the database must `lock` resources while they are being used in a transaction, so that other users cannot change data that are being used in another user's transaction. For example, while you are paying your $6000 to me for my saxophone, another creditor of yours cannot take your monthly payment, and update your balance, at the same time. The transaction will take only a few milliseconds, so it is not a problem to lock the resources for this time.

This implies that the application must do all the components of each transaction in the minimum possible time. We don't want the application to lock some resources at the start of a transaction, go off and do other work for half an hour, and then come back to finish the transaction. Users do this, of course, they start booking their tickets and then have a long discussion with the people who are traveling with them, to check that it is convenient for everybody, and then finish the transaction. This is why most booking websites will hold your choice for only a few minutes before you complete the transaction, and otherwise you must start again.

Your application should collect all the data necessary for a transaction and, only then, `start` the database transaction, apply the changes, and `commit` the transaction. This approach also makes it easier to keep all the commands in one transaction on the same connection (that is, the same database user session). The application is in charge of the interaction with the user and the application can decide on the optimum time to give the user to complete her business transaction.

Most databases support a `set transaction` statement. What these commands do varies from one database to another. A common use of `set transaction` is to control the `isolation level`. This relaxes the isolation rule (in the `ACID` properties described above). For example, we might allow any user to `select` values even if they are being changed in a transaction, with no guarantee that the values will be the same at the end of the `select`. When reading through a long list of account balances, for example, the report could read the balance on your account before you send me your $6000 dollars and then read the balance on my account after your $6000 has arrived in my account. If this happened then the $6000 would be counted twice. For some applications this would be acceptable; for others it would be a serious error. Making the entire list of account balances consistent would need to lock the whole dataset while running the long `select` for the report. I do wonder, though, why anyone would want a detailed report if the details were potentially inconsistent.

As with **savepoints** and **named transactions**, I would challenge the design of an application that needed to change isolation levels; it would have to have a very good reason.

Chapter 12 - Database Migrations That Preserve Data

For Agile Developers, this is the most important chapter because it shows you how to migrate your database, safely, from one state to another. This means that you can embrace change. You can refactor your database, to make it better on every new application release, rather than letting it descend into bloated chaos, which is what does happen in many traditional database developments.

In *Chapter 4 - Database Migrations In SQL on page 97* we looked at database migrations using SQL and we took the simplistic view that we could migrate the database structure and ignore the data. During our initial development we could rebuild all our test data every time. This is realistic for the first few iterations. But we soon get to the point at which we want to keep the data. Certainly, after the first live release, every further development will normally require us to keep the data that is already in the system.

If we are changing the structure then we must migrate the data to the new structure without losing any content and without breaking any relationships.

There is traditionally a fear of changing anything in the database structure, because it is perceived to be difficult and it might break some existing process. It is enormously important to get over this fear. What happens as a result of this fear is that we end up with alternative versions of the same data and that we contort the new development to be compatible with the mistakes we made earlier. This causes many databases to descend into an unreliable, bloated, inefficient mess. We must not be afraid to refactor our databases so that they improve in every aspect over time.

We can mitigate our fear by doing proper testing and by knowing that what we release is what we tested. There are two very important issues in the last sentence. Many database developers do not build proper test suites and do not use scripted migrations, let alone source code control, so they can never repeat a job that they did previously with certainty that it is exactly the same job. It is not such a big leap to get to a tested repeatable process. We just have to do it.

Yes we can restructure data in relational databases, and yes we can do it safely. Let's see how.

In this chapter, we assume that all data in the database must be migrated to the new structure for every iteration. The purpose is to show some techniques for building safe migrations. It does make the migration code a bit longer, of course. It is absolutely worth doing.

The Process

The process we need to follow is:

- Define the migration
- Build tests
- Write scripts
- Run the scripts and the tests in the development and test environments
- When all the tests pass, in the development and test environments:
    - revoke all user access to the live database (at least the tables affected in the migration).
    - take a backup copy of the live database.
    - run the migration scripts and the tests in the live environment.
    - restore user access to the live database.

Any command that changes the structure of the database must be tested with a batch of tests that ensure that it is doing what is intended and doing it correctly. When all the tests pass, and only then, can the script be run against the live database, and then we don't have to worry about it because we know that it will work.

The scripts need to be run using the SQL command line tool. For PostgreSQL you type psql on the command line, for MySQL it is mysqlsh, for Oracle it is sqlplus, for Microsoft SQL Server it is sqlcmd, for IBM DB2 it is db2. Every relational database has a SQL command line tool.

We always use the command line to run scripts and we always automate them. We have a single command that makes the changes and runs the tests. We do not type in the separate commands because, however diligent we are, we will make mistakes.

If you use a graphical user interface tool then you have no record of what you did; this makes it very difficult to identify mistakes if the test does not run correctly. Also, you can never be sure that the sequence of tasks you do in development will be the same as those you do in the test environment or the sequence you do in the live environment. We cannot accept such uncertainty in what we deliver to the live environment.

So do not use a graphical user interface to change your database, not ever. Your vendor may tell you how easy it is to administer your database with the admin tool. Easy, yes, but it is more important to be reliable and repeatable. These tools are OK in read-only mode - they may have some nice charts - but never use them to change anything. Never!

In *Chapter 3 - An Agile Database - Step by Step on page 70* and again in *Chapter 4 - Database Migrations In SQL on page 97* we worked through three iterations. We will go through those again, using SQL to perform the migrations and assuming that we want to preserve all the data that we had at the end of the previous iteration.

Iteration 1

In Iteration 1 we started with a new database. We had to define and create the tables that our first iteration would use. This is exactly the same this time because there is no data to migrate. Iteration 2 gets a bit more interesting.

Iteration 2

In *Chapter 3 - An Agile Database - Step by Step, Iteration 2 on page 89* we needed to make the following changes:

- Add make, model and year to the `vehicle` table
- Create a new table to hold incidents, with `date_and_time_of_incident` and `description_of_incident`
- Remove `date_and_time_of_incident` and `description_of_incident` from `claim` table
- Link `incidents` to `claims`

We will use this example to show the sorts of things that need to be considered and how we can implement this specific case. Some of the techniques used in this case are applicable to many migrations, but every migration is unique so you will need to pick out the parts that are useful and add some specific code to handle your particular case. The process is always the same; the details change for each case.

The Vehicle Table

Adding make, model and year to the `vehicle` table is easy. There is no data in the existing database for these three fields, so nothing needs to be migrated. We just alter the table to add the three new columns, and these columns will be `null` until we populate them. The SQL script is shown again below.

download: alter_vehicle.sql

```
alter table vehicle
    add column make                 varchar(40),
    add column model                varchar(40),
    add column year_first_licensed  integer;
```

There are some cases where using the `alter table` command can make your database less efficient. An example would be adding columns (as we have done here) or making a `varchar` column longer, and then updating existing rows to add data in the new columns or increase the length of strings stored in `varchar` columns. The updated record might not fit back in the physical page that it was in before, so the database would have to put it in a new page and link to that. If you did this on a large scale it could have a noticeable impact on performance. If your system is a large transaction-processing application then you should recreate the table instead. In the next part of the migration we see an example that involves recreating tables.

Separating Claims and Incidents

Shifting incidents into a separate table is a bit more complicated. Here is the migration story:

> *I, as the person responsible for keeping the data model honest, want to take the incident timestamp and description from the* `claims` *table and put it into a new* `incident` *table. When we have done that, we want to link*

each claim to its incident, if it has one, by putting the incident_id *as a foreign key in the* claims *table. This is so that the database reflects the reality that an incident can exist without a claim and a claim can exist without an incident.*

Having captured the story we must define some tests. Our tests need to prove that:

- We have not lost any claims
- We have not lost any incidents
- All incidents are linked to their claims
- We have not duplicated any claims
- We have not duplicated any incidents

Our strategy for the migration will be:

1. To rename the existing claim table to old_claim
2. To build the new claim and incident tables from the old_claim table
3. To run our tests
4. When the tests are OK, to drop the old_claim table

Step 4, dropping the old_claim table is really important. This is the point in time at which we have most confidence that we do not need the old_claim table any more. If we leave it for a while, just to make sure everything is OK, then eventually we will find that our database is full of zombie tables and nobody is sure why they are there and nobody is brave enough to drop them, just in case. I have seen a multi-national organization go through an expensive proof-of-concept with four vendors, and buy a new database server, which cost millions of dollars, simply because over half their existing database space was taken up with zombie tables. Things rapidly get out of hand if we are not highly disciplined about taking out the rubbish.

On the other hand, we could make a mistake. Despite our careful testing, we might miss something. The way to mitigate this remaining risk is to make sure that we have reliable database backups and to schedule a backup just before we do the migration in the production system.

Having the old_claim table during the migration is very useful for testing, so we will use it in our tests and then drop it.

The Tests

First we write the tests. The first one, below, tests that we have not lost or duplicated any claims, solely based on the counts of `claim` rows before and after the migration.

download: test_claim_counts.sql

```sql
select
    case
        when count_before = count_after
        then 'Success. Claim counts OK'
        when count_before > count_after
        then 'Fail. ' || (count_before - count_after) || ' Claims lost.'
        else 'Fail. ' || (count_after - count_before) || ' Claims duplicated.'
    end as test_result
from
    (select count(*) as count_before from old_claim) x,
    (select count(*) as count_after from claim) y;
```

As we noted in *Chapter 10 - Select From Many Tables, Case Expressions on page 211* the `when` clauses in a `case` statement are tested in order and the first one that is found to be true gives the answer; no further `when` or `else` clauses are checked once we have found one true result.

The next example tests that we have not lost or duplicated any incidents, solely based on the counts or rows containing incident data before and after the migration. We don't want to create incident rows in cases where both the incident description and the incident timestamp are `null`; in these cases there is no incident to migrate.

download: test_incident_counts.sql

```sql
select
  case
    when count_before = count_after
    then 'Success. Incident counts OK'
    when count_before > count_after
    then 'Fail. ' || (count_before - count_after) || 'Incidents lost.'
    else 'Fail. ' || (count_after - count_before) || 'Incidents duplicated.'
  end as test_result
from
  (
    select
      count(*) as count_before
    from
      old_claim
    where
      date_and_time_of_incident is not null or
```

```
      description_of_incident is not null
) x,
(
  select count(*) as count_after from incident
) y;
```

Next we want to test, at the field level, that we have not lost any data. Note that we use the set-level **except** function, which is very useful for tests across complete data sets. The **except** function (like **intersect** and **union**) treats **nulls** in different sets as being equivalent. This is important for such tests. We don't want our tests to be invalidated by silently ignoring null values. (See *Chapter 7 - Nulls*, section *...and Set Operators on page 156.* for a reminder about the behavior of set operators with nulls.)

download: test_no_data_lost.sql
```
select
    case
        when count(*) = 0 then 'Success. No data lost in migration'
        else 'Fail. ' || count(*) || ' rows lost in migration'
    end as test_result
from
(
    select
        policy_id,
        person_id,
        first_notification_of_loss,
        date_and_time_of_incident,
        police_reference,
        photos_to_follow,
        sketch_to_follow,
        description_of_weather,
        description_of_incident,
        description_of_property_damage
    from
        old_claim
    except
    select
        a.policy_id,
        a.person_id,
        a.first_notification_of_loss,
        b.occurred_at                   as date_and_time_of_incident,
        a.police_reference,
        a.photos_to_follow,
        a.sketch_to_follow,
        a.description_of_weather,
        b.description                   as description_of_incident,
        a.description_of_property_damage
    from
```

```
            claim a
            left outer join
            incident b
            on a.incident_id = b.id
    ) x;
```

We also want to test, at the column level, that we have not duplicated any data. Again we use the set-level **except** function to do this. Note that this is simply the reverse of the previous test; the previous test looked for rows in the old table that did not have matching rows in the new tables, and this test looks for rows in the new tables that do not have matching rows in the old table. Both tests must be successful.

download: test_no_data_duplicated.sql

```
select
    case
        when count(*) = 0
        then 'Success. No spurious data in migration'
        else 'Fail. ' || count(*) || ' spurious rows created in migration'
    end as test_result
from
(
    select
        a.policy_id,
        a.person_id,
        a.first_notification_of_loss,
        b.occurred_at            as date_and_time_of_incident,
        a.police_reference,
        a.photos_to_follow,
        a.sketch_to_follow,
        a.description_of_weather,
        b.description            as description_of_incident,
        a.description_of_property_damage
    from
        claim a
        left outer join
        incident b
        on a.incident_id = b.id
    except
    select
        policy_id,
        person_id,
        first_notification_of_loss,
        date_and_time_of_incident,
        police_reference,
        photos_to_follow,
        sketch_to_follow,
        description_of_weather,
```

```
            description_of_incident,
            description_of_property_damage
        from
            old_claim
    ) x;
```

Finally we want to test that we have reset the sequences properly for claims and incidents. If we failed to do this then the next inserts into these tables would fail with duplicate IDs. They won't of course because we have taken care of that and now we are testing that we really did take care of that. Here are the test scripts.

download: test_claim_sequence_and_id.sql

```
select
    case
        when y.next_sequence > x.max_id
        then 'Success. Claim sequence reset correctly.'
        else
            'Fail. Max claim.id = ' ||
            x.max_id ||
            ', next sequence = ' ||
            next_sequence || '.'
    end as test_result
from
    (select max(id) as max_id from claim) x,
    (select nextval('claim_id_seq') as next_sequence) y;
```

download: test_incident_sequence_and_id.sql

```
select
    case
        when y.next_sequence > x.max_id
        then 'Success. Incident sequence reset correctly.'
        else
            'Fail. Max incident.id = ' ||
            x.max_id ||
            ', next sequence = ' ||
            next_sequence || '.'
    end as test_result
from
    (select max(id) as max_id from incident) x,
    (select nextval('incident_id_seq') as next_sequence) y;
```

So, these are the tests, and we will run them after we have done the migration to ensure that it worked correctly. When these tests pass in Development we will promote the migration to the Test environment and run the migration and the tests again. If they fail in the Test environment then we will need to think very carefully about what we did wrong and go

Chapter 12 - Database Migrations That Preserve Data

back to Development. When we have solved the problem in Development we will promote the migration and tests to the Test environment again. (We will not patch our migration in test, of course.) When we have a clean run in Development, and a clean run in Test, then we will promote the migration and tests to the Live environment. Then we can run our migration with confidence.

The Migration

Having written the tests, we can now develop the migration and test it.

Before we rename `claim` to `old_claim` we need to drop the constraints that refer to the `claim` table, and the sequence that is attached to the `id` in `claim`. (For an explanation of sequences, see *Chapter 8 - Keys on page 164*) If we don't do this, the existing names for these things will be attached to `old_claim` and we will not be able to use the names we want for the new `claim` table because they will already exist. Also, the foreign keys pointing to `claim` will be pointing to `old_claim`, which is not what we want, and we would not be allowed to drop `old_claim`.

As we mentioned, in *The Process on page 245*, we will revoke user access and backup the databases, before we run the live migration. Once we have tested the migration we will know how long the downtime will be so we can plan for that. For systems that are never supposed to be down it is a bit more difficult. Nobody likes downtime, but in almost all systems a short and predictable downtime is acceptable.

The next script removes the constraints that rely on the `claim` table. We are using `PostgreSQL` here, so getting rid of the serial column is done by dropping the default on `id`, and dropping the sequence that supports it: `claim_id_seq`. Note that if you are using `PostgreSQL` then just typing `\d claim` tells you the tables that refer to `claim`, as an essential part of the useful information. If you are using `Oracle` it is more difficult; have a look in the `user_constraints` view that `Oracle` provides. It is possible to work out the information you need from that.

download: drop_claim_constraints.sql

```
alter table claimant drop constraint foreign_key_claimant_claim;
alter table witness drop constraint foreign_key_witness_claim;
alter table damage drop constraint foreign_key_damage_claim;
alter table claim drop constraint primary_key_claim;
alter table claim alter column id drop default;
drop sequence claim_id_seq;
```

Now we can safely rename `claim` to `old_claim`, keeping all the data in `old_claim` to be used in the rest of the migration and for the tests, and then dropped. This is a straightforward command:

download: rename_claim_to_old_claim.sql

```
alter table claim rename to old_claim;
```

We then need a script to create the new `incident` table.

download: create_incident_table.sql

```
create table incident
(
    id                                  serial          not null,
    occurred_at                         timestamp,
    description                         varchar(2000),
    created_at                          timestamp       not null default now(),
    updated_at                          timestamp,
    constraint primary_key_incident primary key (id)
);
```

I've made the judgment that `description` no longer needs to be qualified with the `_of_incident`; and that `date_and_time_of_incident` would be better named as `occurred_at`. Qualified by the table name, this name will be `incident.occurred_at` which seems unambiguous to me. Improving the names of things is an important part of refactoring. A minute's thought now could save hours of confusion later.

And what if there is code that refers to `date_and_time_of_incident`? Well, it will need to be changed. This is not a big deal. If you keep your code in plain text files then you can use simple search tools to make sure you have found every occurrence. This is all a lot easier if you are working on a `UNIX` system. The visual programming tools, although they claim to increase productivity, actually make this much more difficult.

We now need a way to link rows in this new table back to their matching rows in the claims table. We could try using the incident timestamp and the description. These are probably unique, but "probably" is not good enough. If either of these is null then the chance of duplication is higher. If timestamps have been added as date only with the default time of 00:00:00 then the chance of duplicates becomes higher still. But even a small chance of duplication is too big.

So, we want to use the claim.id, which we have controlled to be unique by specifying it as the primary key. This is what primary keys are for: identifying individual rows precisely.

In old_claim the id identifies both the claim and the incident. We will use the old_claim.id values as the id of both the new claim table and the new incident table. This isn't always the right thing to do, but it works in this case.

Practically, it is important to understand that the serial column in PostgreSQL uses the sequence value as a default. If we specify a value for the id when we insert a row, then the sequence is ignored. Also, by defining the id as the primary key, we do ensure that it is unique, so if we try to insert the same value twice then the insert will fail.

We will use this behavior to set the ids in the new claim and incident tables. We will then adjust the sequences to make sure that new rows added after the migration will take values that are not already in those tables.

Here is the part of the script that populates the incident table from old_claim records that had either an incident description or an incident timestamp, or both.

download: populate_incident_table.sql

```
insert into incident
(
    id,
    occurred_at,
    description,
    created_at,
    updated_at
)
select
    id,
    date_and_time_of_incident as occurred_at,
    description_of_incident as description,
    created_at,
```

```
        now() as updated_at
from
    old_claim
where
    date_and_time_of_incident is not null or
    description_of_incident is not null;
```

Next we need a script to create the new `claim` table. All very straightforward: we have removed the incident columns and added a foreign key (`incident_id`) to point to the incident data in the new `incident` table.

download: create_new_claim_table.sql

```
create table claim
(
    id                              serial      not null,
    policy_id                       integer,
    person_id                       integer,
    incident_id                     integer,
    first_notification_of_loss      timestamp,
    police_reference                varchar(40),
    photos_to_follow                boolean,
    sketch_to_follow                boolean,
    description_of_weather          varchar(2000),
    description_of_property_damage  varchar(2000),
    created_at                      timestamp   not null
                                       default now(),
    updated_at                      timestamp   not null,
    constraint primary_key_claim            primary key(id),
    constraint foreign_key_claim_policy     foreign key (policy_id)
                                       references policy(id),
    constraint foreign_key_claim_person     foreign key (person_id)
                                       references person(id),
    constraint foreign_key_claim_incident   foreign key (incident_id)
                                       references incident(id)
);
```

The new `claim` table then needs to be populated with data from the `old_claim` table and the correct ids for the related incidents in the new `incident` table.

download: populate_new_claim_table.sql

```
insert into claim
(
    id,
    policy_id,
    person_id,
    incident_id,
    first_notification_of_loss,
```

```
        police_reference,
        photos_to_follow,
        sketch_to_follow,
        description_of_weather,
        description_of_property_damage,
        created_at,
        updated_at
)
select
    a.id,
    a.policy_id,
    a.person_id,
    b.id                                as incident_id,
    a.first_notification_of_loss,
    a.police_reference,
    a.photos_to_follow,
    a.sketch_to_follow,
    a.description_of_weather,
    a.description_of_property_damage,
    a.created_at,
    now()                               as updated_at
from
    old_claim a
    left outer join
    incident b
    on a.id = b.id;
```

We made things easy for ourselves by using the ids from the old_claim table as the ids for both the new claim table and the new incident table. At this point these ids let us join the two new tables with 100% reliability. As soon as the migration is finished, when the live system is switched on and new transactions start arriving again, the claim.id and the incident_id will go their separate ways. All this is OK so long as we understand what we are doing.

We need to do an outer join between claim and incident to set the incident_id to the correct value where an incident exists and to make the incident_id null in the cases where there is a claim without an incident. Claim to incident is an optional relationship. If the incident_id in claim is populated then it must point to an existing incident; the foreign key constraint enforces this. And if the incident_id in a claim record is null it means that there is no incident data for this claim (yet). This happens in the real world, so our database must be able to record both possibilities.

Now we need to make sure that the sequences are set correctly.

Columns with the data-type `serial` have their values taken from a sequence which is linked to the table, by default. If you drop and recreate the table then the sequence will be reset to 1. If you are reloading data, then you need to reset the sequence to start with a number higher than any value already in this column in the table, to avoid clashes with existing values.

In this case we chose to override the defaults and set the `ids` from reliable values that we already had. Now we must reset the sequences so that new records inserted into the `claim` and `incident` tables are given `id` values that do not clash with values already used.

The `serial` data-type is very useful, but we need to be careful with it on migrations. Most other databases work in a similar way in this area, so this warning is not only for `PostgreSQL`.

The next two scripts show how to reset the sequences for the `claim` and `incident` tables, using `PostgreSQL`.

download: reset_claim_sequence.sql

```
\set script_file `date +%Y%m%d%H%M%S`.sql
\t
\o :script_file
select
    'alter sequence claim_id_seq restart ' || max(id) + 1 || ';'
from
    claim;
\o
\t
\i :script_file
```

download: reset_incident_sequence.sql

```
\set script_file `date +%Y%m%d%H%M%S`.sql
\t
\o :script_file
select
    'alter sequence incident_id_seq restart ' || max(id) + 1 || ';'
from
    incident;
\o
\t
\i :script_file
```

You will see that these scripts use several commands that are specific to the command line tool itself. In `PostgreSQL` these commands start with a backslash ("\").

The \set command gives a variable a value. In this case, the variable is script_file and we are generating a file name that will be unique. The code between back-ticks ("`") is executed by the operating system, which is UNIX in this case.

The \t command toggles the column headings, and only prints the actual query output. The first \t switches the headings off; the second \t switches them back on.

\o :script_file says: "send the output to the file identified by the variable :script_file."

\o says: "stop sending the output to the file and send it to the standard output as before."

\i :script_file executes the SQL statement(s) in the script_file. In this case we have generated a script file with only one statement in it. We generate a statement that resets the sequence to the highest id currently in the table, plus one, and then we execute this statement.

We do the same process for the claim table and then the incident table.

Now that all the data is where it should be, we can reinstate the foreign keys that point to the claim table, as shown below.

download: reinstate_foreign_keys.sql
```
alter table claimant add constraint foreign_key_claimant_claim
    foreign key(claim_id) references claim(id);
alter table witness add constraint foreign_key_witness_claim
    foreign key(claim_id) references claim(id);
alter table damage add constraint foreign_key_damage_claim
    foreign key(claim_id) references claim(id);
```

I have shown each step separately here. In practice I want to execute all these scripts with a single command, to minimize the possibility of missing a step or making any other mistake in the process. It must be a repeatable process, otherwise it is not safe.

These steps could all go into one long script file, but I would create separate files and then write another one that executes each separate file in sequence. The script to execute almost all of the migration is shown below.

download: migration_preserve_data.sql

```
\i drop_claim_constraints.sql
\i rename_claim_to_old_claim.sql
\i create_incident_table.sql
\i populate_incident_table.sql
\i create_new_claim_table.sql
\i populate_new_claim_table.sql
\i reset_claim_sequence.sql
\i reset_incident_sequence.sql
\i reinstate_foreign_keys.sql
\i test_claim_counts.sql
\i test_incident_counts.sql
\i test_no_data_lost.sql
\i test_no_data_duplicated.sql
\i test_claim_sequence_and_id.sql
\i test_incident_sequence_and_id.sql
\i alter_vehicle.sql
```

When we run this script the results are:

```
claims=# \i migration_preserve_data.sql
ALTER TABLE
ALTER TABLE
ALTER TABLE
ALTER TABLE
ALTER TABLE
DROP SEQUENCE
ALTER TABLE
psql:create_incident_table.sql:9: NOTICE:
    CREATE TABLE will create implicit sequence "incident_id_seq"
    for serial column "incident.id"
psql:create_incident_table.sql:9: NOTICE:
    CREATE TABLE / PRIMARY KEY will create
    implicit index "primary_key_incident" for table "incident"
CREATE TABLE
INSERT 0 6259
psql:create_new_claim_table.sql:23: NOTICE:
    CREATE TABLE will create implicit sequence "claim_id_seq"
    for serial column "claim.id"
psql:create_new_claim_table.sql:23: NOTICE:
    CREATE TABLE / PRIMARY KEY will create
    implicit index "primary_key_claim" for table "claim"
CREATE TABLE
INSERT 0 6726
Showing only tuples.
Tuples only is off.
ALTER SEQUENCE
Showing only tuples.
Tuples only is off.
```

```
ALTER SEQUENCE
ALTER TABLE
ALTER TABLE
ALTER TABLE
        test_result
---------------------------
 Success. Claim counts OK
(1 row)

         test_result
----------------------------
 Success. Incident counts OK
(1 row)

          test_result
-----------------------------------
 Success. No data lost in migration
(1 row)

           test_result
---------------------------------------
 Success. No spurious data in migration
(1 row)

            test_result
-----------------------------------------
 Success. Claim sequence reset correctly.
(1 row)

             test_result
--------------------------------------------
 Success. Incident sequence reset correctly.
(1 row)
```

The only part that is not included in this script is the final removal of the old_claim table. As we said before, it is very important that we remove this, but only after we have checked the results of the tests. If something did go wrong, it would be helpful to have the old_claim table around. However, as soon as we have checked that all the tests have succeeded then we must drop the old_claim table, like this:

```
drop table old_claim;
```

So there you have a very safe database migration. You might say "that's a lot of work." Database tests are important. They need to be developed with care, and that does take some time. We can make our databases agile and robust. The effort is absolutely worthwhile.

The alternative - saving a bit of time on testing at the cost of allowing the database to become more and more incompatible with the real world - is professional negligence. We can make our database better on every release, by being prepared to refactor it every time.

The script shown above runs in a few seconds on typical production volumes. You could do this migration without your customers experiencing any impact.

One other observation: I often hear clients say "we've got thousands of script files...that's a problem...we need a tool to resolve this." Yes, you do. You need a source code control system and a sensible directory structure to store your script files in. What you do not need is an ETL tool where you end up with thousands of unintelligible diagrams showing the bizarre icons that the ETL vendor uses to represent bits of a visual programming language that are similar to bits of SQL, but not as clear, concise and useful as SQL. Despite the promises from the vendors, it is not easy to manage your mappings, migrations and temporary tables using these tools.

You are much better off with plain text files, a good source code control system (such as Subversion[54]) and a well-designed directory structure. Being agile and responsible is much easier (and less expensive!) if you use these simple tools and some discipline.

Iteration 3

Iteration 3 requires us to create the claim_head and transaction tables. We will also need to populate the claim_head table with the 25 or so fixed values that our insurance company uses. We could type these into a csv file and use the bulk loader for our database (`copy` for `PostgreSQL`) or we could write 25 insert statements. Either way it is trivial. There are no other tables to change. We will still write scripts to do this, and we will still test them carefully. These are simple changes but when we move to our Test environment and then to Live, we do not want any embarrassments.

Database migrations are often simple and sometimes non-existent, when the application does not need to change the database. When database changes are needed we should do them willingly and thoroughly. In the

---

54. http://subversion.apache.org

long run this will be less work for everyone involved.

Chapter 13 - When Things Go Wrong

Things do go wrong. We make mistakes, we misunderstand what our users want, we misunderstand the tools we are using, systems run out of resources, and there are many other possible reasons.

Whenever we write some data from our application to any storage mechanism, there is a possibility that it will fail. Even if you are writing a text file to your local hard disk, that disk can become full or corrupted or even permanently broken. With a shared database those things can happen too, but also you may clash with another user or you may be trying to breach some integrity constraint. These are real-world, unavoidable situations. We have described some in *Chapter 11 - Populating Your Database on page 227*. In this chapter we will describe some ways of dealing with these exceptions.

Usually our applications, and the things they depend on, don't fail, but occasionally they will, and this means that we must always check. As Hunt and Thomas say in *The Pragmatic Programmer*[55]:

> "... it is good practice to check for every possible error - particularly the unexpected ones. However, in practice this can lead to some pretty ugly code: the normal logic of your program can end up being totally obscured by error handling ..."

When I worked in a hospital, the managers used to say: "this place would be easy to run if we didn't have any patients." Our code would be easier to write if we didn't have any exceptions. True, but what would be the purpose?

Error handling requires the intervention of a human being - an end user, a database administrator, a system manager or a developer. It is the program's responsibility to give the human being relevant information in enough detail so that the problem can be resolved without further research.

Exceptions are reported in different ways by different programmers - some of these are more useful than others. Here are the main styles we have come across:

---

55. See Bibliography [Hunt&Thomas]

- silent failure
- "something went wrong"
- the wild goose chase
- crying "wolf!"
- the useful message

Silent Failure

This is the very worst kind of error handling. The program is coded to ignore errors. It says that everything is OK when something has failed. The user finds out about the exception later - often months later - when the damage may be extremely hard to put right.

An example I experienced was caused by the failure to validate dates on input and by the storage of these dates in a text field. This saves a lot of bother with nasty messages about dates which aren't quite right, but... Eventually we discovered that some dates had been entered in UK format (dd/mm/yy) and some in US format (mm/dd/yy). For dates where the day is between 1 and 12 it was impossible to determine the correct value from the data alone. For example "12/04/2014" could be 12th April or 4th December. The only solution was to go back to the source documents and check every date that was ambiguous. The cost of doing this for tens of thousands of records was enormous. If the dates had been validated, at least we would have found out as soon as we hit day 13 and tried to interpret it as a month. But, in fact, the errors continued to accumulate in the database for many months after that.

Another kind of silent failure is something that you should never do with SQL, and that is to select a result set and then only look at the first row returned. If there is meant to be only one row, then you should make sure that there is only one. I once came across a particularly bad example of an application that did this. It was selecting the products installed at a customer's site and working out which products were most profitable. But it only looked at the first product for each customer and allocated all the revenue from that customer to that product. For customers that had several products installed, the results were completely misleading. As a result the company discontinued some products that were actually profitable and continued with some that were losing money. The company went out of business with the loss of thousands of jobs and major impacts on its customers and shareholders.

But one consultant insisted that it was *best practice* to read the first row returned and then ignore any others, because this did not alarm the users. I asked him if he put duct tape over the warning lights on his car dashboard, and to my amazement he said that he did, because the oil light kept coming on but he "knew" that it was actually OK. I never found out if he ended up stranded by the side of the road with a blown engine. If so, I hope it was raining.

Always check possible error conditions, and let the users know that something has failed. As Hunt and Thomas say in *The Pragmatic Programmer*, "Crash, Don't trash"[56].

"Something Went Wrong"

This isn't as bad as the silent failure - at least we know that there is a problem, but the error report is so vague that it is extremely hard to track down and fix the underlying problem. As a result there may be no-one with the time and expertise to actually resolve it.

The exception handling built into many languages, including Java, Ruby and `Oracle`'s `PL/SQL` makes it easier to handle exceptions without messing up your code too much.

The Java syntax works like this:

download: java_exception.java
```
    try
    {
      resultSet = statement.executeQuery(query);
    }
    catch (SQLException e)
    {
      e.printStackTrace();
    }
```

This shows an example of the `try...catch...` construct, using the java.sql package. In this case, the message shown as a result of `e.printStackTrace` gives us the precise location of the error in the application, what was happening at the time, and a useful message. I often find that this `SQLException` class gives me enough information

---

56. See Bibliography [Hunt&Thomas]

to find the cause of the problem. However, we do need to think about what could have happened and sometimes write specific code in the application to show current values of relevant fields to make it easier to debug.

If you have Java code in your systems, it is worth scanning for empty `catch` blocks. I have found some in some popular open source code. An empty `catch` block is a silent failure.

Here's an example from an application that executes `SQL select` statements provided by the user. If one of these fails, it is very helpful to have the `SQL` query text as well as the exception reported by the `SQLException` class.

download: java_exception_extra.java

```
try
{
  measureResultSet = selectMeasureStatement.executeQuery(query);
}
catch(SQLException sqle)
{
  logFile.logMessage
    ("Failed to execute query " + query + ". " + sqle.toString());
}
```

The `try...catch...exception` syntax is very useful, but it can be misused, as illustrated below.

download: java_exception_bad.java

```
try
{
  // All my dodgy code ...
  // pages ...
  // and ...
  // pages ...
  // of ...
  // it ...
  // NEVER DO THIS!
}
catch (Exception e)
{
  System.out.println("Something went wrong! Ha! Ha! Ha!");
}
```

I have come across applications written like this. In fact I have had to debug them. It isn't fun. In such programs there is the start of a `try...catch` block at the beginning of the program and the `catch` part right at the end. All the code is in between so any exception will be caught, but you won't know where the error occurred, except that it occurred somewhere in the program. This happens in Java and very often in Oracle's PL/SQL.

Handling exceptions properly does make your code longer, but you really must put the `try...catch...exception` blocks around every statement that can cause an exception. That's the way it is; you can't make it any simpler for yourself without seriously inconveniencing your colleagues (or possibly yourself six months later).

When I say "every statement that can cause an exception" what does that mean? How can you tell which statement might cause an exception and which will not. One good guide is the set of exceptions built into Java. By looking at the Java documentation[57] you can see which classes throw exceptions and the types of things they check. Anything that accesses a file, a network or a database can potentially throw an exception because the resource it is trying to access may not be accessible. Any attempted conversion of a string value into a strong data-type (int, date, boolean, etc.) will raise an exception if the string value does not make sense as that data-type. If the value was entered by a user, and not already checked by your application it may fail. Anything that assumes the format of something (such as `XML`, `URI`, `JSON`, etc.) will raise an exception if the format is invalid. If the string you are processing has come from outside your application then you cannot assume that it is correct until you have validated it. You should always check such things.

You do not need to check the operation of the programming language you are using. If you assign an integer value to another integer, that will work. You can also assume that your database will operate as specified[58].

The Wild Goose Chase

In *The Wild Goose Chase*, the program reports a particular error with apparent confidence, when in fact the problem is something completely

---

57. http://docs.oracle.com/javase/8/docs/api/. There may be a later release by the time you read this.
58. unless your "database" is Hive.
    See http://www.thedatastudio.net/hive_for_sql_developers.htm

different. When you've spent half a day trying to find the reported problem and you stumble across the right one, you'll understand why this is so bad.

Many products and many applications do this, so I don't want to suggest that Oracle is the only culprit. But I did come across this example when using Oracle and it was a wild goose chase. I was migrating some JDBC code from another database to Oracle 11g. A JDBC query that worked fine in the other database gave this error in Oracle:

```
ORA-00911: invalid character
```

I copied the query from the Java code and pasted it into SQL*Plus, where it worked fine.

So I looked up the error in the Oracle documentation and this is what it said:

> "*Cause: identifiers may not start with any ASCII character other than letters and numbers. $#_ are also allowed after the first character. Identifiers enclosed by double quotes may contain any character other than a double quote. Alternative quotes (q'#...#') cannot use spaces, tabs, or carriage returns as delimiters. For all other contexts, consult the* SQL *Language Reference Manual.*"

It was hard to know where I might look in the SQL Language Reference Manual because I had just proved that the SQL statement was correct by running it in SQL*Plus. So I checked the JDBC documentation. No help there. I ran the statement text through the UNIX command od -cx to make sure that there were no invisible characters (tabs, nulls, no-break spaces, etc.). All OK. Eventually I tried removing the semi-colon at the end of the statement. I don't know what made me think of this as a possible cause, because the semi-colon is part of the statement, and without it we cannot tell, in many cases, that a statement is complete. Maybe it was because Oracle SQL*Plus allows a slash ("/") on a new line as a signal to execute the query without a semi-colon. Including the semi-colon in most JDBC implementations is fine, but not with Oracle. That was, indeed, the problem.

We have all come across wild goose chase errors and wasted many hours trying to understand how the problem we are witnessing relates to the message we received. Let's all try to avoid inflicting such frustration on our users.

Crying "Wolf!"

Sometimes errors are reported, but they don't matter, or maybe they are not errors at all.

This happened in batch installation scripts for one database I have worked with, where the scripts attempt to delete old versions of database objects (tables, synonyms, procedures, etc.) and report an error if the object does not exist. Well, of course this doesn't matter because we didn't want the object to exist anyway. But when there is a 30-page log file with dozens of error messages that are actually OK, how do you find the one important message that is in there somewhere? You don't even know that there is a genuine error.

As we know from the story of the boy who cried "wolf!", when there really was a wolf, no-one believed him.

Why do developers write programs which behave so badly?

There can be many reasons. Software development is quite difficult, and having to deal with all the possible exceptions makes it more so. Often, pressures of deadlines encourage developers to take short cuts. Sometimes, though not often in my experience, developers are just lazy. And sometimes developers have been trained and advised badly.

Many developers I know will fight to be allowed to do a thorough job and will put in long hours to go beyond what their managers want them to do. Whether we are developers or managers, we all need to focus on what is important, not just what is urgent. Our applications generally run for a few years and it cannot be good business to build systems that fail inexplicably just days after going live.

The Useful Message

In both interactive and batch programs, the developer must give the user relevant information about the problem and how to resolve it.

Interactive Applications

With an interactive system, the program can present the user with one message at a time, and prevent the user from moving on until the problem is resolved. The context of the problem should be quite obvious so the program only has to provide the specific details, and may suggest possible approaches to resolving it. This happens a lot in good web forms. They insist that you provide all the necessary data. They can check your address and your car license number and show you extra data (the rest of your address, or the make and model of your car) so that you can confirm that it is correct. Life is so much easier when the data is accurate and complete from the start.

Batch Systems

With batch systems it is quite different. Error messages must be stored somewhere and delivered to the users after the batch run is finished. We must consider:

- Diagnosis of the problem. Most errors are caused by some data value that the application did not expect. Which field was in error? What value did it have? What rules should it obey? Do these rules depend on other fields in the record?

- Identifying the erroneous data to the user. Which file or table was it in? How can we find the specific record in this file or table?

- Routing of errors to the appropriate audiences. Who is affected by it? Who can resolve it?

- Management of widely varying numbers of errors. Do we abandon a file or a whole batch run if the number of errors exceeds some threshold?

- Recycling of corrected records. How do we get the correct data into the system? Has bad data already been stored in the database, and if so, how do we clean or remove it?

If you ever get the chance to work with a Netezza system (now bought by IBM and being quietly buried) make sure that you run the `nzload` command and see how that reports any errors in the data file you are loading. `nzload` tells you exactly what you need to know. It gives you the line number in the file and the character position in that line, plus a good attempt to describe what the problem is. You can go directly to the problem character in the file, however big that file is. I try to provide a comparable level of information in the character encoding profiler described at http://www.thedatastudio.net/character_encoding_profile.htm

Exception handling is part of our job as developers. We should take pride in handling exceptions thoroughly and gracefully, rather than treating them as something that gets in the way of our grand design.

Chapter 14 - Tuning

Modern relational databases running on modern hardware are blindingly fast. However, once again, Wirth's Law[59] kicks in: the more powerful our computer systems become, the more powerful (or inefficient) applications we use them for and the capacity of our new computers soon gets used up. It is possible to ask a relational database to do something big and complicated and find that it isn't as fast as we want.

Sometimes we can solve the problem by buying more hardware. That is usually a simple solution, and often cheaper than getting a team of clever people to re-design the software, but hardware is not the only cost involved. A Proof of Concept exercise can easily cost more than solving the performance problem by tuning your database or your application.

I am amused by the plethora of `in-memory` databases being peddled, as if in-memory were something new.

For the most part this is just marketing fluff and you should be very skeptical. There is one exception that I am aware of and that is `VoltDB`[60], a database with an architecture designed specifically to achieve spectacular transaction processing performance by using systems with main memory large enough to hold the entire database. This is now feasible and affordable for applications where very high-speed, totally reliable transactions are required. `VoltDB` is based on sound research by Michael Stonebraker and his team[61].

Databases have always used a memory cache to hold data likely to be needed again soon. This includes the system catalogs (all the metadata), which is comparatively small and is referenced all the time, then there is recently-used data, anticipated data (reading ahead through a long list you have selected), part or all of indexes, and other categories of data that you are likely to need. What all good databases try to do is to arrange for more of your data accesses to be satisfied from memory rather than disk. Some "in-memory" databases were designed to run in memory and then had `persistence` grafted on later. The databases that were designed to make optimal use of disks and memory from the start are

---

59. Wirth attributes this to Martin Reiser. See Bibliography [Reiser]
60. https://www.voltdb.com
61. See Bibliography [Stonebraker&Cetintemel] and [Malviya&Others]

generally better designed and run well. The sheer scale, of both disk and memory, changes dramatically over time and the relative performance of disk and memory changes too. The recent wide availability of solid-state disks (SSDs) has shifted this balance very significantly.

If you have any of the leading relational databases discussed in this book, then most "in-memory" databases are trying to sell you something that you have already.

You will also be told that `scale-out architecture` is what you need, or a `key-value store` is what you need, or some other jargon-loaded promise. Be very skeptical!

In this chapter we discuss some things that you can do to make the most of the high performance of your existing relational database system.

Do Not Use Abstract Data Models

I have seen systems that were so hopelessly inefficient that no amount of hardware could make them perform well. The two that come to my mind as the worst offenders were both using abstract data models. These are discussed at length in *Chapter 16 - Universal Data Models on page 299*.

The lesson I have learned is that trying to tune an abstract data model is simply throwing good money after bad. The best approach is not to start with an abstract data model in the first place. If you inherit one, then replace it right now. The longer you wait the worse it gets. We did replace one on a project I was leading. It took us two months. The conversion to a proper data model was successful. We migrated all the data and fixed the applications. The performance was several orders of magnitude better after we had finished.

On the other hand I have seen a company try to make the best of an inherited abstract data model for several years. The effort that went into keeping this behemoth going was enormous, many person-years more than it would have taken to migrate to a proper data model. The continuing slow running and data integrity failures caused many justified customer complaints as well as difficulties with the auditors and the investors.

When I say replace any abstract data model right now, I am not joking.

Chapter 14 - Tuning

The abstract data model may have cost a lot, but as accountants tell us, "sunk costs are always irrelevant". Redesigning the database will be cheaper in the long run than trying to persuade an abstract data model to perform at an acceptable level.

Keep Database Navigation in the Database, Not in the Application

Second place in the bad performance league is database navigation in the application rather than the server. This is the most common reason that I see for poor performance in online applications. The solution is very simple and I will explain it after I explain the problem in more detail. Let's look at an example.

Suppose that a developer has been asked to produce a report from the claims database (see *Chapter 3 - An Agile Database - Step by Step on page 70*). The report will be for any specified person, for whom the user supplies surname and first name. The report must show the surname, first name, the claim head (for example: "Third-party Vehicle Damage") and the amount of each transaction.

The developer correctly works out that he needs to:

1. Start by finding the person with the specified name
2. Use the `id` of the person to find the cases where this person has been a claimant, if there are any.
3. Having found each claimant, use the `id` of the claimant to find the transactions for this claimant. That will give the amount of each transaction.
4. Finally, use the `claim_head_id` from each transaction to look up the `claim_head` description.

So, the developer implements the solution shown below. This solution is logically correct and produces the right results, but it is hopelessly inefficient. Why is it so slow?

download: database_navigation_bad.java

```java
import java.sql.Connection;
import java.sql.ResultSet;
import java.sql.SQLException;
import java.sql.Statement;
import java.util.Date;

public class PullUp
{
  public static void main(String[] args)
  {
    String familyName;
    String firstName;
    Connection connection;
    DatabaseConnection databaseConnection;
    Statement personStatement;
    Statement claimantStatement;
    Statement transactionStatement;
    Statement claimHeadStatement;
    ResultSet personResultSet;
    ResultSet claimantResultSet;
    ResultSet transactionResultSet;
    ResultSet claimHeadResultSet;
    Date startDate;
    Date endDate;
    long startTime;
    long endTime;


    familyName = new String(args[0]);
    firstName = new String(args[1]);

    databaseConnection = new DatabaseConnection();
    connection = databaseConnection.get();

    startDate = new Date();
    startTime = startDate.getTime();

    try
    {
      personStatement = connection.createStatement();
      personResultSet = personStatement.executeQuery
      (
        "select * from person " +
        "where family_name = '" + familyName + "' and " +
        "first_name = '" + firstName + "';"
      );
      while (personResultSet.next())
      {
        claimantStatement = connection.createStatement();
        claimantResultSet = claimantStatement.executeQuery
        (
          "select * from claimant " +
          "where person_id = " + personResultSet.getInt("id") + ";"
        );
```

```java
            while (claimantResultSet.next())
            {
              transactionStatement = connection.createStatement();
              transactionResultSet = transactionStatement.executeQuery
              (
                "select * from transaction " +
                "where claimant_id = " + claimantResultSet.getInt("id") + ";"
              );
              while (transactionResultSet.next())
              {
                claimHeadStatement = connection.createStatement();
                claimHeadResultSet = claimHeadStatement.executeQuery
                (
                  "select * from claim_head " +
                  "where " +
                    "id = " + transactionResultSet.getInt("claim_head_id") + ";"
                );
                while (claimHeadResultSet.next())
                {
                  System.out.println
                  (
                    "Family name: " +
                    personResultSet.getString("family_name") + ", " +
                    "First name: " +
                    personResultSet.getString("first_name") + ", " +
                    "Claim head: " +
                    claimHeadResultSet.getString("description") + ", " +
                    "Amount: " +
                    transactionResultSet.getBigDecimal("amount")
                  );
                }
              }
            }
        }
        catch (SQLException e)
        {
            e.printStackTrace();
        }

        endDate = new Date();
        endTime = endDate.getTime();
        System.out.println("Elapsed time: " + (endTime - startTime));

    }
}
```

(As with other examples, this one is greatly simplified, ignoring many aspects, to show only the navigation logic. The code works, but is lacking in error handling, in particular. Also, the database connection class is not shown - it is all standard JDBC.)

Let's look at the data we are reporting on.

The following table shows the claimants, and numbers of transactions, for a person called Oliver Soloman. There is only one person with this name and his id is 20371. He's quite a prolific claimer though, appearing as a claimant six times in our database. We can also see from the number_of_transactions column, that he has a total of 74 transactions.

```
 person_id | claimant_id | number_of_transactions
-----------+-------------+------------------------
     20371 |       14416 |                     15
     20371 |        6784 |                     10
     20371 |        3258 |                      9
     20371 |        6801 |                     22
     20371 |        3813 |                     11
     20371 |        3304 |                      7
(6 rows)
```

So, the application as written needs to run:

- 1 SQL query to find the person
- 1 SQL query to find the claimants
- 6 SQL queries to find the transactions
- 74 SQL queries to find the claim head descriptions

That's a total of 82 queries.

Every time the application executes a query, it sends a message from the machine where the application is running to the server where the database is running and gets a response back. If each message between the application and the server takes 40 milliseconds then this process will take 7 seconds, plus the time spent in the database and the time in the application. The messaging time is going to be by far the biggest part of the total elapsed time.

For an online application, this is an obvious problem. (For a batch process it might be less obvious, but still a problem.) We should process this volume of data in a fraction of a second and get the response back to the user in under a second. I have seen many cases where web applications were timing out, and giving the user an error message, precisely because the application was using this nested iteration approach.

Let's now look at how this should be written (again, this example works, but is much simplified). There is just one query, so one pair of messages between the application and the server. If our messages take 40 milliseconds each, we have an 80-millisecond overhead instead of a 7-second overhead. The Java code is shorter and simpler in this version. All the joins are done in the database.

download: database_navigation_good.java

```java
import java.sql.Connection;
import java.sql.ResultSet;
import java.sql.SQLException;
import java.sql.Statement;
import java.util.Date;

public class PushDown
{
  public static void main(String[] args)
  {
  String familyName;
  String firstName;
    Connection connection;
    DatabaseConnection databaseConnection;
    Statement statement;
    ResultSet resultSet;
    Date startDate;
    Date endDate;
    long startTime;
    long endTime;

    familyName = new String(args[0]);
    firstName = new String(args[1]);

    databaseConnection = new DatabaseConnection();
    connection = databaseConnection.get();

    startDate = new Date();
    startTime = startDate.getTime();

    try
    {
      statement = connection.createStatement();
      resultSet = statement.executeQuery
      (
        "select " +
          "a.family_name, " +
          "a.first_name, " +
          "d.description as claim_head, " +
          "c.amount " +
        "from " +
          "person a " +
          "join " +
          "claimant b " +
          "on a.id = b.person_id " +
          "join " +
```

```
            "transaction c " +
            "on b.id = c.claimant_id " +
            "join " +
            "claim_head d " +
            "on c.claim_head_id = d.id " +
          "where " +
            "a.family_name = '" + familyName + "' and " +
            "a.first_name = '" + firstName + "' " +
          "order by " +
            "claimant_id, " +
            "claim_head_id;"
        );
        while (resultSet.next())
        {
          System.out.println
          (
            "Family name: " + resultSet.getString("family_name") + ", " +
            "First name: " + resultSet.getString("first_name") + ", " +
            "Claim head: " + resultSet.getString("claim_head") + ", " +
            "Amount: " + resultSet.getBigDecimal("amount")
          );
        }
      }
      catch (SQLException e)
      {
        e.printStackTrace();
      }

      endDate = new Date();
      endTime = endDate.getTime();
      System.out.println("Elapsed time: " + (endTime - startTime));
    }
  }
```

Databases have been optimizing joins for over 40 years and they are now very good at it. You don't stand much chance of beating the database performance by writing your own code to do database joins.

You will probably hear talk of **push-down** strategies used by database tools. This is what we are doing in our recommended approach above. Push-down means pushing the database navigation logic down to the server where the database can execute the SQL very efficiently. This approach is a feature that has been added to ETL (Extract, Transform and Load) tools in particular.

Select Exactly the Columns You Need and No More

You may also notice that our recommended navigation code specifies exactly the columns it wants, rather than saying select * , as the first example does. This is also a fault in the design of the code in the first example. By saying select * we clutter up the result set with all the columns that we are not interested in, increasing the size of the messages, and using more memory in our application. Don't say, "memory is cheap"! As soon as you say that, your application becomes a memory-hog. Always specify exactly the columns you need in your select statements, and no more.

Use the Database Tools to Collect Statistics for the Optimizer

When the database receives a SQL statement to execute, the first thing it does is to work out the best way to get what you are asking for. If you are looking for one specific row based on its key, then the optimizer will have an easy job and the query will be quick. If you are joining six tables, using aggregates and sub-queries, then the optimization is far more complex but the database can still do this far better than any client application, so long as it has the information it needs.

Modern query optimizers look at many factors and have many strategies to choose from. They may access via an index or scan a whole table. They may join by reading one table and looking up the matching rows in another. They may hash the join columns and match them in memory before looking up the non-key data in the rows. There are many join algorithms with different performance characteristics, and choosing the best one for the job can make a very big difference.

Where there are multiple joins, the order in which they are done can make a huge difference too.

You do not make these choices; the query optimizer does that. Given the right information the optimizer can do an excellent job of finding the fastest way to service the query. In almost all cases, the query optimizer does a much better job than you or I could do.

The information the optimizer uses starts with the metadata that the database keeps anyway: the tables, columns, data-types, primary key constraints, indexes, not-null constraints, and so on. (See *Chapter 15 - Metadata on page 288*.)

The next level is the statistics that are recorded by most leading relational databases. The statistics collected include the number of rows in each table and some characteristics of the physical storage: number of disk blocks, number of levels in an index, density of data and so on. The statistics may also describe the distribution of data values.

The following table shows the commands used in the leading databases to collect statistics that are used by the query optimizer. Generally, these are not recorded automatically. Some databases perform some limited gathering of statistics but you must build and run the scripts to collect statistics in order to get the maximum benefit.

Database Product	SQL Command	Alternative recommended by vendor
PostgreSQL	analyze <table name>;	
Oracle	analyze <table name>;	dbms_stats package
MySQL	analyze <table name>;	
Microsoft SQL Server	update statistics <table_name>;	stored procedure sp_updatestats
Sybase	update statistics <table_name>;	
DB2 UNIX	runstats	
DB2 zOS	runstats	

Some of these statistics-gathering commands have many, many options. In all but extreme cases, you can just take the defaults and use the commands in their simplest form.

On a production system, statistics for all the tables that may have their content changed should be collected, typically once a day, ideally at a quiet time of day, if there is a quiet time for your database. Statistics collection is a read-only process for the table being analyzed, so it can be scheduled to run at the same time as other work if necessary. Analyzing one table at a time is unlikely to have a serious impact on the overall resource use.

Jobs that make bulk changes to the database should also include steps to analyze the tables that have had significant change, immediately after making that change. This includes jobs such as loading a batch of new data, deleting out-of-date data, and creating or dropping an index or a constraint.

If you have a thorough statistics collection regime in place then everything should work well. In rare cases when a query still takes too long then you need to look at other options. In most databases it is possible to find out what `query execution plan` the optimizer generated and that may help you to see what other tuning options may be helpful.

Indexes

Some databases create some indexes automatically, on primary keys, for example. Do not remove these because they are used to ensure that primary keys are unique, and to do this efficiently.

You can add indexes on any column or combination of columns so long as the columns have sensible data-types - not blobs or `XML` or large text fields. You are not going to use silly data-types (such as blobs and `XML`) are you? See *Chapter 6 - Data Types on page 125*.

Do not add indexes on small tables, because they can actually make access slower. A full table scan is not a bad thing especially if the table is small enough to fit in memory. Really! A scan is often the most efficient way to get at the data. Try it and measure the results.

For large tables, indexes improve the speed of access to specific rows, based on a particular key or a range of keys. However, indexes also make `inserts`, `updates` and `deletes` slower, because the database must adjust the index as well as adjusting the data.

Indexes can be useful, but they are generally over-used. If you add an index, measure the improvement you get in selecting the data and measure the cost the index imposes on `inserts`, `updates` and `deletes`, compared to the relative frequency of the different operations. You can then make an informed decision about whether the index is worth having or not.

There are different types of indexes and different storage structures for the data. Some databases offer a `column-store` structure (also known as an `inverted index`). Some databases provide `hash indexes` which are not really indexes but create a hash value from the key and use that to store the record in a specific disk block. They can then find that record very quickly by hashing the required key and going straight to the block where the record is stored. Some databases have a special type of index that is optimized for accessing spatial data (geographic locations, latitude and longitude, for example). Some databases have `bitmap indexes` that are ideal for data where the same value can exist in many records and where this data is rarely updated.

If you have a choice of index types and storage methods, this can help you to get the very best performance for particular applications. Once again it is important to measure the impact of any change to indexes and storage structures. Typically some accesses to the data will get faster and some will get slower as the result of adding an index. With measurements on typical volumes and distribution of data, as well as typical access patterns, you can make an informed decision about your tuning options. Be sure to measure the impact on `inserts`, `updates` and `deletes` as well as on selects.

Transactions

In *Chapter 11 - Populating Your Database on page 227*, we explained multi-statement transactions. The database needs to lock data that is being changed until the transaction is completed (`committed`) or abandoned (`rolled back`). Locking restricts access to the data records that are in an indeterminate state, until the intended change is completed. It can therefore cause delays to other users who are waiting to use the same records. Booking systems are a good example of this. The seat at a concert must be locked from the time one user chooses it until she has either paid for the seat or decided not to take it. Banking transactions are another classic case where each transaction requires (at least) two accounts to be updated so that the payer withdraws money and the recipient receives the money, or no change is made.

For best overall performance, for all users, the application should collect all the information it needs to do the transaction, then start the transaction (which starts locking the resources), apply the changes, and `commit`, without doing any other work, so that resources are locked for the shortest possible time.

Collect the data then apply the whole transaction - don't do part of the transaction before an interaction with the user and the rest afterwards; the user may take a long time and block several other users.

Don't Use Object-Relational Mapping systems (ORMs)

This will no doubt invoke some fury, especially by the suppliers of ORMs.

I have to say that ActiveRecord is better than most ORMs because it maintains a close relationship between the structure in the database and the structure in the model held in the application. This is how it should be.

However, I have seen some ORM implementations where the mapping between the database and the application is horribly complex, difficult to build and difficult to maintain. Then the ORM drags whole object trees into memory, doing thousands of unnecessary database accesses. The concept of an object tree is inherently mistaken because it implies a single hierarchical structure. Both relational databases and object-oriented applications have a network of objects. There can then be many valid trees depending on where you start and what you are trying to achieve. These trees must be accessed only as they are needed. The database is working hard to give the best performance by minimizing actual disk accesses. If your applications pulls in unnecessary data then it wastes time, uses more memory, and misleads the database about what data is needed, making the whole system inefficient.

With Java, I use JDBC and never touch an ORM because the ORM only makes the application more complex and less efficient. Where is the benefit in that?

Perceived Performance

In many cases, the perceived performance is more important than the raw performance. If you are getting a long list of records from the database and presenting them on a web page, for example, the user will judge your performance by the response time of the first page, and the time taken to scroll forwards and backwards through the pages.

Typically (in Java with JDBC for example) you will be iterating through a result set (just one, not a nest of them). As soon as you have the first page complete, present it to the user. You can be preparing the next page while the user is looking at the first one. You can also keep earlier pages in memory when the user has moved on so that you can scroll back quickly.

Rewrite Complex Queries

In most cases the query optimizer can identify logical equivalents for the query you have written and it may automatically find a more efficient one. Some databases are better at this than others.

If that doesn't give the performance you need, then you can consider rewriting complex queries. There are usually different ways to express the same query so try some alternatives and measure the results.

For very complex queries it is sometimes beneficial to produce tables of intermediate results so that you can split the query into two or more stages. Again you should measure the performance change. There is a cost in creating intermediate tables because you then have to manage them. It is worthwhile sometimes, but check that you really are getting a significant and necessary performance improvement before doing this. Always drop the intermediate tables when the query is finished; never leave them lying around in the database. Many databases are filled up with intermediate results and performance suffers as a result.

Advanced Database Tuning

There are some systems that require extreme measures. I am thinking in particular of a mobile telephone system that collected 100 million call data records (CDRs) every day. In `Oracle` (a few years ago) the only way to give access to these was by partitioning the CDR table into one partition per day. This did make it possible to perform queries on a single day's CDRs but it was still practically impossible to report over CDRs for a month, say. The partitioning technique adds quite a lot of administration overhead, so it was not very satisfactory. Eventually the mobile telephone company installed a `Netezza` data warehouse appliance and then we could run queries on all the CDRs that were stored (a few months' worth) and get results back in seconds. The `Netezza` appliance would not have been usable for the operational systems but it was excellent for querying vast amounts of data. This was a better solution than the partitioning, but at a cost.

For the very largest systems, more advanced techniques are required and there is bound to be some trade-off. If you work on one of these systems you must be prepared for this, but most of us do not. For most applications, we can happily avoid these advanced techniques altogether.

Chapter 15 - Metadata

You may be new to a particular database, or you may be revisiting one that has changed since you last worked on it. Help is at hand. The database will tell you all about its structure and content whether the documentation is up-to-date or not. What the database tells you is `metadata`.

We think of data as being simply the values of things. In fact, those values are not much use without something to say what the values mean. Is 15 the time in minutes to get to my office, the height of my house in meters or the age of my grandson or the cost of a meal in a restaurant?

Basic Metadata

As soon as we give a value a name then we have `metadata`. The name is just one piece of the metadata. Metadata is all the information about a data value. This may include data-type, length, range of values, whether the data item must have a value or can be unknown (null), whether the item is used as a key, whether it is indexed for fast access and many other characteristics. Creating rich metadata helps us to have reliable and accurate data. When we come across an existing database that we need to understand, the metadata tells us a lot about how that database works.

In relational databases, each cell (the intersection of a row and a column) contains a value and those values are data. The names of the columns, the names of the tables they exist in, their data-types, sizes and constraints are all metadata.

In an object-oriented system it is usual to be able to examine the metadata of an object. This is called `reflection` or `introspection`. It will usually show the metadata as well as the current data values, or "state" of the object.

All relational databases let you see the metadata which they store to describe the data in the database. This is usually implemented by `system catalog views` which let you run queries to examine whatever part of the metadata you are interested in. Most systems have some shorthand for the common things. `Oracle` has the `describe` command for basic information about tables, etc. Here's an example:

```
SQL> describe person
 Name                           Null?    Type
 ------------------------------ -------- ----------------------------
 ID                             NOT NULL NUMBER(38)
 FAMILY_NAME                             VARCHAR2(40)
 FIRST_NAME                              VARCHAR2(40)
 TELEPHONE_NUMBER                        VARCHAR2(16)
 EMAIL_ADDRESS                           VARCHAR2(200)
 ADDRESS_LINE_1                          VARCHAR2(60)
 ADDRESS_LINE_2                          VARCHAR2(60)
 CITY                                    VARCHAR2(60)
 STATE                                   VARCHAR2(2)
 ZIP_CODE                                VARCHAR2(5)
 DATE_OF_BIRTH                           DATE
 APPROXIMATE_AGE                         NUMBER(38)
 NAME_OF_INSURANCE_COMPANY               VARCHAR2(60)
 POLICY_NUMBER                           VARCHAR2(40)
 CREATED_AT                     NOT NULL TIMESTAMP(6)
 UPDATED_AT                     NOT NULL TIMESTAMP(6)
```

`PostgreSQL` has `backslash commands` to describe tables and most other objects. (Type "\?" at the `PostgreSQL` command line for a list.) Here's an example:

```
claims=# \d person
                                     Table "public.person"
          Column           |          Type          |                     Modifiers
---------------------------+------------------------+----------------------------------------------------
 id                        | integer                | not null default nextval('person_id_seq'::regclass)
 family_name               | character varying(40)  |
 first_name                | character varying(40)  |
 telephone_number          | character varying(16)  |
 email_address             | character varying(200) |
 address_line_1            | character varying(60)  |
 address_line_2            | character varying(60)  |
 city                      | character varying(60)  |
 state                     | character varying(2)   |
 zip_code                  | character varying(5)   |
 date_of_birth             | date                   |
 approximate_age           | integer                |
 name_of_insurance_company | character varying(60)  |
 policy_number             | character varying(40)  |
 created_at                | timestamp without time zone | not null default now()
 updated_at                | timestamp without time zone |
Indexes:
    "primary_key_person" PRIMARY KEY, btree (id)
Referenced by:
    TABLE "claim" CONSTRAINT "foreign_key_claim_person" FOREIGN KEY (person_id) REFERENCES person(id)
    TABLE "claimant" CONSTRAINT "foreign_key_claimant_person" FOREIGN KEY (person_id) REFERENCES person(id)
    TABLE "driver" CONSTRAINT "foreign_key_driver_person" FOREIGN KEY (person_id) REFERENCES person(id)
    TABLE "passenger" CONSTRAINT "foreign_key_passenger_person" FOREIGN KEY (person_id) REFERENCES person(id)
    TABLE "policy" CONSTRAINT "foreign_key_policy_person" FOREIGN KEY (person_id) REFERENCES person(id)
    TABLE "track_latitude_longitude" CONSTRAINT "foreign_key_track_person" FOREIGN KEY (person_id) REFERENCES person(id)
    TABLE "witness" CONSTRAINT "foreign_key_witness_person" FOREIGN KEY (person_id) REFERENCES person(id)
```

`Oracle`, `PostgreSQL` and all the other serious relational databases document their system catalogs, and offer views to see the metadata in convenient forms.

Accessing Metadata In an Application

If you're using JDBC to access your database then you have a much more consistent interface whatever database brand you are using. This is a good thing.

I very often encounter existing databases that are poorly documented and have poor data quality. I use a data profiling application[62] to get a picture of the database I'm dealing with. There are also several commercially available products to do this.

Most relational databases organize tables in groups called schemas within a database. So I start by finding out what schemas we have in the database. The next example is a minimal Java class to list the schemas in a database.

download: list_schemas.java

```java
import java.sql.Connection;
import java.sql.DatabaseMetaData;
import java.sql.ResultSet;
import java.sql.SQLException;
public class ListSchemas
{
  public ListSchemas(Connection connection)
  {
    DatabaseMetaData databaseMetaData = null;
    ResultSet schemaNames = null;
    try
    {
      databaseMetaData = connection.getMetaData();
      schemaNames = databaseMetaData.getSchemas();
      while (schemaNames.next())
      {
        System.out.println
        (
          "Schema: " +
          schemaNames.getString("table_schem")
        );
      }
      schemaNames.close();
    }
    catch (SQLException e)
    {
```

---

62. You can get details of this data profiling application at http://www.thedatastudio.net/data_profiling.htm

Chapter 15 - Metadata

```
            e.printStackTrace();
        }
    }
}
```

In all the Java examples in this chapter I am showing simplified code. It all works, but I would not, for example, put a whole series of statements in one `try...catch...` block in a real application because that gives the "something went wrong" type of error (see *Chapter 13 - When Things Go Wrong on page 264*. I would also do something more useful (but a little more complicated) than using `System.out.println` to list the schemas. All I am trying to do here is to show the basics of how to use the `DatabaseMetaData` class, so I've pared everything else down as much as possible.

Unfortunately, in my real application, I still have to use the column name `table_schem` because that is specified in the interface. What possesses someone to name a field `table_schem` when it is actually the `schema_name`? It is a database schema, not a table schema, and what benefit is there in abbreviating "schema" to "schem"? How do you pronounce it now? (See *Chapter 5 - Naming Things on page 114*.)

We must always mitigate things we cannot change, in this case by hiding the bad naming at the lowest possible level and providing the best presentation we can at higher levels. But when we choose names we must do much better than this.

The results of our schema query are shown below.

```
Schema: information_schema
Schema: pg_catalog
Schema: pg_toast_temp_1
Schema: public
```

In `PostgreSQL: information_schema, pg_catalog` and `pg_toast_temp_1` are standard schemas that contain system information. They are interesting, but not for my purpose of finding out what the user-defined database looks like. In this case, the user tables are in the `public` schema; very often they will be in a schema with a name that describes the system being modeled.

So, the next thing to do is to find out what tables exist in the public schema. To do this we call the method getTables with 4 parameters, like this:

```
databaseMetaData.getTables(null, "public", null, tableTypes)
```

to get the list of table names in the `public` schema. I have set `tableTypes` to the String array: `{"TABLE"}` so that I only get only real tables.[63]

Using Metadata To Profile Your Database

Having got the list of tables, I then build a `SQL` statement for each one to find out how many rows it has, like this:

```
query = new String
(
    "select count(*) as row_count from " +
    tableName[i] + ";"
);
```

I then execute the query, and (for this simplified version) print out each table name and the number of rows it has.

download: list_tables.java

```java
import java.sql.Connection;
import java.sql.DatabaseMetaData;
import java.sql.ResultSet;
import java.sql.SQLException;
import java.sql.Statement;

public class TableList
{
  public TableList(Connection dataConnection, String schema)
  {
    DatabaseMetaData databaseMetaData = null;
    ResultSet tableNames = null;
    String query;
    Statement statement = null;
    ResultSet rowCount = null;
    int numberOfTables = 0;
    int numberOfRows =0;
    int i = 0;
    String[] tableName;
    String[] tableTypes = {"TABLE"};

    try
    {
      databaseMetaData = dataConnection.getMetaData();
    }
    catch (SQLException e)
```

63. http://docs.oracle.com/javase/8/docs/api/ for the full list of what is available.

Chapter 15 - Metadata

```
    {
      e.printStackTrace();
    }

    try
    {
      tableNames =
         databaseMetaData.getTables(null, "public", null, tableTypes);
    }
    catch (SQLException e)
    {
      e.printStackTrace();
    }

    tableName = new String[1024];
    try
    {
      i = 0;
      while (tableNames.next())
      {
        tableName[i] = new String(tableNames.getString("table_name"));
        i++;
      }
    }
    catch (SQLException e)
    {
      e.printStackTrace();
    }

    numberOfTables = i;
    System.out.println("Number of tables: " + numberOfTables);
    for (i = 0; i < numberOfTables; i++)
    {
      query = new String
          ("select count(*) as row_count from " + tableName[i] +';');
      try
      {
        statement = dataConnection.createStatement();
      }
      catch (SQLException e)
      {
        e.printStackTrace();
      }
      try
      {
        rowCount = statement.executeQuery(query);
      }
      catch (SQLException e)
      {
        e.printStackTrace();
      }
      try
      {
        if (rowCount.next())
        {
          numberOfRows = rowCount.getInt("row_count");
```

```
          }
        }
        catch (SQLException e)
        {
          e.printStackTrace();
        }
        System.out.println
        (
          "Table: " +
          tableName[i] +
          ", Row count: " +
          numberOfRows
        );
      }
    }
  }
```

The results are shown below. It can be very useful to get an initial view of what is in the database. You may often find tables with dates and/or people's initials in the name, indicating that these are some temporary work and not part of the core system. Such tables should be removed, of course, but it isn't always so easy. Another thing you may see is a large number of tables that have zero rows. These are often present in packaged software that has many tables that are not used in a particular installation. Being able to eliminate these from your initial analysis and to focus on only the tables that contain data can help you get a picture of what is really happening.

```
Number of tables: 14
Table: claim, Row count: 6726
Table: claim_head, Row count: 23
Table: claimant, Row count: 16211
Table: damage, Row count: 0
Table: driver, Row count: 6093
Table: incident, Row count: 0
Table: passenger, Row count: 573
Table: person, Row count: 12537
Table: policy, Row count: 4739
Table: posting, Row count: 5
Table: track, Row count: 6
Table: transaction, Row count: 170127
Table: vehicle, Row count: 11253
Table: witness, Row count: 4074
```

You must be careful doing this analysis. Some tables in real systems are so large that simply taking a count of the number of rows will take minutes or even hours, and may affect the performance of the system. You have to feel your way carefully when analyzing large production systems. But you do need this information. Talk to the DBAs and try to find

Chapter 15 - Metadata

a quiet time to run big queries if you are working on a very large system.

Having found the schemas and then the tables in a schema that we are interested in, we can go much further. I want to know what the columns are in each table: their names, data-types, maximum length and whether they are allowed to be null or not.

The Java code fragment below shows you how to do this.

download: list_metadata.java

```
try
{
  tableColumns = databaseMetaData.getColumns(null, schemaName, tableName, null);
}
catch (SQLException e1)
{
  e1.printStackTrace();
}

new MetaDataColumns(tableColumns);

System.out.println
(
    "Ordinal position\t" +
    "Column Name\t" +
    "Nullable?\t" +
    "Data-type\t" +
    "Column size"
);

try
{
  while(tableColumns.next())
  {
    if (tableColumns.getString("TABLE_SCHEM").equals(schemaName))
    {
      columnElement = new ColumnElement();
      columnElement.setColumnId(tableColumns.getInt("ORDINAL_POSITION"));
      columnElement.setColumnName(tableColumns.getString("COLUMN_NAME"));
      columnElement.setDataLength(tableColumns.getInt("COLUMN_SIZE"));
      if (tableColumns.getString("IS_NULLABLE").equals("NO"))
        columnElement.setNullable("N");
      else
        columnElement.setNullable("Y");

      dataTypeCode = tableColumns.getInt("DATA_TYPE");

      dataTypeName = JDBCType.valueOf(dataTypeCode).getName();

      System.out.println
      (
        tableColumns.getInt("ORDINAL_POSITION") + "\t" +
```

```
            tableColumns.getString("COLUMN_NAME") + "\t" +
            tableColumns.getString("IS_NULLABLE") + "\t" +
            dataTypeName + "\t" +
            tableColumns.getInt("COLUMN_SIZE")
        );
        columnElement.setDataType(dataTypeName);

        this.add(columnElement);
      }
    }
  }
  catch (SQLException e1)
  {
    e1.printStackTrace();
  }
```

You can see that this gives us the ordinal position of the column in the table. This should not be relevant because, unless you use select * (which I advise against) your queries will work whatever the sequence of the columns in the table. I keep it mainly to make it easy to present my data profile report with the columns in the order that the DBAs expect.

The column name is obviously important.

The column size is tricky because it has a different meaning depending on the data-type. For numeric data, it is the maximum number of digits. For character data, it is the length in characters. For other types it is not very interesting for the purposes of data profiling. The Java API[64] does define exactly what it means for various data-types.

The nullable attribute tells us whether not null was specified when the table was created (or subsequently altered).

The data-type is specified using the Java constant from java.sql.Types and needs to be translated. We can do this with the JDBCType.valueOf(dataTypeCode).getName() methods as shown in the above code.

Having captured this information about the columns, we can construct queries to find, for each column:

- minimum value
- maximum value
- the percentage of null values (for nullable columns)

64. http://docs.oracle.com/javase/8/docs/api/

Chapter 15 - Metadata

- how many distinct values there are in the column
- maximum actual length (for strings: `varchar` columns)
- the frequency distribution of values in the column (for non-unique columns)
- the patterns in character data and their frequency distribution
- whether the values stored in character columns are actually numbers or dates

Patterns can classify characters into alphabetic, numeric, punctuation, currency symbols, etc. Patterns can be used to check whether the column contains valid values or not and whether it is stored in the most appropriate data type.

All this data profile information[65] is very valuable when looking at an existing database. I have yet to see one that did not surprise its managers by containing "impossible" data.

The term "metadata" is now becoming a much more widely used term. We hear it from politicians and news media. It describes, for example, the information held about most photographs we can find on the Internet, information such as date, time and location where the photo was taken, what kind of camera was used, the exposure time and aperture, the image type and resolution.

In databases we create, the metadata controls how the data is used, what can be stored in each field, and other parameters that help to guard the quality of our data and the performance of the system. When we work on an existing database we can use the metadata to find out many things about how the data is used. Metadata is good stuff.

---

65. See http://www.thedatastudio.net/data_profiling.htm to learn more about data profiling

Part E - Some Common Traps To Avoid

You will come across some misguided design ideas. You will be subjected to the vendors' preferences and these may not always be the best for your project. This part is intended to help you avoid the mistakes that many others have made, and to make the best choices for your project.

Not everything in this part is always bad. Some of the practices described here should always be avoided, the rest should be treated with caution. We'll explain as we go along.

Chapter 16 - Universal Data Models

The three sections in this chapter look at different examples of the unbounded desire to build one generic solution to all data processing problems. They are all expensive. They are the opposite of agile development, since they try to build one grand design that encompasses all needs, rather than constructing a system piece by piece, carefully understanding each piece until the whole represents exactly what the users need and want.

The abstract data model has been tried many times. The intention is to make one part of the system very simple, but in the end this causes huge complexity and inefficiency for the system overall. You might get away with this for a tiny database, but almost always this will end in tears.

The Enterprise Resource Planning ("ERP") systems and Industry Standard Data Models are big business. There are vast amounts of money to be made by vendors and consultants around these products. There have been many spectacular failures using them. Some organizations do, somehow, make them work, but always at a huge cost.

Abstract Data Models

This one is a poisoned apple. You should not even take a little bite. Always avoid abstract data models.

An **abstract data model** is an attempt to simplify building databases by reducing all the different data entities to a few generic tables and fields.

The basic idea behind abstract data models is that relational data models are difficult and complex, so it would be better to have one data model that supports any application you can think of.

In my experience, there is no escape from the need to understand the data model that your application is dependent on. Whether you use an abstract data model or a relational model, you must analyze the relationships and attributes of your data; this takes work, but it is unavoidable. Once you understand the data model then it is easy to build it using a relational database. When you need to change your data model (as you will) then it is easy to do with a relational database.

By contrast, abstract data models are difficult to understand and difficult to change, and they have some unfortunate side effects.

What Is An Abstract Data Model?

There are several variants of abstract data models, but generally they look something like the data design below.

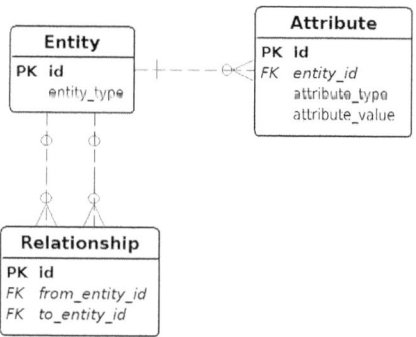

Every entity has a row in the `Entity` table. Because there are not separate tables for different entity types, every entity row must have an attribute - the `entity_type` - to say what kind of entity it is.

Chapter 16 - Universal Data Models

Every attribute has a row in the **Attribute** table. Again this table must have an attribute - the **attribute_type** - that says what kind of attribute it is. It also has a link back to the entity it belongs to, and it has the value of the attribute. Because all attributes are in the same table they have to have the same data-type so they must all be stored as strings.

Every relationship between entities is stored in the **Relationship** table.

You have to admit that it is a simple data model, but it is already confusing. Did you have to do a double-take to work out what I was talking about when I said *attribute*?

Let's look at some data in these tables and see if it makes more sense then.

The **Entity** table shown below doesn't look too difficult: we have three party entities, three vehicle entities and three policy entities.

```
id | entity_type
----+-------------
  1 | party
  2 | party
  3 | party
  4 | vehicle
  5 | vehicle
  6 | vehicle
  7 | policy
  8 | policy
  9 | policy
(9 rows)
```

The next table shows the attributes for these nine entities. You can link the two tables together by matching the foreign key **entity_id** in the **Attribute** table back to the **id** in the **Entity** table.

```
id | entity_id |   attribute_type    |   attribute_value
----+-----------+---------------------+--------------------
  1 |         1 | first_name          | Wendy
  2 |         1 | family_name         | Smith
  3 |         1 | date_of_birth       | 1973-12-10
  4 |         2 | first_name          | Michael
  5 |         2 | family_name         | Jones
  6 |         2 | date_of_birth       | 1967-03-21
  7 |         3 | first_name          | Janice
  8 |         3 | family_name         | Green
  9 |         3 | date_of_birth       | 1982-07-16
 10 |         4 | make                | Jeep
 11 |         4 | model               | Renegade
 12 |         4 | year_first_licensed | 2005
```

```
 13 |         4 | license_number       | EEF 212
 14 |         5 | make                 | Toyota
 15 |         5 | model                | Prius
 16 |         5 | year_first_licensed  | 2012
 17 |         5 | license_number       | 118 598
 18 |         6 | make                 | Nissan
 19 |         6 | model                | Armada
 20 |         6 | year_first_licensed  | 2013
 21 |         6 | license_number       | UQBZLAQ
 22 |         7 | policy_number        | SMI/100345
 23 |         7 | inception            | 2014-04-02 12:00:00
 24 |         7 | premium              | 456.35
 27 |         8 | policy_number        | SMI/100763
 28 |         8 | inception            | 2014-05-31 09:00:00
 29 |         8 | premium              | 728.50
 32 |         9 | policy_number        | SMI/100425
 33 |         9 | inception            | 2014-06-22 00:00:00
 34 |         9 | premium              | 1035.26
(30 rows)
```

For completeness let's also look at the data in the Relationship table.

```
 id | from_entity_id | to_entity_id
----+----------------+--------------
  4 |              7 |            1
  5 |              7 |            6
  6 |              9 |            3
  7 |              9 |            4
  8 |              8 |            2
  9 |              8 |            5
(6 rows)
```

An easier way to link up the entities with their attributes is to write some SQL to do it for us. The SQL would look like this:

download: find_entity_attributes.sql

```
select
    a.entity_type,
    b.entity_id,
    b.attribute_type,
    b.attribute_value
from
    entity a
    join
    attribute b
    on a.id = b.entity_id
order by
    a.entity_type,
    b.entity_id,
    b.attribute_type;
```

Chapter 16 - Universal Data Models

And the results are shown below.

```
 entity_type | entity_id |    attribute_type   |    attribute_value
-------------+-----------+---------------------+---------------------
 party       |         1 | date_of_birth       | 1973-12-10
 party       |         1 | family_name         | Smith
 party       |         1 | first_name          | Wendy
 party       |         2 | date_of_birth       | 1967-03-21
 party       |         2 | family_name         | Jones
 party       |         2 | first_name          | Michael
 party       |         3 | date_of_birth       | 1982-07-16
 party       |         3 | family_name         | Green
 party       |         3 | first_name          | Janice
 policy      |         7 | inception           | 2014-04-02 12:00:00
 policy      |         7 | policy_number       | SMI/100345
 policy      |         7 | premium             | 456.35
 policy      |         8 | inception           | 2014-05-31 09:00:00
 policy      |         8 | policy_number       | SMI/100763
 policy      |         8 | premium             | 728.50
 policy      |         9 | inception           | 2014-06-22 00:00:00
 policy      |         9 | policy_number       | SMI/100425
 policy      |         9 | premium             | 1035.26
 vehicle     |         4 | license_number      | EEF 212
 vehicle     |         4 | make                | Jeep
 vehicle     |         4 | model               | Renegade
 vehicle     |         4 | year_first_licensed | 2005
 vehicle     |         5 | license_number      | 118 598
 vehicle     |         5 | make                | Toyota
 vehicle     |         5 | model               | Prius
 vehicle     |         5 | year_first_licensed | 2012
 vehicle     |         6 | license_number      | UQBZLAQ
 vehicle     |         6 | make                | Nissan
 vehicle     |         6 | model               | Armada
 vehicle     |         6 | year_first_licensed | 2013
(30 rows)
```

But this is not what we want to see. No user wants to be bothered with the way we have stored the data in this abstract data model; our users want to see their data in tables. To reconstruct the data as it is expected, we have to write SQL like that shown below.

download: reassemble_table.sql

```
select
    a.entity_id,
    a.attribute_value as policy_number,
    b.attribute_value as inception,
    c.attribute_value as expiry,
    d.attribute_value as cancellation,
    e.attribute_value as premium
from
    (
        select
```

```
                entity_id,
                attribute_value
        from
            entity x
            join
            attribute y
            on
                x.entity_type = 'policy' and
                y.attribute_type = 'policy_number' and
                x.id = y.entity_id
    ) a
    left outer join
    (
        select
            entity_id,
            attribute_value
        from
            entity x
            join
            attribute y
            on
                x.entity_type = 'policy' and
                y.attribute_type = 'inception' and
                x.id = y.entity_id
    ) b
    on a.entity_id = b.entity_id
    left outer join
    (
        select
            entity_id,
            attribute_value
        from
            entity x
            join
            attribute y
            on
                x.entity_type = 'policy' and
                y.attribute_type = 'expiry' and
                x.id = y.entity_id
    ) c
    on a.entity_id = c.entity_id
    left outer join
    (
        select
            entity_id,
            attribute_value
        from
            entity x
            join
            attribute y
            on
                x.entity_type = 'policy' and
                y.attribute_type = 'cancellation' and
                x.id = y.entity_id
    ) d
    on a.entity_id = d.entity_id
```

```
        left outer join
        (
            select
                entity_id,
                attribute_value
            from
                entity x
                join
                attribute y
                on
                    x.entity_type = 'policy' and
                    y.attribute_type = 'premium' and
                    x.id = y.entity_id
        ) e
        on a.entity_id = e.entity_id;
```

The results would look like this:

```
entity_id | policy_number |      inception      | expiry | cancellation | premium
----------+---------------+---------------------+--------+--------------+--------
        7 | SMI/100345    | 2014-04-02 12:00:00 |        |              |  456.35
        8 | SMI/100763    | 2014-05-31 09:00:00 |        |              |  728.50
        9 | SMI/100425    | 2014-06-22 00:00:00 |        |              | 1035.26
(3 rows)
```

Did you breathe a sigh of relief? I did. But this is just the `policy` entity. We would have to do something similar for the `party` and `vehicle` entities, plus more SQL to show which policies and vehicles belong to which parties. Already it is getting complicated, and this is an extremely simple data model.

So let's see how it should have been done. Here is the normalized data model that is hidden in the abstract model.

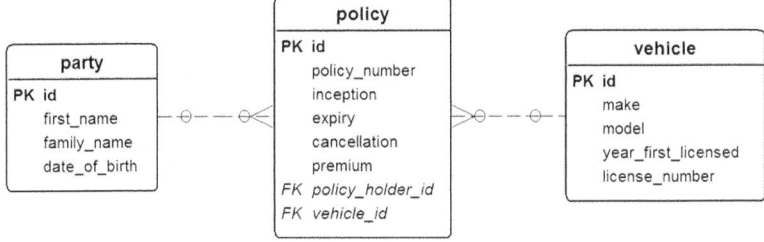

In this data model, the tables and their data are shown below.

```
# select * from party;
 id | first_name | family_name | date_of_birth
----+------------+-------------+---------------
  1 | Wendy      | Smith       | 1973-12-10
  2 | Michael    | Jones       | 1967-03-21
  3 | Janice     | Green       | 1982-07-16
(3 rows)

# select * from vehicle;
 id | make   | model    | year_first_licensed | license_number
----+--------+----------+---------------------+----------------
  4 | Jeep   | Renegade |                2005 | EEF 212
  5 | Toyota | Prius    |                2012 | 118 598
  6 | Nissan | Armada   |                2013 | UQBZLAQ
(3 rows)

# select * from policy;
 id | policy_number |      inception      | expiry | cancellation | premium | policy_holder_id | vehicle_id
----+---------------+---------------------+--------+--------------+---------+------------------+-----------
  7 | SMI/100345    | 2014-04-02 12:00:00 |        |              |  456.35 |                1 |          6
  8 | SMI/100763    | 2014-05-31 09:00:00 |        |              |  728.50 |                2 |          5
  9 | SMI/100425    | 2014-06-22 00:00:00 |        |              | 1035.26 |                3 |          4
(3 rows)
```

Now we can use a straightforward SQL statement to get the policy data, with the vehicle and the policy holder in a form that might be useful to someone taking a call from the customer.

download: select_policy_data.sql

```
select
    a.policy_number,
    b.first_name || ' ' || b.family_name            as policy_holder,
    c.make || ' ' || c.model                        as vehicle,
    c.license_number,
    cast(date_trunc('day', a.inception) as date)    as inception_date,
    a.premium
from
    policy a
    left outer join
    party b
    on a.policy_holder_id = b.id
    left outer join
    vehicle c
    on a.vehicle_id = c.id;
```

```
 policy_number | policy_holder |    vehicle     | license_number | inception_date | premium
---------------+---------------+----------------+----------------+----------------+---------
 SMI/100345    | Wendy Smith   | Nissan Armada  | UQBZLAQ        | 2014-04-02     |  456.35
 SMI/100763    | Michael Jones | Toyota Prius   | 118 598        | 2014-05-31     |  728.50
 SMI/100425    | Janice Green  | Jeep Renegade  | EEF 212        | 2014-06-22     | 1035.26
(3 rows)
```

The extra complexity of the abstract data model approach is not simply a case of having to write longer SQL statements. Proponents of this approach always say that it is more flexible because you never have to change the data model. But there *is* a data model and it is buried in the entity_types, the attribute_types, and the relationships. The real proof of this folly is when you ask the people who have provided such a

Chapter 16 - Universal Data Models 307

system to make a change. Then you find out that it is not flexible at all.

Abstract data models cause many other problems too:

- They do not enforce uniqueness.
- They do not enforce the presence of mandatory fields.
- They do not enforce relationships between entities.
- They hide their own metadata and make the metadata that is maintained by the database system useless.
- They destroy the ability of the database to deliver good performance.
- They do not use the strong data types built into the database management system.

We have looked at the reasons why these points are important in *Chapter 1 - Learning to Drive Your Database on page 32*. It's a lot to give up for the sake of having a very small number of tables. In my experience, it is not so hard to learn how to use a relational data model, and when you do, you get all these good things for free.

Using an abstract data model is like taking your shiny new car, with its superb road-holding, economy, comfort, performance and safety features, and using this car to drive a home-built wagon.

Industry Standard Data Models

The leading Data Warehouse tools vendors provide what they call **industry standard data models**. The price for the model is generally in six figures. These models are so difficult to use that you need a small army of very expensive consultants to work out how to fit your data into their scheme. When that is done, you need more consultancy to explain to the developers how to use it.

These industry standard models are highly generalized. This is done with the stated intention that any business model can be fitted in to this very general structure. This is terribly misguided. Every organization is unique. Even organizations in the same business sector have their own products, their own terminology and their own processes.

The most difficult part of any data-modeling job, and the most important, is to understand the structure of the organization and the processes that it operates. Once these are understood, designing a data model to support these structures and processes is comparatively easy. Fitting the real model into a highly generalized model is much more difficult, and the difficulty is repeated for everyone working with the model for as long as it survives.

A further problem is the very bland names used in standardized models. The data model design process should result in tables that represent recognizable objects in the organization we are trying to help. Tables called: account, product, or address are more usable than tables with abstract names such as: arrangement, condition, resource item and business direction. One of the leading vendors is not satisfied with this level of difficulty and compounds it by abbreviating every table name to two letters!

It would be so much better to design the database that the organization actually needs, using rigorous, database principles to ensure integrity, consistency, the greatest simplicity that is compatible with the actual use of the database, and performance.

Enterprise Resource Planning (ERP) Systems

I'm Sorry, I Haven't a Clue is the name of a radio series on the UK's BBC Radio 4. One of the games on this show is called *One Song to the Tune of Another*. The BBC describes it like this:

> "It is hard to explain the rules of this particular game, involving as it does the combination of the lyrical or rhythmic component of one piece of music, with the libretto of another; the couplets of the latter being matched to the cadences of the accompaniment to the former in order to create a new, and occasionally harmonious, whole. [...] the result is as often sublime as ridiculous. Did you know, for example, that it is possible to sing Jerusalem to the tune of The Birdie Song?"[66]

This game can be very funny in an excruciating kind of way.

An Enterprise Resource Planning (ERP) system is a range of

---

66. The quotation is from *h2g2 The Hitchhiker's Guide to the Galaxy: Earth Edition*. Accessed on 24-Aug-2017. I think this may have been on the BBC website originally, but it is now on h2g2.

applications with a shared database. The vendors promise that these applications are integrated. They typically cover the functions of large corporations needing systems for finance, human resources, manufacturing, distribution, etc.

ERP systems are complex. They typically have tens of thousands of tables in their databases; 60,000 tables is not unusual. There is a significant failure rate with these implementations, and when they do fail companies lose tens of millions of dollars.

Organizations that do make these systems work take the package as it is and change their processes to match the package. At least this way, the tune and the words match.

Unfortunately, most implementations of these systems are customized. This really is taking the lyrics of your business and trying to sing them to the song of the ERP package. This may be excruciating, but it isn't funny.

Once again, a simple, clear data model that reflects the actual objects that the organization uses is the best way to go. Many smaller, more specific software packages do a much better job.

Chapter 17 - Big Data

From the amount of noise in the market you might think that Relational Databases are dead and that Big Data tools have superseded them. This is not true. This chapter explains what Big Data Tools are good for and what Relational Databases are good for; they are complementary. I hope this chapter will help you if you have to explain to your boss why you are not using the latest, coolest technology, but rather the one that is best for the job that you need to do.

When I say "Big Data Tools" I am referring mainly to the **Hadoop** "ecosystem", which is an open source project managed by **Apache**[67], and is packaged and aggressively marketed by several large vendors. There are over 20 products each covering part of the job that a relational database does and many of them overlapping with one another. Big Data is a complex initiative. While it may be delivering some successful systems, it is also soaking up huge development resources and training developers in a muddled architecture.

Unfortunately, Big Data, like relational databases and many other software initiatives in the past, has the potential to make some people very, very rich. The tools themselves are free, but the hardware and the expertise that are needed to make them work are a long way from being free. When that much money is involved, things get distorted. Products get sold for purposes that they are not suitable for. Features get added because a customer with a lot of money can be persuaded that he needs them. A few people get rich and, by the time these people have gone to relax on their monster yachts, systems have failed and products have become bloated with inappropriate features.

The Big Data vendors are just the latest to say:

> "There is too a Silver Bullet - AND HERE IT IS!"

The quotation is from Frederick P. Brooks, in his wonderful book *The Mythical Man-Month*[68]. In the 20th Anniversary edition, Brooks notes that he received many communications about the view he expressed in the first edition, that there would be "No Silver Bullet." He goes on to say

---

67. http://hadoop.apache.org

68. See Bibliography [Brooks]

that these communications:

> "...assert that there is indeed a silver bullet for the software beast, which the author [of the tool] has invented. As I reread the early responses today [in 1995], I can't help noticing that the nostrums pushed so vigorously in 1986 and 1987 have not had the dramatic effects claimed."

Brooks is always the gentleman in his writing.

Big Data tools have a number of places where they can make a very positive contribution. They are not, however, a universal panacea for the challenges of data management. In particular, they are nowhere near being the best solution for all systems with a lot of data.

Unfortunately, Big Data has become a brand, which means that people recognize the brand and suppose that they know what substance is behind it, just from the name. Already, there are people who know nothing more about Big Data than the name, and they have constructed an image of that brand as being the thing you need if you have a lot of data. *"I think you'll find it's a bit more complicated than that"*[69]

What are Big Data tools good for?

Big Data tools are good for data that is complex in its format. Typically this is text, particularly very informal text, such as text messages on mobile phones, Twitter feeds, postings on blogs and social media in general, crime reports (especially witness statements), insurance claim reports, in fact anything written by people or transcribed from their speech. In addition, other multi-media sources may be handled well by Big Data tools. These include sound files, photographs, scanned images of documents, and video.

These sources are all difficult for traditional tools. Now, image processing has improved so much that computers can detect car license numbers, faces, signatures, landmarks, and many other things from images. For sound files, as recorded by most call-centers, it is possible to interpret speech and turn it into useful text files. We can also translate text from any human language to any other with a level of reliability that is beginning to be useful.

69. See Bibliography: [Goldacre]

Image and sound processing now enable us to find data in these complex sources.

This is all far more like the way our own brains work than the precise, predictable data processing carried out by traditional computer systems. Big Data tools can find patterns in this complex data, and the patterns can be used to benefit human beings. One good use of this kind of data is to pick up looming crises in the text messages of large populations:[70]

> "At the most general level, properly analyzed, these new data can provide snapshots of the well-being of populations at high frequency, high degrees of granularity, and from a wide range of angles, narrowing both time and knowledge gaps. Practically, analyzing this data may help discover what Global Pulse has called 'digital smoke signals' -- anomalous changes in how communities access services, that may serve as proxy indicators of changes in underlying well-being. Real-time awareness of the status of a population and real-time feedback on the effectiveness of policy actions should in turn lead to a more agile and adaptive approach to international development, and ultimately, to greater resilience and better outcomes."

Big Data can also be used to bombard me with advertisements for shoes, just because I happened to browse some shoes in an online shopping site. I guess that is a good thing for the advertisers.

Big Data systems typically distribute data over large numbers of low-cost servers. They also let you add and remove servers easily without losing data. So if your business is very seasonal and this results in widely varying loads on the system throughout the year, you can save money by having only the number of servers you need today and scaling out to the number of servers you need in the three weeks before Christmas, when you get most of your sales, for example. You then only need to pay for the extra servers when you need them, rather than paying to keep them idle for the rest of the year. In my experience, any saving will be far outweighed by the cost of dealing with the inherent complexity and poor reliability of Big Data systems.

---

70. http://www.unglobalpulse.org/sites/default/files/BigDataforDevelopment-GlobalPulseMay2012.pdf. Accessed on 9-Jan-2016. UN Global Pulse is an initiative based in the Executive Office of the Secretary-General United Nations.

What are Relational Databases good for?

Relational Databases are good for processing structured data. This includes all the traditional record-keeping that we rely on in our everyday lives. We want our bank to keep track of our money accurately and not go losing chunks of it. We want our telephone company to track the calls we make and charge us only for our own calls, not for the calls made by someone else. We want our railways to accurately measure the track that the trains roll on and to pinpoint faults so that they can be fixed before the train bounces off the track. There are millions of systems in which very precise numbers must be tracked and recorded accurately and reliably.

These are the systems where relational databases shine. And they can be very, very big. There are real databases of several petabytes. A petabyte is 1,000,000,000,000,000 bytes. That is very hard to imagine. It's about two billion books, or one book for every three people on the planet. It is still hard to imagine, but it is definitely big data, even if it isn't Big Data.

The `Internet of Things` is already dramatically increasing the amount of data we record. Overwhelmingly, the devices currently in the Internet of Things produce highly structured data.

One example of the Internet of Things, which I worked on, was a car insurance system that used a device in each policyholder's car to monitor the position, speed, acceleration, engine state, etc. Every single item of data in the feed from this device was a number, a timestamp or a Boolean variable. There was no text and nothing vague. There were degrees of precision, of course, but even these were self-monitoring. The positioning numbers were given as latitude and longitude along with a value (called `Horizontal Dilution of Precision`) that gave a measure of the accuracy of the position information, so we could tell if the position was accurate to within 10 meters or 250 meters, with many steps in between.

The point of this is that it is consistently structured data. Structured data is ideally supported by a relational database system. That relational database system enabled us to match the position of the car with a map so that we could tell where the car was down to which side of which road the car was driving on. Of course, SatNav does this all the time, even telling you when to change lanes. We were using this data to reward safe drivers (those who did not habitually exceed the speed limit for example).

And this data was big. By its fourth year, the insurance company had about 4GB of policy data. Just think of all the questions your insurer asks you when you insure a car and it isn't too hard to see how you get to 4GB in four years. In the same period, this same insurance company accumulated over 5TB (that's 5,000GB) of data from the devices in the cars.

The data from the devices was growing much faster than the policy data too. Once your policy data is recorded it doesn't grow much: a change of car, a renewal each year, maybe a claim, but most drivers do not make claims. The device data keeps growing though; every time you drive the car, it adds more data. The insurance company needs to keep this for several years because people can make claims several years after an incident and the insurance company wants to check what your car was doing at the time of the claim. Also, after four years, we started installing the second-generation devices. The first generation devices collected a sample of data every 30 seconds; the second generation collected a sample every five seconds. When there was a big acceleration event (which could possibly be a crash) the first generation reported accelerations every 100th of a second for the few seconds around the crash; the second generation reported every 1000th of a second and over a bigger window of time from a few seconds before the crash to a few seconds afterwards.

This is typical. In the Internet of Things, devices will deliver more and more data over time as the technology becomes more and more sophisticated.

Relational databases are very good at this kind of big data.

What are the downsides of relational databases?

You don't have to be the most perceptive person in the world to work out that I am a big fan of relational databases. I have had a very interesting career, most of which was dependent on my knowledge of relational databases. I do think they are great. I have been involved in some very exciting projects that delivered real benefit to the organizations I worked for, and to their clients. As well as enabling me to earn a living, delivering systems that help people has been very rewarding. My views are also significantly influenced by my having experience of what computer systems were like before relational databases. (Don't ask me unless you want a long diatribe about `COBOL`.)

As I have said, relational databases are very good at processing structured data that has a high requirement for accuracy and reliability. They are not so good at processing free text and multi-media or any big blobs of data with variable content. There have been attempts to add features into relational databases to deal with the less structured data but they have been failures. I have used these features, and you can sort-of make them work, but it is very inefficient and expensive.

Cost is often cited as a big downside of relational databases. If you let Oracle, IBM, Microsoft or another big vendor take over your computer systems, sure, you should expect to pay high costs, but don't blame the relational database. You can get very good relational databases for nothing.

In summary, for the appropriate job, a relational database is the best tool you can use to manage the data and it is worth the investment. Not every job is appropriate, but most are.

What are the downsides of Big Data tools?

Currently (July, 2017) the biggest downside of Big Data tools is the complexity. The number of tools you need to get familiar with is daunting. While you can do some amazing things, you do have to write a lot of code to make it all work. `Tagging Engines`, which separate out the data you are interested in from the noise, require skill and hard work. Translation and image and speech recognition are well-known techniques now, but you do have to integrate them into your system.

Although Big Data systems run on "low-cost" hardware, you can easily spend millions on this hardware. But the hardware is only the beginning. You will pay a lot for support and consultancy from the supplier of the open-source Big Data software too. Then you pay enormous costs to get developers who can make the Big Data tools work, as far as that is possible. "Low cost" is not a term that can honestly be applied to Big Data tools.

Don't be fooled into thinking that Big Data tools are easier than relational databases. They are not. They are definitely harder to access; *MapReduce* is a much lower-level interface than SQL. The SQL interfaces to Big Data are currently unusable, unless you like spending a lot of time on workarounds. Administration of Big Data systems can be quite demanding too.

Also, because Big Data tools are designed to handle unstructured data they do not have the emphasis on completeness and accuracy that relational databases have. Losing a record from a Big Data system is not usually a serious problem. Not being able to make sense of a particular field value in a Big Data system is not usually a problem. If you expected a date and you get a text string or the field is missing, it will not usually be the end of the world. As a result, Big Data tools do not focus on data integrity and data quality, and the data stored in them is usually of lower quality. So long as most of it makes sense, that is OK for most Big Data jobs. Those systems that add advertisements to your web pages need to get good hit rates, in the high 90s in percentage points, but if they miss the odd one it just doesn't matter. In contrast, if your bank missed the odd payment into your account, it certainly would matter. That is why banks use relational databases for keeping your accounts.

Big Data tools are not necessarily fast. They are very scalable, but you may not get consistently good performance from a Big Data system.

In general, because relational databases focus on absolute transaction consistency, they are good at it. Big Data systems focus on scalability and handling unstructured data, and they are good at that.

Which Approach Should You Use?

It really depends on the needs of the applications you are building. The discussion in the last few paragraphs should help you to decide whether a conventional relational database or a Big Data solution is best for your application. You should not use a relational database just because that is the tried and tested approach and you should not use a Big Data solution just because that is the new and trendy approach, nor because you have a lot of data.

Relational databases have been around for over 40 years; Big Data tools for less than half that time. Perhaps Big Data tools will mature and address their weaknesses. Hopefully the relational database vendors will not try to shoehorn Big Data capabilities into their products. There would be some serious internal re-engineering to make that work. The resulting products would become overblown with features that most users would not use.

In January 2008, David J. DeWitt and Michael Stonebraker bravely stuck their heads above the parapet, to argue that the MapReduce upstart was a wannabe Emperor, very lacking in clothes [71]. The response was furious. Nine years later we can see that the upstart has indeed made a lot of money, but, as I have experienced recently, still does not work well for most applications.

We owe DeWitt and Stonebraker a debt of gratitude for their courage in taking a critical look at this technology bubble early on.

When I wrote the first draft of this chapter, about two years ago, I tried to strike a fair balance between the Relational Database and Big Data worlds. I have spent most of the intervening time working on a Big Data project. I was shocked. This chapter now reflects my conclusions. You would need a very special application for me to recommend using the Big Data tools and you would need to be prepared for a huge investment. Most systems involving large quantities of data would do much better to use a real relational database. I will never work on a Big Data project again because I like to deliver systems that work.

---

71. See Bibliography: [DeWitt]

Chapter 18 - Database Features To Be Wary Of

Why Not Use All The Features?

If you look at the marketing literature from any of the big database vendors you will see words like: "cloud", "simplicity", "scale", "insights", "ease", "rapid". Do those words give you any idea about what these products do? The marketing literature is aimed at the people with the authority to spend huge sums of money, and if you are reading this book you are probably not one of those. Rather, you are probably someone who wants to build systems that do something useful for your users or customers. When you look at the documentation of the database, to check how to do something practical, something that gives the right answer every time, you really have to dig deep to get to the precise statement of what code you have to write to get to a correct and efficient solution. After a while your favorites or bookmarks list is full of specific links to pages buried several layers down in the vendor's website, something that is actually useful.

Because of the marketing arms race, many features have been added to databases. Some of them have been good: case statements, window functions, alternative storage structures and the invisible improvements in query optimization and transaction efficiency, for example. But many of the features have made things worse. They damage what Fred Brooks calls, "Conceptual Integrity" and as David Heinemeier-Hansson says, "flexibility is not free". Part of being "On Rails" is to avoid the features that may seem like a quick fix today, but will cost you time and effort tomorrow and for months and years to come.

Here we will look at just four features that I use very rarely, or avoid altogether. They are:

- Views
- Stored-Procedure Languages
- Create Table As Select
- Visual Database Tools

I hope this chapter will help you to resist some of the quick fixes that your manager might want you to employ and, instead, to build more robust, efficient applications that will be easy to maintain and enhance over many years.

Views

SQL Views are saved queries. You might have a query that `joins` three tables. If you create a view using this query, the view looks just like a table, and every time you `select` from the view it runs the underlying query and gets the latest data from the underlying tables.

The big selling point for views is that they enable you to change the database without changing your application. For example, if you delete a column in your database, you can create a view that puts a dummy column where the deleted column used to be, so that the query returns the number of columns that your application expects. This is a very bad idea, even if it works. You should keep your applications and databases in step with one another at all times. When you release a new version of your application you should migrate your database to match it and vice versa.

Where views are used in an attempt to insulate against change, this rarely works. The system will change in ways that make us change the view. We may change a system to fix a bug, or to make the structure match the real world a little better, but usually we will change it to add features that users have asked for. These features will be in the forefront of the users' minds and they will want to use them. The data that supports the new features will not be represented in the existing view so we have to change it anyway.

We must always be ready to make changes. "Embrace Change" says Kent Beck in the title of his book *Extreme Programming Explained: Embrace Change*[72]. Trying to defend against change is doomed to failure and the techniques used to defend against change generally make the system worse. Many databases are clogged with views that present old versions of tables. After a while, the database looks like a hoarder's garage and nobody can sort the useful, accurate data from the out-dated junk. In such an environment users make mistakes and customers suffer inconvenience or worse. It really is less expensive to clear up our junk as we go along rather than keeping everything because it might be useful one day.

---

72. See Bibliography [Beck]

Another use of views is to transform data so that it can be delivered to another system, perhaps a data warehouse. People do this because their `ETL` (Extract, Transform and Load) tool is difficult to use and inefficient, and it is easier to do the transformation in `SQL`. Well, it is true that `SQL` is much better for transforming data than any `ETL` tool. Worse than using an `ETL` tool is using the `ETL` tool for some of the work *and* using `SQL` for other parts of the work. Then, when you maintain the system, you have to look in two places to see what to change, and make sure your changes work together. The best solution is to use `SQL` scripts for all the transformations. This is not complicated and is highly maintainable, so long as you:

- Organize the scripts in a sensible directory structure representing the jobs you run
- Manage them in a source code control system
- Automate the running of the scripts
- Trap any exceptions in the automation and deal with every exception

Views will not help you do any of this.

Another, very important, reason for not using views is that they are often significantly less efficient than accessing the underlying tables. People build queries on top of views because the views look just like tables. That seems a reasonable thing to do, but then we end up with the `joins` and `where` clauses built into the view as well as the `joins` and `where` clauses being done in the query. There can be redundancy or conflict between the view and the query built on it. In practice we see generally worse performance when we use views, often spectacularly worse.

It is possible to update some views, subject to some restrictions. You should *never* do this; you should always update the underlying tables. We carefully design the database to make updates safe, unambiguous and efficient, so don't subvert this good work by trying to update the view.

Madness is layered on top of madness with `materialized views`. A materialized view is one that is saved as a physical table. There are many options for when to refresh materialized views. A materialized view is really a table with some transformation and scheduling logic built in. So now when we have to see what our system does and when it does it we have to look in the proper transformation code and job schedule *and* in the view definitions. Please do not make life so hard for yourself.

All-in-all, there isn't much to recommend views, and I would suggest that you avoid them.

User-Defined Functions and Stored Procedures

SQL is a non-procedural language. It says what to do, not how to do it. There are no loops or conditional branching constructs (if ... then ... else ...) in SQL.

Most relational databases provide a procedural language as well as SQL. There is a standard for these (SQL/PSM) but it is not followed. In fact, the standard was derived from the existing languages and there is no realistic chance that they will ever converge. Each database procedural language is proprietary to the database vendor.

The database procedural languages are interpreted by the database server. This is a big advantage for little snippets of programming that need to be applied to values in a row as it is being processed inside the database. If, for example, the snippet is applying some validation the result of which is then used to select the rows to be returned, then it can make the process more efficient by reducing the amount of data that has to be sent back across the network to the client process.

Let's work through an example of the good use of a user-defined function. If your company is processing credit card data, it must be very, very careful with credit card numbers. And, let's suppose that you are loading some data into a table for later analysis and that data contains a field which is a long number. You need to make sure that this number is never a credit card number, because it would be bad to put unencrypted credit card numbers into the analytics system where they could be seen by many people.

There are three things that can tell us if any random integer is possibly a credit card number or not. In fact, these rules apply to all payment cards:

- Payment card numbers are between 12 and 19 digits long
- The first six digits of any payment card number is the IIN (Issuer Identification Number)[73]
- The final digit is a check digit calculated using the Luhn algorithm[74]

---

73. https://en.wikipedia.org/wiki/ISO/IEC_7812

74. https://en.wikipedia.org/wiki/Luhn_algorithm

In a set of random long numbers, only a tiny percentage will be possible payment card numbers. If we select every number from the database, transfer them all to our application and check them in our application, that will be a costly process. If we can check the numbers in the database and send back to our application only those that could be valid payment card numbers then we will save a lot of traffic across the network from the database to the application. In this case it will be worth the cost of building a function to do the Luhn check and combining that with standard SQL to restrict the number of rows that need to be processed. Here is such a function written for `PostgreSQL`:

download: luhn_check_passed.sql

```
create function
luhn_check_passed(possible_pan varchar)
returns boolean
as
$body$
    declare
            i               integer;
            j               integer;
            check_digit     integer;
            last_digit      integer;
            c               char;
            even            boolean;
            sum_digits      integer;

    begin
        if possible_pan is null
        then
            return null;
        end if;
        i := length(possible_pan);
        c := substring(possible_pan from i for 1);
        begin
            last_digit := cast(c as integer);
        exception
            when others then return null;
        end;

        sum_digits := 0;
        even := true;
        i := i - 1;
        while i > 0 loop
            c := substring(possible_pan from i for 1);
            begin
                j := cast(c as integer);
            exception
                when others then return null;
            end;
            if even
            then
```

```
                j := j * 2;
                if j > 9
                then
                    j := 1 + j - 10;
                end if;
            end if;
            even := not even;           -- toggle true/false
            sum_digits := sum_digits + j;
            i := i - 1;
        end loop;

        if (sum_digits % 10) = 0
        then
            check_digit := 0;
        else
            check_digit := 10 - (sum_digits % 10);
        end if;

        if check_digit = last_digit
        then
            return true;
        else
            return false;
        end if;
    end;
$body$
language 'plpgsql'
immutable
leakproof
strict
cost 100;
```

This function is similar to most of the built-in functions in relational databases, because:

- It returns a single value with a simple data-type every time you call it. In the jargon, it returns a "scalar" result (rather than a "vector").
- It does not access any data in the database. It does not do any `selects`, `inserts`, `updates` or `deletes`.
- It does not preserve its state from one call to the next. In other words, the function behaves in exactly the same way every time we call it; no information is passed from one call to the next.
- It does not communicate with the outside world except through its input parameter and its single result value.

Small simple functions like the Luhn check make good sense in many cases. These functions may have more than one parameter (as the substring function has in all the leading databases) but they always have a single result value.

In `PostgreSQL`, functions can be labeled in various ways to let the query optimizer assess the performance impact, and to determine possible interactions with the security system. Functions that follow the list above will not cause any problems; those that do not can make things much more complex and inefficient. The `PostgreSQL` labels that can be used with functions behave according to these rules are: `immutable`, `leak-proof`, `strict` and (from version 9.6) `parallel safe`. These labels are described in the `PostgreSQL create function` documentation[75].

There is another good use of stored procedures and this is in very high-performance transaction-processing systems. Putting each whole transaction, possibly changing several tables, in one stored procedure ensures that nothing interferes with the sequence of statements in the transaction. This improves performance since there is only one message from the client to the server, to execute the stored procedure, and one reply. This is compatible with my suggestion that we should collect all the data necessary for a transaction and then submit it to the database without any intervening processing, so that each transaction is completed as fast as possible. (See *Chapter 11 - Populating Your Database: Transactions on page 238*). Also this is one of the options appropriate to *Chapter 14 - Tuning: Advanced Database Tuning on page 286*.

If these are good uses of database procedural languages why am I saying that we should be wary of them?

The problem occurs when whole applications are written in the database procedural language. This happens a lot in Oracle with PL/SQL and in Microsoft SQL Server with Transact-SQL. The vendors are very keen that you should use their proprietary tools to access the database.

The Oracle stored procedure language - PL/SQL - is a nicely structured language, absolutely fine for writing user-defined functions. But a whole industry has grown up around the development of complete applications in PL/SQL. In my experience, this is not the best way to build applications.

Microsoft does not distinguish the SQL Server stored procedure language from the rest of Transact-SQL so it is harder to set a boundary. Again, in my experience it is better to use the stored-procedural language

---

75. https://www.postgresql.org/docs/10/static/sql-createfunction.html

elements only for small simple functions, and avoid being tempted to write whole applications in Transact-SQL.

I resist the wide use of database stored procedure languages, because:

- They muddle the clear purpose of the relational database
- They do not provide modern facilities found in good development languages
- As they are proprietary, they lock you into one particular product
- They pretend to present an object-oriented image, but they are no such thing

Of course, vendors will tell you that you can build any application with their favorite language. That may be true, but what you can do, and what it is best to do, are not the same thing.

Defining the boundaries between the application and the databases is controversial. Some developers try to do everything in the application, and just treat the database as a fairly dumb file server. On the other hand I see database developers who want to do all the development in their chosen database product. I have worked on such projects. I have written quite large applications in Oracle's `PL/SQL`. It can be done, but it is a mistake and I promise never to do it again.

The database is responsible for being the ultimate repository of trusted data, and `SQL` is the interface through which all data must be accessed. This book defines that interface in detail and, that, I believe, is the best place to draw the line between what is best done in the database and what is best done in the application.

The best tools for developing applications consist of languages (Ruby on Rails, Java, Python, etc.), source code control, development environments (or just a good editor), testing tools, and so on. These things are responsible for the user interface and the business rules. They are also responsible for integration with the web, and with the latest network and interface protocols. When these tools want to store and retrieve data they should send a message to the relational database to do it.

Create Table As Select

The data returned from a `SQL` query is called a `result set`. In fact you can create a table directly from the result set of a query, as shown below.

download: create_table_as_select.sql

```sql
create table person_basic as
select
    city,
    state,
    family_name,
    date_of_birth
from
    person;
```

Having run this statement, we can ask `PostgreSQL` (in this example) what the table looks like. Here is the result.

```
# \d person_basic
            Table "public.person_basic"
    Column     |         Type          | Modifiers
---------------+-----------------------+-----------
 city          | character varying(60) |
 state         | character varying(2)  |
 family_name   | character varying(40) |
 date_of_birth | date                  |
```

`Create table ... as select` even has an acronym - `CTAS` (pronounced "see-tass").

I never use `create table ... as select` because I want full control over `primary key` constraints, `not null` constraints, data-types, and so on. Generally, constraints do not get copied to the new table.

Also, we do not want to be creating lots of ad-hoc tables. The risk in creating ad-hoc tables is that your system becomes littered with large numbers of tables that were used once and did not get deleted because no one was sure whether they were still needed. This is expensive, and you should avoid it.

So, write a proper migration (see *Chapter 12 - Database Migrations That Preserve Data on page 244*) including tests, to create your new table and to populate it. Then drop the old tables. This is a tiny bit more code now but you will get the new table you want and save a lot of work later.

Visual Database Tools

There are managers who believe that their teams are made up of stupid lazy people who need to be put in their place and get on with churning out code. This description does not fit you, does it? You have already proved that you are miles ahead of such managers because you are reading a book. If you are working for such a manager, I do hope you can find a better job. There are some good managers out there and you deserve to be working for one of them.

For as long as I have been working people have been trying to make programmers redundant. They aren't even looking in the right place. Coding is not the problem. The problem that we have to solve every day in our work is to determine exactly what is needed. Once you know what is needed it is comparatively easy and quick to turn that need into code, and it's fun! Maybe that is the issue. I have met managers who believe that work should involve suffering, and writing neat code must therefore be not real work.

The mistaken beliefs of the bad managers is an open goal for the sales and marketing arms of the vendors. Here is a quote from the marketing literature for one visual programming tool:

> *Write and edit queries without expertise. A customizable UI automates formatting and speeds editing.*[76]

That is a bad manager's dream. Since he has such a low opinion of his team, he will pay money for a product that claims to do the work for them. He is so wrong!

It says *"without expertise"*! I have seen the results of using the tool that this quote is promoting. The result was wrong. The customer wrongly lost a bonus payment and was rightfully angry. It took a bit of analysis (by me) to find and fix the problem but far more important was the loss of that customer and the damage to the company's reputation caused by the customer exposing the mistake publicly.

Sometimes "without expertise" someone could get the right answer, but that is just "programming by coincidence" as described in *The Pragmatic Programmer* [77]. Good developers do not program by coincidence; they

---

76. https://www.quest.com/products/toad-data-point/

make sure they know what they are doing. Most times, work done "without expertise" gives a random plausible answer that is wrong.

It is not possible to do our job "without expertise". Would you want someone fixing your car "without expertise"? Would you want a surgeon operating on your daughter to be "without expertise"?

This quote also suggests that formatting and editing are mindless tasks that need to be automated away. When I'm writing code, the act of editing and formatting is part of what I do to make sure that I understand what I am doing and that the code reflects the solution that is in my head.

One day, perhaps, artificial intelligence will have advanced to such a level that systems can create themselves. I will accept that my inability to imagine such a world is possibly a failing of mine; I will not accept that we are anywhere near there already.

I believe that visual programming tools are not the most effective way to develop code. The great programming languages we have now are more effective, by a long way. I also believe that the visual programming tools are not easier. They look good in demonstrations when there are five objects on the screen, but in the real world where you have 50 objects, the diagram is unintelligible. And, finally, visual programming tools sometimes have their own version control, but it is never as good as the general purpose source code control tools we use (such as `Subversion` and `Git`) and they cover only the visual programming artifacts.

Visual programming tools may impress a gullible manager, but they really are something you should avoid.

77. See Bibliography [Hunt&Thomas]

Part F - Wrapping Up

Some closing thoughts.

Chapter 19 - Wrapping Up

I hope that you have learned that relational databases can be fun. For me, that is certainly true. I get a kick out of delivering a system that delights its users, and especially when we can use the database to tell them things that they didn't know and that they never thought would be possible to find out.

We have learned that some discipline is needed to use relational databases effectively. We have to learn how they work and apply our knowledge consistently. But we can have the discipline without the bureaucracy. Database projects can be agile projects. In fact database projects *must* be agile projects. The cost and waste created by `waterfall` projects is just as large with database projects as it is with any other.

We have learned that testing and refactoring can keep our database as shiny as new, even after many iterations and many releases. There is no need for the database to descend into chaos, as many have before.

We have learned how to make our database friendly to the developers who come after us, so that they are never left wondering what the column `tran_ind` means.

We have learned how to structure our data so that it makes sense to the data scientists who are using amazing analytics and visualization tools to extract new, exciting, and most of all accurate meanings from it.

We have learned how to avoid some popular myths, so that our projects do not repeat the errors of the past, but live long and serve their users well.

Bibliography

[Beck] Kent Beck. *Extreme Programming Explained: Embrace Change*. Addison-Wesley Longman, Reading, MA, 2000.

[Beck&Fowler] Kent Beck and Martin Fowler. *Planning Extreme Programming*. Addison-Wesley, Reading, MA, 2001.

[Agile-Manifesto] Kent Beck, Mike Beedle, Arie van Bennekum, Alistair Cockburn, Ward Cunningham, Martin Fowler, James Grenning, Jim Highsmith, Andrew Hunt, Ron Jeffries, Jon Kern, Brian Marick, Robert C. Martin, Steve Mellor, Ken Schwaber, Jeff Sutherland & Dave Thomas. *Manifesto for Agile Software Development*. Web article: http://agilemanifesto.org Accessed 8-Jan-2016

[Brooks] Frederick P. Brooks Jr. *The Mythical Man-Month: Essays on SoftwareEngineering*. Addison-Wesley, Reading, MA, Anniversary edition, 1995.

[Date] C.J. Date. *An Introduction to Database Systems*. Addison-Wesley Longman,Reading, MA, 7th edition, 2000.

[DeMarco&Lister] Tom DeMarco and Timothy Lister. *Peopleware: Productive Projects and Teams*. Dorset House, New York, NY, USA, Second edition, 1999.

[DeWitt] David J. DeWitt. *MapReduce: A major step backwards*. Web article: https://homes.cs.washington.edu/~billhowe/mapreduce_a_major_step_backwards.html Accessed 11-Aug-2017.

[Fowler-evodb] Martin Fowler. *Evolutionary Database Design*. Web article: https://www.martinfowler.com/articles/evodb.html Accessed 11-Aug-2017.

[Fowler] Martin Fowler. *Patterns of Enterprise Application Architecture*. Addison-Wesley Longman, Reading, MA, 2003.

[Fowler&others] Martin Fowler, Kent Beck, John Brant, William Opdyke, and Don Roberts. *Refactoring: Improving the Design of Existing Code*. Addison-Wesley, Reading, MA, 1999.

[Gawande] Atul Gawande. *The Checklist Manifesto: How To Get Things Right*. Profile Books, 2010.

[Goldacre] Ben Goldacre. *I Think You'll Find It's A Bit More Complicated Than That*. Fourth Estate, http://www.4thestate.co.uk, , 2014.

[Harold] Elliotte Rusty Harold. *Effective XML*. Addison-Wesley, Reading, MA, 2003.

[Heinemeier Hansson] David Heinemeier Hansson. *Secrets Behind Ruby on Rails*. Web article: http://web.archive.org/web/20130729205858id_/http://itc.conversationsnetwork.org/shows/detail658.html Recorded 2005. Accessed 11-Aug-2017.

[Hunt&Thomas]	Andrew Hunt and David Thomas. *The Pragmatic Programmer: From Journeyman to Master*. Addison-Wesley, Reading, MA, 2000.
[Malviya&Others]	Nirmesh Malviya, Ariel Weisberg, Samuel Madden, Michael Stonebraker. *Rethinking Main Memory OLTP Recovery*. Web article: *http://hstore.cs.brown.edu/papers/voltdb-recovery.pdf*. Accessed 6-Oct-2017.
[Mason]	Mike Mason. *Pragmatic Guide to Subversion*. The Pragmatic Bookshelf, Raleigh, NC, and Dallas, TX, 2010.
[Reiser]	Martin Reiser. *The Oberon System*. Addison-Wesley, Reading, MA, ,1991.
[Ruby]	Sam Ruby. *Agile Web Development with Rails 4*. The Pragmatic Bookshelf, Raleigh, NC, and Dallas, TX, 2013.
[Stonebraker&Cetintemel]	Michael Stonebraker and Uğur Çetintemel. *"One Size Fits All": An Idea Whose Time Has Come and Gone*. Web article: *https://cs.brown.edu/~ugur/fits_all.pdf*. Accessed 6-Oct-2017.

Index

A

abbreviate, 45, 52, 72, 93, 117, 118, 120, 134, 179, 195, 291, 308
abstract data model, 274-275, 299-307
accounting, 14, 15, 35, 40, 42, 92, 93, 128, 142, 227, 275
accuracy, 15, 25, 36, 57, 59, 60, 68, 85, 87, 89, 96, 114, 123, 124, 125
ACID, 239, 242
acronym, 239, 326
ActiveRecord, 59, 62, 234, 285
actuary, 84
adjacent, 187
administration, 98, 210, 264, 286
aggregate, 154, 182, 183, 184
agile, 15, 25, 26, 30, 31, 56, 98, 113, 261, 262, 299, 312, 330
Agile Manifesto, 11, 18, 20
algorithm, 281, 321
alphabetic, 37, 114, 297
alter, 97, 107, 247
American, 22, 116, 126, 137
analyst, 19, 70, 114, 173, 174, 177, 184, 185, 189, 190, 213, 216, 225, 294, 321, 327
analytics, 16, 25, 27, 28, 171, 172, 185, 321, 330
analyze, 28, 199, 218, 225, 282, 294, 300, 312
annual, 125
anomalous, 148, 312
ANSI, 126, 129
Apache, 310
API, 296

appliance, 104, 225, 231, 286
approximate, 17, 86, 88, 130, 232, 233, 289
architect, 107, 273, 274, 310
archive, 146, 145, 192
arithmetic, 127, 130, 152, 218
array, 36, 37, 139, 142, 147, 292
artifacts, 328
asc, 179, 184, 190, 191, 212
ASCII, 269
assert, 9, 311
assign, 27, 42, 93, 162, 174, 268
atomic, 37, 68, 84, 86, 88, 100, 139, 142, 146, 147
attribute, 45, 52, 64, 116, 117, 123, 150, 179, 273, 296, 300, 301
audio, 140
audit, 234
auditors, 227, 274
author, 11, 18
auto, 106, 168
autocommit, 239, 240
automate, 19, 69, 79, 114, 135, 143, 168, 229, 245, 282, 283, 286, 320, 327, 328
average, 154, 180, 182, 183, 190, 191
axis, 148

B

backslash, 259, 289
backup, 245, 248, 253
bandwidth, 145
bank, 15, 21, 47, 49, 59, 117, 123, 124, 128, 164, 166, 238, 240, 313,

316
batch, 245, 270, 271, 278, 282
BBC, 308
bcp, 231
Beck, Kent, 11, 18, 19, 52, 319
Beedle, Mike, 11
begin transaction, 240
belong, 12, 13, 42, 52, 53, 60, 62, 64, 65, 67, 83, 84, 85
benefit, 9, 16, 20, 51, 62, 99, 106, 107, 128, 140, 282, 285, 286, 291, 312, 314
best practice, 9, 115, 266
bfile, 140
Big Data, 18, 22, 29, 117, 141, 239, 310, 311, 312, 313
BigDecimal, 95, 129
bigint, 86, 106, 127, 128
bigserial, 168
bill, 15
binary, 126, 130, 132, 140
biology, 16
Birdie Song, 308
bitmap, 284
blank, 78, 108, 150
blob, 126, 140, 141, 283, 315
blogs, 192, 311
bookmarks, 318
books, 7, 9, 20, 30, 45, 122, 192, 313
boolean, 126, 133, 134, 268
bordereau, 92, 93
bottleneck, 167
brackets, 105, 108, 122
brains, 312
branching, 175, 321
brand, 132, 162, 290, 311
breach, 91, 264
break, 28, 39, 124, 139, 142, 165, 209, 239, 244, 269
breakdown, 72
broken, 19, 208, 210, 264
Brooks, Frederick P., 148, 310, 311, 318
browse, 173, 312
budget, 93, 118
bug, 19, 136, 137, 319
bulk, 227, 230, 231, 237, 238, 262, 282
bundled, 139
bureaucracy, 8, 10, 18, 34, 57, 68, 330
byte, 127, 132, 133, 135, 166, 313
bytea, 140

C

cache, 273
calculate, 15, 86, 128, 138, 155, 179, 181, 185, 188, 189, 190, 321
CamelCase, 121, 122
camera, 297
candidate, 47, 213
capability, 14, 15, 317
capacity, 92, 273
capitals, 2, 108
capture, 18, 32, 43, 54, 71, 72, 74, 75, 76, 77, 78, 79, 81, 92
cardinality, 197
Cartesian Product, 203, 204, 217
cast, 130, 218
catalog, 16, 273, 288, 289, 291
catch, 238, 266, 267, 268, 291
Celko, Joe, 192
cell, 17, 32, 33, 34, 36, 46, 142, 146, 147, 150, 288
cents, 128
century, 137
char, 70, 84, 87, 95, 108, 114, 115, 118, 119, 121, 125, 130, 134
charge, 23, 49, 242, 313
charts, 246
cheap, 10, 18, 141, 155, 174, 214, 273, 275, 281
check, 32, 86, 107

Index

checklist, 8, 26, 56, 57, 68, 69, 72, 81, 84, 85, 95
chronological, 184
chunks, 313
cidr, 139, 140
circle, 131, 138
cited, 23, 315
classify, 16, 60, 213, 297
clause, 45, 160, 174, 175, 179, 180, 183, 184, 187, 189, 194, 195, 200
clean, 12, 26, 51, 54, 56, 120, 226, 236, 253, 271
client, 18, 33, 100, 135, 262, 281, 314, 321, 324
clob, 140
close, 7, 17, 49, 55, 108, 130, 131, 139, 285, 329
cloud, 318
clutter, 281
coalesce, 159, 203
COBOL, 13, 122, 315
Cockburn, Alistair, 11
Codd, E.F., 45
cohesion, 12, 13
collaboration, 11
colleagues, 28, 268
colon, 105, 108, 138, 269
column-store, 283
combine, 47, 49, 107, 141, 166, 169, 180, 184, 205, 283, 308, 322
comma, 105, 108, 143, 230
command, 28, 83, 85, 89, 97, 98, 104, 107, 193, 201, 210, 232, 233, 238, 240, 241
comment, 46, 152, 153, 229
commercial, 12, 47, 125, 132, 150, 290
commit, 163, 168, 240, 241, 242, 284
communicate, 20, 58, 92, 118, 137, 310, 323
compare, 25, 35, 37, 125, 126, 135, 141, 151, 161, 162, 189, 222, 236, 283
compatible, 13, 129, 204, 207, 244, 308, 324
complex, 7, 10, 18, 21, 32, 33, 34, 36, 59, 64, 96, 98, 114, 127, 134, 136
complying, 148
component, 13, 60, 100, 123, 139, 148, 193, 239, 242, 308
composite, 142, 148
compound, 49, 68, 84, 142, 169
compress, 118, 125, 145
concatenate, 38, 217
conceptual, 10, 57, 68, 148
concrete, 74, 116, 198
condition, 28, 73, 77, 173, 180, 184, 185, 194, 195, 200, 203, 212, 213, 214, 216, 217, 266, 308, 321
conditional, 174-175, 321-325
configuration, 62
confirm, 67, 72, 238, 271
conflict, 9, 19, 121, 142, 147, 320
conform, 42
connection, 2, 241, 242, 277
consistent, 16, 26, 29, 38, 42, 59, 62, 97, 105, 115, 122, 126, 128, 146, 147, 176, 195, 224, 241
consists, 122
constant, 230, 296
constrain, 59, 66, 79, 87, 91, 105, 106, 107, 109, 132, 155, 169, 208
construct, 15, 43, 51, 141, 179, 184, 187, 198, 204, 224, 266, 296, 299, 311, 321
consultant, 9, 73, 266, 299, 307, 315
consuming, 25
contact, 10, 151, 175, 193, 200
context, 119, 164, 269, 271
convention, 47, 61, 62, 114, 115, 118, 119, 122, 137, 198, 316
conversion, 137, 268, 274

convert, 22, 54, 122, 125, 135, 158, 159, 176, 184, 189, 217
coordinates, 129, 131
copy, 9, 11, 30, 73, 98, 99, 115, 118, 117, 118, 120, 157, 174, 230, 231, 245
core, 126, 149, 294
corporate, 15, 23, 120, 170, 309
corrupted, 264
cost, 8, 10, 18, 29, 35, 40, 57, 58, 72, 98, 114, 116, 124, 126, 141
count, 19, 29, 34, 39, 219, 221, 242, 249, 261
crash, 14, 72, 238, 239, 314
criterion, 76, 77, 78, 79, 115
cross join, 203
cryptic, 27, 115, 118, 121
csv, 32, 143, 145, 230, 231, 262
CTAS, 326
Cunningham, Ward, 11
currency, 128, 297
customer, 12, 14, 15, 20, 27, 46, 47, 48
customize, 309, 327

D

DASD, 117
dashboard, 266
data scientists, 330
data-type, 125-149, 300-307
database, 7-8, 13-15, 32-56
database administrator, 20, 294, 296
DatabaseMetaData, 291
Datanamic, 83
dataset, 242
date of birth, 12, 86, 136, 137, 150, 165
DDL, 97, 109, 240
debug, 240, 267, 268
DEC, 137
decimal, 95, 127, 128, 129, 130, 132, 133
declaration, 11
decode, 216
deduplicate, 205
default, 106, 109, 121, 137, 150, 162, 166, 168, 169, 170, 179, 184, 189, 194, 205, 229, 233, 253, 255
define, 10, 26, 27, 45, 49, 51, 57, 66, 68, 81, 83, 85, 87, 92, 97
definitive, 100
defunct, 137
delete, 28, 52, 54, 55, 162, 209, 210, 227, 237
delimiter, 35, 269
DeMarco, Tom, 10
depend, 15, 16, 51, 52, 53, 55, 64, 68, 69, 84, 86
desc, 179, 180, 184, 190, 191, 212, 244, 330
describe, 288-289
deserialize, 117, 118, 120
design, 7, 8, 12, 15, 20, 21, 25, 26, 27
DeWitt, David J., 317
diagram, 58, 61, 67, 83, 84, 196, 206, 262, 328
digit, 79, 86, 124, 128, 132, 133, 137, 138, 140, 166, 177, 296, 321
directory, 141, 262, 320
discipline, 18, 21, 25, 35, 36, 55, 68, 92, 125, 248, 262, 330
discover, 92, 265, 312
disk, 14, 100, 117, 146, 203, 238, 264, 273, 282, 283, 285
distinct, 183, 297
distribute, 125, 139, 166, 282, 284, 297, 309, 312
divide, 38, 97, 128, 153, 154, 217
DML, 28, 43, 97
document, 10, 9, 11, 29, 43, 61, 99, 100, 107, 123, 124, 135, 138, 139, 143, 146, 147

dodgy, 135, 153
domain, 17
dot notation, 61
double, 105, 132, 133, 206, 269, 301
drop, 97, 110, 248, 253, 254, 258, 261, 282, 286, 326
duplicate, 14, 15, 37, 46, 47, 49, 51, 52, 54, 55, 58, 166, 183, 189, 191, 205

E

edit, 27, 85, 89, 98, 99, 172, 175, 178, 229, 325, 327, 328
efficient, 12, 26, 29, 33, 59, 95, 97, 98, 125, 135, 141, 185, 213, 216, 247, 280, 283, 285
elapsed, 278
element, 13, 17, 28, 35, 40, 42, 146, 147, 186, 229, 325
embedded, 38, 165
Embrace Change, 319
empty, 91, 96, 101, 160, 161, 162, 267
enable, 9, 12, 28, 43, 51, 58, 59, 62, 67, 106, 147, 184, 185, 225, 227, 312, 313, 314, 319
encoding, 135, 272
enforce, 49, 59, 106, 125, 138, 155, 208, 210, 221, 257, 307
enhance, 25, 149, 318
enter, 73, 177
entity, 17, 65, 80, 81, 120, 149, 300, 301, 302, 303, 305
environment, 109, 111, 112, 117, 164, 210, 216, 225, 245, 246, 252, 262, 319, 325
ePub, 143
ERP, 299, 308, 309
error message, 175, 221, 270, 278
escape, 15, 300

estimate, 86, 114, 173
ETL, 119, 262, 280, 320
evaluate, 218
event, 116, 240, 314
except, 34, 108, 157, 205, 208, 212, 250, 251, 268, 323
exception, 28, 118, 123, 163, 226, 234, 264, 265, 266, 267, 268
exclude, 34, 121, 211
execute, 91, 104, 219, 259, 260, 267, 269, 278, 280, 281, 283, 292, 324
executeUpdate, 234
Extreme Programming (XP), 18, 52, 319

F

false, 133, 134
FastLoad, 231
First Normal Form, 45
First Notification of Loss (FNOL), 71, 72, 75, 76
fix, 10, 25, 47, 52, 71, 74, 84, 95, 123, 134, 146, 177, 225, 262, 266, 274, 313, 318, 319
flag, 120, 134
flexible, 19, 33, 36, 42, 58, 62, 138, 143, 148, 149, 306, 318
float, 129, 130, 131, 132
Foreign Key, 61, 65, 85, 208
Formula, 17
Fowler, Martin, 11, 20, 60, 213
fraction, 98, 129, 278
function, 17, 37, 106, 114, 125, 126, 127, 138, 139, 146, 147, 153, 154, 158, 176
functionality, 19, 54, 74, 75, 149, 193

G

Gartner, 148
Gawande, Atul, 69
generate, 14, 47, 49, 58, 84, 85, 86, 88, 89, 90, 128, 139, 140, 143, 166, 168
generic, 116, 299, 300
geographic, 138, 284
geometric, 126
getName, 296
getTables, 291, 292
gigabytes, 133
Git, 100, 328
Goldacre, Ben, 7, 311
GPS, 129, 138, 185
graphical, 198, 232, 238, 245, 246
Grenning, James, 11
group by, 180-185
guess, 27, 61, 64, 75, 81, 86, 115, 117, 124, 167, 198, 312
GUID, 139

H

Hadoop, 9, 310
Harold, Elliotte Rusty, 22
hash, 166, 281, 283
having, 16, 19, 47, 54, 58, 84, 93, 98, 106, 116, 120, 124, 135, 176, 184, 216, 240
header, 34
heading, 26, 33, 34, 38, 71, 144, 223, 259
Heinemeier Hansson, David, 45, 60, 147, 149
hexadecimal, 140
hierarchy, 193, 285
Highsmith, Jim, 11
history, 100, 117
Hive, 117, 268
hoarder, 319
hog, 281
host, 140
Hunt, Andrew, 11
hyphen, 122, 140, 166, 229

I

IBM, 117, 161, 231, 236, 240, 245, 271, 315
id, 38, 47, 49, 55, 59, 66, 75, 76, 85, 88, 92, 93, 106, 119, 127, 128
identity, 106, 168
if-then-else, 174-175, 321-325
ignore, 14, 20, 46, 107, 133, 183, 244, 250, 255, 265, 266, 277
IIN, 321
immutable, 324
impact, 24, 213, 225, 247, 262, 265, 282, 284, 324
impedance, 11
implement, 19, 23, 40, 60, 64, 65, 67, 80, 104, 122, 139, 168, 176, 193, 201, 212, 214
import, 142, 231
include, 12, 19, 20, 39, 42, 52, 60, 64, 70, 104, 106, 108, 120, 126, 133, 137, 138, 139
increment, 57, 106, 148, 168
independent, 9, 53, 64, 148, 149, 184
indeterminate, 284
indicate, 116, 119
inet, 139, 140
infile, 231
infrastructure, 15
ingest, 231
Ingres, 150
inner (nested) query, 188
inner join, 194, 196, 199, 201
input, 25, 126, 140, 231, 235, 265, 323
insert, 227-231

Index

insights, 318
inspect, 19, 39
instance, 17, 97, 117, 150, 178
instrument, 202, 203, 207
integer, 125-128
integrate, 20, 309, 315, 325
integrity, 15, 18, 59, 70, 106, 148, 208, 210, 264, 274, 308, 316
interface, 12, 13, 62, 89, 104, 107, 108, 193, 213, 232, 238, 245, 246, 290, 291, 316, 325
intermediate, 197, 286
internal, 127, 139, 142, 317
international, 86, 126, 312
internet, 7, 13, 58, 59, 92, 130, 185, 297, 313, 314
intersect, 150, 156, 206, 250, 288
interval, 189
intervening, 317, 324
introspection, 288
invalid, 108, 250, 268, 269
invisible, 269, 318
invoke, 285
IP, 117
IPv, 140
IRMI, 92
ISO, 126, 139, 143, 321
isolate, 239, 242
issue, 23, 25, 27, 45, 114, 135, 225, 226, 244, 327
item, 11, 25, 36, 43, 58, 77, 108, 142, 147, 288, 308, 313
iterate, 19, 25, 26, 28, 31, 32, 56, 57, 64, 70, 71
iTunes, 65

J

jargon, 17, 71, 116, 274, 323
Java, 8, 37, 95, 108, 121, 122, 129, 149, 163, 193, 234, 266, 267, 268, 269
JDBC, 108, 163, 233, 234, 269, 277, 285, 290
JDBCType, 296
Jeffries, Ron, 11
job, 7, 9, 12, 19, 20, 23, 34, 78, 79, 93, 115, 142, 164, 236, 244, 265, 270, 272, 281
join, 193-204
joins and nulls, 155-159
JSON, 142, 147, 268

L

lag, 187, 189
language, 7, 8, 9, 12, 16, 22, 25, 29, 37, 46, 59, 62, 70, 97, 107
latitude, 129, 130, 131, 133, 139, 186, 284, 289, 313
left outer join, 200, 201, 219, 220
legacy, 122
length, 87, 115, 134, 135, 139, 247, 274, 288, 295, 296, 297
letter, 2, 52, 117, 118, 121, 134, 165, 166, 176, 195, 269, 308
Levenshtein, 178
license, 9, 12, 32, 35, 39, 47, 72, 76, 109, 165
like, 177-178
linestring, 138, 139
link, 26, 27, 30, 49, 54, 61, 81, 86, 89, 92, 121, 141, 164, 167, 170
Linux, 161
list, 66, 201, 228
Lister, Tim, 10
ListIterator, 193
literal, 159, 175, 233
load, 7, 15, 29, 32, 126, 137, 144, 146, 210, 227, 230, 231, 262, 272, 274
lob, 140
local, 99, 100, 166, 195, 264
location, 59, 118, 139, 186, 187,

188, 266, 284, 297
lock, 148, 242, 284, 325
log, 100, 270
logic, 149, 154, 264, 277, 280, 320
logical, 10, 57, 58, 68, 97, 137, 167, 275, 286
long, 18, 19, 22, 23, 24, 28, 99, 114, 115, 118, 121, 126, 138, 140, 157, 163, 166, 207, 216
longitude, 129, 130, 131, 132, 133, 139, 186, 284, 289, 313
loop, 175, 185, 192, 321
loss, 10, 14, 15, 32, 53, 55, 86, 87, 92, 110, 118, 121, 122, 136, 138, 144, 199, 200, 227
lowercase, 105, 121, 122, 176
lowest, 18, 44, 291
Luhn, 321, 322, 323

M

MAC, 140
macaddr, 139, 140
Machanic, Adam, 192
mainframe, 114, 117
mandatory, 69, 77, 79, 106, 116, 198, 307
map, 42, 95, 129, 138, 148, 262, 285, 313
MapReduce, 316, 317
Marick, Brian, 11
markup, 9
Martin, Robert C., 11
mask, 123
Mason, Mike, 100, 178
materialized view, 320
mathematics, 16, 130
maximum, 87, 128, 135, 154, 182, 183, 282, 295, 296, 297
measure, 19, 95, 133, 190, 283, 284, 286, 313
media, 140, 141, 297, 311, 315

median, 190-192
megabytes, 146
Mellor, Steve, 11
memory, 14, 203, 273, 274, 281, 283, 285, 286
metadata, 288-297
metaphone, 178
methodology, 10, 11, 57
methods, 10, 13, 17, 148, 284, 296
Microsoft, 14, 22, 122, 136, 137, 139, 140, 162, 168, 175, 231, 236, 239, 240, 245, 282, 315, 324
migration, 70-96, 97-112, 244-263
minimum, 154, 182, 183, 231, 242, 296
minus, 122, 150, 153, 206
missing, 77, 88, 107, 151, 153, 166, 208, 216, 217, 218, 259, 316
MOBI, 143
mobile, 47, 164, 286, 311
model, 10-11, 57-69, 80-96, 97-111, 299-309
money, 9, 18, 35, 42, 92, 95, 98, 114, 115, 128, 129, 132, 180, 227, 238
multiply, 128, 213
MySQL, 162, 168, 181, 231, 236, 240, 245, 282
mysqlimport, 231

N

naming, 114-124
navigation, 58, 127, 129, 138, 142, 196, 275, 277, 280
nchar, 134
nclob, 140
nest, 211, 214, 216, 220, 225, 278, 285
Netezza, 104, 162, 231, 271, 286
network, 126, 140, 145, 185, 268,

Index

285, 321, 322, 325
newline, 108, 107, 229
Normal Form, 45, 46, 51, 53, 54, 55, 57, 59, 64, 147
normalize, 54, 57, 58, 64, 68, 142, 305
ntile, 189
null, 68-69, 84-95, 105-111, 150-163, 164-170, 182-184, 194-203, 229-239, 246-257, 288-297
NuoDB, 162
nvarchar, 134, 136
nvl, 203
nzload, 231, 271

O

object, 11-15, 59-60, 142-148, 285-285
operational, 286
optimize, 29, 280, 281, 282, 283, 284, 286, 318, 324
Oracle, 104, 108, 121, 122, 127, 130, 134, 135, 137, 150, 160, 161, 166, 168, 180, 203, 216, 231, 235
order by, 45, 179, 183, 184, 187, 191, 205, 212
ordinal, 179, 189, 296
organization, 7, 8, 9, 14, 15, 26, 68, 99, 114, 115, 117, 124, 128, 138, 164, 198
organize, 12, 25, 26, 33, 34, 58, 59, 97, 290
ORM (Object-Relational Mapping), 59, 285
outer join, 199, 200, 201, 202, 203, 219, 220, 257
owner, 60, 165, 167

P

padded, 134, 135
panacea, 311
paradigm, 193
parent, 16, 60, 63, 65, 107, 198
parentheses, 105, 155, 180, 217, 219
parse, 35, 37, 146, 193
partition, 58, 187, 189, 286
patch, 253
pattern, 28, 46, 47, 56, 57, 58, 62, 113, 173, 177, 178, 284, 297, 312
Peopleware, 10
percentage, 216, 296, 316, 322
percentile, 189
performance, 15, 16, 27, 28, 93, 133, 168, 185, 192, 201, 225, 226, 247, 273, 274, 275
persistence, 14, 15, 17, 273
petabyte, 313
physical, 10, 43, 44, 57, 58, 68, 229, 247, 282, 320
pivot, 222, 223
plain english, 120
plain text, 98, 99, 175, 254, 262
playlist, 65, 66
plural, 92, 104, 121
polygon, 138, 139
populate, 28, 91, 96, 97, 106, 109, 114, 168, 204, 226, 229, 234, 247, 255, 256, 257, 262, 312
position, 43, 129, 130, 131, 132, 166, 179, 186, 189, 216, 272, 296, 313
PostgreSQL, 100-111
Pragmatic Programmer, The, 39, 99, 100, 115, 198, 264, 266, 327
precision, 95, 128, 129, 132, 133, 313
prefix, 37, 38, 64, 79, 115, 119, 120
preserve, 91, 96, 109, 246, 260,

323
previous, 37, 46, 92, 163, 186, 187, 188, 189, 210, 224, 227, 240, 244, 246, 251
Primary Key, 46-55, 59-69, 164-170
procedural, 321, 324
productive, 29, 33, 36, 254
professional, 12, 262
profile, 174, 272, 290, 296, 297
program, 2, 12, 35, 148, 193, 241, 264, 265, 268, 270, 271, 327
programmer, 7, 11, 12, 13, 19, 23, 62, 70, 98, 107, 116, 117, 119, 121, 122, 129, 133, 136
project, 15, 18, 19, 22, 23, 26, 33, 56, 98, 104, 108, 114, 115, 135
proof, 248, 306, 324
property, 13, 17, 72, 73, 117, 123, 131, 148, 178, 180, 197, 198, 242
proprietary, 9, 127, 149, 321, 324, 325
psql, 245, 260
Python, 149, 325

Q

quality, 8, 13, 23, 27, 45, 113, 114, 125, 128, 134, 140, 177, 290, 297, 316
quartile, 189
quote, 24, 105, 175, 269, 327, 328

R

Rails, 32-56, 70-96
raise, 71, 110, 234, 268
rank, 189, 190
rectangle, 138, 213
refactor, 26, 28, 31, 50, 113, 213, 244, 254, 262, 330
referential integrity, 208, 210

reflection, 288
Reiser, Martin, 273
relationship, 57-68
release, 8, 15, 25, 42, 96, 111, 227, 244, 262, 268, 319, 330
reliable, 7, 12, 16, 28, 33, 35, 36, 37, 42, 86, 97, 133, 165, 173, 239, 246, 248, 253, 257
relvar, 45
rename, 135, 207, 248, 253, 254
repeat, 34, 38, 39, 40, 46, 51, 68, 84, 86, 88, 119, 144, 210, 221, 244, 246
reset sequence (key generator), 14, 169, 252, 258, 261
restrict, 36, 68, 84, 86, 89, 94, 115, 125, 126, 180, 201, 212, 284, 320, 322
restructure, 32, 37, 40, 51, 245
robust, 27, 31, 33, 46, 62, 113, 149, 210, 261, 318
role, 15, 81, 88, 89, 93, 143, 149
rollback, 234, 240, 241
round, 128, 129, 217, 218
Ruby, 21-22, 59-67, 70-96
runstats, 282

S

SAP, 136, 137, 231
SatNav, 129, 130, 313
savepoints, 241, 243
scaffold, 81, 83, 90, 93, 94
scalable, 316
scalar, 323
scale, 21, 128, 143, 147, 155, 247, 274, 312, 316, 318
schema, 58, 290, 291, 292, 295
Schwaber, Ken, 11
scm, 100
script, 2, 23, 83, 98, 104, 107, 109, 110, 111, 112, 228, 232, 237,

Index 343

238, 244
scroll, 119, 285, 286
Second Normal Form, 55
select, 172-192, 193-225
sequence (key generator), 166-169, 252-263
sequence (sort order), 42-45, 178-180
SerDe, 117
serial, 106, 109, 117, 168, 229, 253, 255, 258, 260
serialize, 117, 120
session, 28, 240, 241, 242
SGML, 143
silent failure, 250, 265, 266, 267
silver bullet, 29, 310, 311
skill, 15, 16, 28, 35, 36, 98, 315
slash, 269
smallint, 127, 128
smartphone, 16, 73, 78
sound, 19, 62, 85, 198
sound-bite, 18
soundex, 178
spatial, 126, 138, 139, 148, 284
specialist, 10, 20
speech, 311, 315
spell, 22, 115, 116, 120, 137, 167
spreadsheet, 21, 28, 33, 34, 70, 71, 72, 73, 74, 114, 144, 174, 214, 216, 224
SQL, 97-111, 172-192, 193-225, 227-243, 244-263
SQL/PSM, 321
sqlcmd, 245
SQLException, 266, 267
SQLite, 162
square, 105, 122
SSD, 274
stateless, 13
statistics, 185, 189, 190, 282, 283
status, 10, 123, 312
Stonebraker, Michael, 273, 317
storage, 10, 14, 58, 117, 129, 132, 133, 141, 198, 264, 265, 282, 283, 284, 318
stored procedure, 29, 270, 282, 318, 324, 325
string, 125-137, 160-162
strong data-type, 89, 125, 134, 136, 179, 268
substring, 17, 180, 323
Subversion, 100, 99, 100, 262, 328
sum, 125, 154, 181, 182, 183, 213
Surrogate Key, 167
Sutherland, Jeff, 11
Sybase, 136, 137, 168, 231, 236, 282
symbols, 297
symptoms, 225
syntax, 70, 97, 162, 168, 195, 235, 236, 240, 266, 267

T

tab, 107, 269
Tableau, 84, 224
tableTypes, 292
telematics, 59, 166
temporary, 262, 294
Teradata, 168, 231
terminate, 108, 120
test, 231-238, 244-263
Third Normal Form, 51, 53, 54, 55, 57, 59, 64
timestamp, 137-138
Transact-SQL, 324
transaction, 238-243
trap, 28, 29, 320
truncate, 135, 238
try, 9, 16, 17, 20, 21, 71, 130, 132, 151, 163, 166, 175, 185, 209, 239, 255, 266
tuning, 28, 58, 198, 273, 283, 284, 286, 324

tuple, 17, 45

U

unchanged, 164, 165, 233
undo, 209, 239
union, 204, 205, 250
unique, 46-49, 164-170
UNIX, 136, 141, 231, 236, 254, 259, 269, 282
unstructured, 316
update, 231-237, 283-284
updatestats, 282
uppercase, 114, 121, 122, 176
URI, 268
URL, 30, 141
UUID, 126, 139, 140, 166

V

van Bennekum, Arie, 11
varchar, 125-138
vargraphic, 134
VAX, 137
vector, 323
vendor, 9, 22, 29, 33, 62, 98, 115, 117, 126, 135, 146, 149, 168, 231, 246, 248, 262
Venn, 206
video, 127, 140, 311
view, 29, 114, 119, 214, 244, 253, 288, 289, 294, 310, 315, 319, 320
visual programming tools, 29, 98, 254, 262, 318, 327, 328
visualize, 25, 27, 58, 172, 224, 330
voice, 23, 141

volume, 14, 21, 59, 78, 146, 167, 168, 204, 205, 225, 230, 262, 278, 284

W

Walker, David, 22, 59
warehouse, 29, 59, 114, 225, 230, 234, 286, 320
warning, 258, 266
wasNull, 163
waste, 11, 18, 19, 20, 46, 51, 52, 56, 57, 115, 119, 135, 147, 162, 229, 269, 285, 330
waterfall, 10, 25, 57, 98, 330
website, 2, 14, 64, 72, 224, 242, 308, 318
wiki, 116, 122, 136, 321
wikipedia, 136, 321
window function, 186
Wirth, Niklaus, 273

X

xml, 9-10, 21-21, 34-56, 142-148

Y

YAGNI (You Ain't Gonna Need It), 52

Z

ZIP Code, 47, 52, 53, 55, 86, 87, 122, 139, 177, 234
zOS, 282